FOUR
CENTURIES

Edinburgh University Life
1583–1983

FOUR CENTURIES

Edinburgh University Life

1583-1983

Edited by
GORDON DONALDSON
Historiographer Royal for Scotland

9010187901

THE UNIVERSITY OF EDINBURGH

1983

© University of Edinburgh 1983
Edinburgh University Press
22 George Square, Edinburgh
Printed and bound by
Clark Constable (1982) Ltd
Printers to the University

British Library Cataloguing
in Publication Data

Four Centuries
1. University of Edinburgh – History
I. Donaldson, Gordon
378.413/4   LF1041
ISBN 0 85224 467 3

over. Upper Library Hall

CONTENTS

ABBREVIATIONS
used in the References

AUL   Aberdeen University Library

Bower   Alexander Bower, *The History of the University of Edinburgh*, 3 vols (Edinburgh 1817)

Craufurd   Thomas Craufurd, *History of the University of Edinburgh from 1580 to 1646* (Edinburgh 1808)

DNB   *Dictionary of National Biography*

EUL   Edinburgh University Library

Grant   Alexander Grant, *The Story of the University of Edinburgh during its first three hundred years*, 2 vols (London 1884)

GUL   Glasgow University Library

Horn   David B. Horn, *A Short History of the University of Edinburgh, 1556–1889* (Edinburgh 1967)

Morgan   Alexander Morgan (ed.), *Charters, Statutes and Acts of the Town Council and the Senatus, 1583–1858* (Edinburgh 1937)

NLS   National Library of Scotland

SHR   *Scottish Historical Review*

UEJ   *University of Edinburgh Journal*

Foreword

JOHN McINTYRE

The title of this volume has been very carefully chosen in order to prevent any initial misunderstanding. For it does not purport to be yet another history of the University of Edinburgh, though perhaps there is a gap there waiting to be filled in an authoritative way. It sets out to describe what it was like to be living and studying and teaching in the University, at different times and in different parts of it, during the four hundred years of its existence. The dangers in such a presentation are immediately obvious. The choice of topics could be idiosyncratic; the descriptions themselves, anecdotic or episodic; while the balance in time could easily be thrown in one period rather than another. In the event, however, the presentation has been controlled by four considerations.

First, there has been a rejection of the idea that the University can either be equated with, or interpreted in terms of, any single element within it. Such an idea would have been an instance of what Whitehead called 'the fallacy of misplaced concreteness', the fallacy of treating a part of an entity as if it were the whole. This fallacy is particularly seductive in the University context, where there is a strong predilection for the single, integrating, unifying principle: such is intellectual tidiness. Recourse may be had to different devices, such as tracing the history of the constitution of the University, or of the buildings constructed, or various faculties' curricula. Even more desperate measures are adopted when some such concept as 'the idea of education', or 'the nature of knowledge', or 'the process of learning' becomes the principle chosen as the interpretative basis for the history. In the present volume, we shall look in vain for any such over-simplifications of how the University has grown and developed.

Secondly, the positive expression of what has just been said: the University is to be regarded as an educational institution which across four hundred years achieves its aims by formulating and implementing its educational principles and criteria within a complex of social structures and a network of personal relationships. So, in the present volume, sometimes the concentration is upon principles and methods, as when Eric Forbes in his essay on 'Philosophy and Science Teaching in the Seventeenth Century' assesses the extent to which the seventeenth-century regents in Edinburgh allowed contemporary scientific developments to affect their teaching in natural philosophy, and how much they could achieve within the Aristotelian-Cartesian-Newtonian framework, by incorporating references to foreign physicists.

The way in which educational principle is shown to be highly determinative both of the attitude of the students to their curriculum, and of the international reputation of the University, is to be seen in J.B. Morrell's account of the principle of *lernfreiheit*, the freedom of choice allowed to students to elect courses from the various offerings and not to be subject to any kind of pastoral guidance. The strong throve on the system, and the weak went under. Morrell's essay describes 'Medicine and Science in the Eighteenth Century', and how Edinburgh attracted students from other countries.

Principles, still educational principles even if of a different sort, are the central subject of the contribution of Sheila Hamilton in 'The First Generations of University Women 1869–1930', in which she traces the hard-fought struggle of women to secure a place in higher education, finding that most opposition came from the Faculty of Medicine, students as well as staff. Even here the principles shade into the background as the personalities come forward to form the story – Sophia Jex-Blake, Francis Melville, Elsie Inglis and Professor Masson, with his statement that until the needs of women's education were fully recognised and fulfilled, 'we persevere in the guilt of a great injustice, and we dawdle on as a nation at but half our possible nobleness and strength' (p.113).

Two other of the essays take us a long way towards understanding how important it is in the history of an institution like the University never to forget how it looks from the point of view of the student. Ian Campbell, writing on 'Carlyle and the University of Edinburgh', gives us a picture not only of how one very perceptive observer registered his impressions both of his fellows and of the staff, but also of the kind of emotional reactions which young students, coming from the country in Carlyle's day, or at any time since, experienced in coming into an emancipating society. It was clear how heavily the Edinburgh system depended on the professorial capacity to make a subject interesting or otherwise, though it ought to be remembered that regents and tutors might be equally dull.

In the following century, and this time in the Faculty of Medicine, another student, belonging to the Ibo tribe in West Africa, graduated in Edinburgh, James Africanus Beale Horton. While in Edinburgh, he embarked upon a programme of writing which was eventually to earn him the reputation of being one of the founders of African nationalism. The African connection is one which the University has always valued and furthered, and no more fitting tribute could perhaps be paid than the comment that the attitude to black students was one 'of companionship and respect' from their white colleagues. George Shepperson in his essay describing 'An Early African Graduate' tells us that Horton was one of a whole series of Edinburgh Graduates who figured prominently in the subsequent history of their land – Omoniyi, Bankole Bright, Hastings Banda and Julius Nyerere.

Pursuing the theme of how the University looks this time to the student who encounters it as new experience, we shall find James Jennings' account of 'The Other Side of the Counter' a good refutation of the slander that administration is equivalent to bureaucracy. The Matriculation Office is the student's first encounter with officialdom, and as the essay protrays it, the reception is friendly and helpful and the achievement of graduation makes the final encounter little short of euphoric. Between these two experiences, the students have, of course, had to find somewhere to live, and Roy Pinkerton records the ambivalent way in which the University has understood its responsibility for housing its undergraduates. Until about a century ago, as he points out in his essay 'Of Chambers and Communities', it was the landladies of the town who provided the board and residence, as well as a good deal of pastoral care and stern discipline, *in loco parentis*, though they would not have thought of themselves in these terms. The development of the Halls system throughout the city – University Hall, Masson Hall, Muir Hall, Cowan House, and later the Pollock Halls – combined with the other arrangement of Student Houses, usually large villas converted into groups of study-bedrooms with a shared kitchen, was a very necessary supplement to the private housing in the city which could never have coped with the vastly increased numbers of students. While they had their own constitution for self-government, they were never in danger of creating a separated group of students with exclusive off-campus interests. The Halls have always been able to remain part of the University, which on the other hand has not been slow to use the amenities they provide.

Attention has been drawn to the way in which the professoriate affects the students in the class-room, and, we could add, in the slightly chilly and tongue-tying conditions of afternoon tea at the professor's home. When, however, the professor is not engaged in his employment, or spending a dreamy hour in Senate or its committees, he has a human face and indulges in human ploys. What these might have been, during the period represented by the century between the second and third centenaries of the University, is portrayed for us in meticulous terms, with menus, prices and reports on behaviour, by C. P. Finlayson, in an entertaining version of 'The Symposium Academicum'. The places of meeting recorded by the author provide us with a 'Good Food Guide' to the nineteenth century. Since the Professor of Divinity was a not infrequent participant in those occasions, perhaps too much ought not to be said, except to remark that some of the verses uttered during or after dinner suggest that MacGonagall may have had a University education.

I have been indicating the ways in which the different essays illustrate what I have called the second controlling consideration of this volume, namely, that the University is an educational institution which across four hundred years achieves its aims by formulating and implementing its educational principles and criteria within a complex of social and personal relationships. The opening and the final essays in the volume provide the framework in which the others have rightly been fitted. Christine Shepherd tells us in the first essay, 'University Life in the Seventeenth Century', about the pastimes of the students, the subjects they studied, how they were taught, how they behaved, and what the aims of the University educational system were, in that period. Gordon Donaldson touches on many of those subjects in 'Some Changes in the Classroom in the Twentieth Century', referring to teachers no doubt known to a host of readers and providing a mature assessment of the changes which have overtaken us in the post-war years of rapid, sometimes unplanned, expansion, and of momentous social change. For the ways in which a member of staff views these conditions we have the benefit of the experience of Denys Hay, in 'Some Changes outside the Classroom over the Last Half Century', which fills in our picture of the terms of staff employment as it has improved over the period, the facilities for staff community life, and the consequences for the scholar of the transfer of the Library and the Arts Faculty to George Square.

The third controlling consideration operating in the series of essays is the implicit claim that this method is a perfectly valid one for understanding an historically evolving and socially complex institution like the University. It is in this kind of evidence, concerning how the institution ticks, rather than in the formal curricula, or the legal constitutional enactments, or even committee minutes, that you have to look to discover the nature of the education provided within this system. The method is one which has by now established itself in a variety of disciplines – from theology to psychiatry – and, often pompously given the description 'phenomenonological', it works on the principle of seeing how the institution operates, how its members behave, react and speak about it, both staff and students. In other words, a collection of essays of this kind is an exercise in self-analysis, and the logical sequel to such a study is to go on to ask ourselves what they tell us about our Scottish, or more precisely, Edinburgh style of education, and the principles it embodies. In such self-analysis, we would investigate the special role of the professor or head of department, and whether the system requires such a hierarchical structure. I can only speak for myself when I say that without the lecture system, I could not have enjoyed the day-by-day training in thinking given by such professors as A.E. Taylor or Kemp Smith. Writing a twelve hundred word essay, to have it mulled over by a tutor, or listening to my peers expressing their immature comments, would have been no substitute for that kind of discipline.

Our self-analysis should also run to asking ourselves whether, given the vast committee system which we now have, too much administration is being done by academics, and whether we are not now due for another attempt to stream-line the system. But we must not try to anticipate what must be the book about the questions which the present volume so sharply raises and for which it so generously equips us.

The final controlling consideration in the essays is the conviction that there is enough evidence still available to make the phenomenological approach truly scholarly. Marjorie Robertson, in 'Manuscript Sources in the Library on the Life of the University', observes that some of the material for a study of the life of the University in the four centuries of its existence is obviously to be found in the University Library's Department of Special Collections, in court, senate and other collections of minutes. But on its own initiative the University Library in 1980, the year of its own Quatercentenary, invited graduates and staff to provide any material which might be thought to be of historical interest, relating to the life of the University. She has listed certain important items that came in as a response to that appeal. But it is admitted that material of this sort is difficult to come by, or to preserve, as every social historian knows; and the invitation given in 1980 has to be freqently repeated.

A year or two ago there was an argument about whether history was 'the remembered past' or 'the past that is worth remembering'. In the present essays we have portrayed for us a past which is not only worth remembering, but which is also worth enjoying. We may also add that it is a past with a future, for it is difficult to resist the conclusion that an institution which has evolved so richly over four hundred years has within it sufficient flexibility, impetus and adaptiveness, to ensure both its survival and its continuing evolution.

over. Old College, Edinburgh

University Life in the Seventeenth Century

CHRISTINE SHEPHERD

Most seventeenth-century students exist only as names in the matriculation and laureation records, and first-hand accounts of what university life was like for them are almost non-existent. However, we do have a great deal of official information, contained in the records of Edinburgh Town Council, the University and the various Commissions appointed during the century to visit the University, about what those authorities expected of the students.[1] Besides, we occasionally get more intimate glimpses of student life in the many students' notebooks which survive.

The Town Council, which maintained a strict control over the University's financial affairs, appointments of staff and educational policy, had definite ideas on what students should and should not do, and a set of rules compiled as a result of deliberations between 1619 and 1628 was nothing if not comprehensive. Students who failed to reconvene on 1 October after the holidays were to be fined two shillings for every day of absence thereafter. On matriculation every student had to swear obedience to the teachers and to the laws and ordinances of the College. Attendance at all lectures and disputations was required, as was daily attendance at the kirk. At public meetings no one was to push another student out of a seat, or claim any seat for his own, but everyone had to content himself with the first empty seat he came to. No one was to go out of the gate after the janitor had locked it, without obtaining permission from one of the regents. Latin had to be spoken at all times, in and out of class. There was to be no swearing, blasphemy or fighting, and the possession of daggers and swords was forbidden. Once students had been dismissed – at any time of day, but especially in the evening – they had to go home to their lodgings directly, and not loiter at the gate or anywhere else. This last rule is an indication that students generally lived outwith the University precincts, and we know that most did so. Student 'chambers' existed, but seem to have been used less as sleeping accommodation than as studies or reading-rooms. There were to be no cards and dice, and students were not to frequent taverns or other unseemly places. No student was to wear long hair. Finally, to guard against any outburst of graduation exuberance, a fine of £40 would be exacted if students held a public banquet before or after laureation or caused any other public disturbance; and to drive the point home, students contravening this regulation would lose their degrees as well as being fined. The Town Council also enacted that students were to wear gowns, but this was never enforced, possibly because influential parents objected.[2]

Clearly, being a student was a serious affair, and in addition virtually every minute of his time was accounted for. The day began at 6 a.m. in winter and 5 a.m. in summer, though in the second half of the century the regime was tempered to 7 in winter and 6 in summer. After the regents had commended themselves and their students to God, they spent the morning in lecturing and the afternoon in questioning students to make sure they had understood the morning's lesson. On play-days in the winter students had two hours of games, followed by further examinations on their lessons: in summer the questions session preceded the games. Saturday mornings were spent in disputation. On Sundays students were required to attend church, for most of the century twice in the day, but by the end of the century only once, and they were examined on the sermons and instructed in the Catechism. In addition to their daily classes, students had to attend public lectures in divinity and mathematics, and the Principal frequently preached and lectured to the whole College.

The fullest statement of the curriculum followed by the students appears in the set of rules already referred to, laid down by the Town Council around 1628:[3]

Year 1: Latin authors, especially Cicero. Translations from Latin into English and from English into Latin. Clenard's *Greek Grammar* to be studied with certain portions of the New Testament. Isocrates. Phocilides. Hesiod. Homer. Ramus's *Dialectic*.

Year 2: Talaeus's *Rhetoric*. Cassander, or something similar. Apthonius's *Progymnasmata*. Exercises in dialectic and rhetoric. Aristotle's *Organon* and other logic works. Porphyrius's *Isagoge*. Compendium of arithmetic.

Year 3: Dialectical and rhetorical analysis of the authors studied. Aristotle's *Posterior Analytics* (2 books), *Ethics* (5 books), *Prior Acroamatics* (3 books). Description of the human anatomy.

Year 4: Aristotle's *De coelo* (especially books 2 and 4). Sacrobosco's *Sphere. De ortu. De meteoris. De anima.* Hunter's *Cosmography*.

The curriculum remained more or less the same throughout the century: Year 1: Greek; Year 2: Logic/Metaphysics; Year 3: Metaphysics/Ethics; Year 4: Physics. However, the authors studied, especially in philosophy and science, changed.[4] A considerable number of students followed their completion of the Arts course by a period of study in divinity.

The main examinations took place at the beginning of each academic year. The student was examined on the previous year's course.[5] Bajans, or 1st year students, were required to turn a piece of Scots into Latin, and any found to be so badly grounded in Latin that there was no hope of their profiting were admonished to return to the study of the Latin tongue until they were more able. The Semibajans, or 2nd year students, had to turn a piece of Latin into Greek and were also examined on Ramus's *Dialectic* and *Ars Syllogistica* and the Greek poets. The examination of the Bachelors, or 3rd year students, consisted of the logical analysis of part of some Latin or Greek author, Porphyrius and the Categories, and Aristotle's works on logic. And the Magistrands, or final year students, were examined on Ramus and on Aristotle's Logic, Ethics and Physics. Students who missed this examination were required to attend a second examination, and if they missed that too they were reprimanded and required to undergo a third examination.

The graduation or laureation ceremony took place some time before the middle of July, when Theses were produced by the regent of the magistrand class to be defended by the students. Probably less importance was attached to this than to the examinations which took place at the beginning of the academic year, but a large gathering of local ministers, advocates and bailies was usually present at the laureation ceremony, and if a candidate excelled himself in debate it could be a passport to a future career. The ceremony seems to have been a grand affair, but during the course of the century laureations became less and less frequent. One reason was the constant political and ecclesiastical changes: when Presbyterians ruled, Episcopalians were unwilling to take the oath required at laureation, and vice versa. But it was also true that many of the students were reluctant either to stay on until the laureation after completing their curriculum in June or to return from their homes for it. In 1633 the Town Council expressed concern at magistrands departing as soon as teaching had finished instead of waiting for laureation, and proposed a fine to stop this practice. The small numbers which appeared at some of the ceremonies were an embarrassment to the regents, so private laureations became more and more frequent.

Once the laureation was over, students were on holiday. In the earliest days of the University students had been allowed only one month's holiday in the year – August – but that had gradually been extended, and for most of the seventeenth century the student was on holiday from mid-July until

1 October. A week's holiday was also allowed between Christmas and New Year.

Teaching was by the regenting system. Instead of having one teacher allotted to each subject as in the professorial system, each regent took his class right through the Arts course, teaching every subject in turn. Various attempts were made during the century to introduce the professorial system, but they were completely successful only after 1708.

The students' programme would seem to leave little time for any extra-curricular pursuits, unless the two hours of games on play-days can be so designated, but in addition to such official provision there were opportunities for students to learn fencing, dancing and riding in the town and also to study subjects not taught at the University, mainly modern languages such as French, Dutch and German.

All this tells us what University life formally involved, but what were the students actually like? Fourteen was the average age at which they entered the University, in view of which the solicitude of the Town Council for every aspect of their lives was perhaps not so overbearing as it might appear. Most of the students came from near Edinburgh, or at any rate from Scotland, but there was also an increasing number of English nonconformists, a few Irish students and, at the beginning of the century, a number of French Huguenots. The reasons for students attending the University were mainly practical, to obtain a degree as an opening to careers in the law, the church or government, and this probably explains why Edinburgh was the most popular of the Scottish universities. Scottish legal and administrative institutions were centred in Edinburgh, there was a parliament there until 1707 and when a general assembly met (which it rarely did in the seventeenth century) it too usually met in the capital. Representatives of the law, the administration and the church attended laureation ceremonies, so students would have been alive to the careers to which attendance at the University might lead. A figure of 320 students at Edinburgh is recorded,[6] and this number may well have increased with the influx of students debarred from the English universities. Certainly the graduation theses frequently list about 30 students in the first half of the century, while the theses at the beginning of the Restoration period have about 50 or 60 names. Natural disasters, such as the plague, affected student numbers, since parents frequently withdrew their sons when the plague was raging. In 1645 the University was forced by the plague to move from Edinburgh to Linlithgow, so that work could continue.

There seems to have been a fair cross-section of society among the students, in line with the egalitarian tradition of Scottish education. In 1610 one of the graduates was William Ker, son of the Earl of Roxburgh. In 1616 John Campbell, then heir of the laird of Lawers and later Earl of Loudon, was commended for his performance in defending and attacking the theses at the laureation ceremony, and the laird of Polwarth, Patrick Home, received similar acclaim in 1620. In the 1630s the sons of Sir Thomas Hope, the Lord Advocate, attended the University. There are two sets of student notes which were taken down by Sir James Hope of Hopetoun from the lectures of Robert Ranken in 1632–4. Sir James's brother Alexander had been the occasion of a certain amount of agitation in 1630: among certain aristocratic fathers who took exception to the practice of listing magistrands' names at the beginning of the graduation theses in order of merit (obviously because their sons' names had come too far down the list) was Sir Thomas Hope, although his son Alexander's position was 'equal to his deserving'.[7] As a result of this complaint, the practice fell more or less into abeyance, and the names were usually listed in alphabetical order until 1643, when the old custom of listing in order of merit was revived. Later in the century, during the 1680s, one of the students was a future Lord Advocate, Thomas Kennedy, son of Thomas Kennedy of Dunure and Dalquharran, who was provost of Edinburgh in 1685 and 1686.[8] Between 1689 and 1693 the son of Sir John Foulis of Ravelston attended the University. Probably many other sons of titled men were at Edinburgh during the century, some of them possibly accompanied by tutors, as the Mackenzies at St Andrews were at the beginning of the eighteenth century.[9] These tutors were responsible for their charges' physical and moral welfare; they had to make sure the boys attended to their studies and were probably required to correspond regularly with their employers, giving an account of their sons' progress and submitting their expenses.

At the other end of the social scale, many of the students were by no means well off, and a kind of rudimentary means test operated in their favour. A wealthy man like Sir John Foulis of Ravelston gave between £20 and £30 each year – quite a substantial sum – to his son's regent during his four years' course. More than once during the century the Town Council decreed that the regents must instruct poor students without such a fee, but, besides the payment normally made to the regents at the beginning of each session, there was also a payment due at the laureation, and one of the reasons why private laureations became more and more common during the century (in addition to those already given) was undoubtedly that some students could not afford the fee for the public ceremonial.

Further information about the social origins of some students comes from the *curricula vitae* of candidates for the office of regent, who were frequently recent graduates.[10] Thus in 1603 one of the candidates was John Douglas, brother of Lord Torthorwald, who had graduated in 1601. In 1611 the candidates were: 'Mr Andrew Stevenson, son to Andrew Stevenson, an honest burges, of an senatorian family; Mr Robert Burnet, son to Burnet of Barns, in Tweddale; and Mr James Ker, son to the laird of Linton'. In 1625 there were eight candidates of whom six were recent Edinburgh graduates, and again their fathers' occupations are given: George Hannay was 'son to an honest burges of the Canongate', John Brown was 'son of Mr William Brown, one of the clerks of Exchequer', Alexander Hepburn was 'son to Mr Thomas Hepburn, parson of Aldhamstoks', John Armour and Robert Ranken were both sons of 'honest burgesses'; we are not told anything about the sixth candidate. Of the seven other Edinburgh graduates who were candidates for the post of regent up to 1646 and for whom details of parental occupation are given, two were the sons of writers, one was a minister's son and four were the sons of the recurring 'honest burgesses'.

An interesting sidelight on the social history of Edinburgh student life is that up to 1635 the College porter was appointed from among the student body, either from the magistrand class or from the new graduates who had gone on to study divinity. At this date, however, it was decided that a student could not adequately carry out a porter's duties, since he was often required to be elsewhere, so the appointment was given instead to someone whose occupation could be carried on in the porter's room, in the first instance to a bookbinder.[11]

We have seen how many regulations were laid down for the guidance of students, but student life was not always in accordance with them. At the beginning of the century students reacted against the rigorous enforcement of the regulations and also against the formidable examinations by leaving Edinburgh and trying to gain admittance to other universities: by 1611 this practice had become so common that an application was made to the privy council to prevent students who had been expelled, or who had deserted, from being admitted elsewhere.[12] However, whatever the reasons behind these student defections, they did not cause a great decline in the numbers attending Edinburgh.

Successive resolutions of the Town Council and University provide ample evidence that student behaviour continued to be a problem. There was the recurrent tardiness of students in returning to the University in October, and the Town Council, which referred to it in 1633, 1635 and 1647, again required that a fine be exacted for each day's absence and stipulated that bursars who returned late were to lose their bursaries. 'Attending a funeral' seems even then to have been too often tendered as an excuse for absence, for in 1635 it was noted that students were spending too much time away from their studies because of attending burials, and in future they were to be allowed to attend the funerals only of benefactors of the University, advocates, other legal dignitaries, or fellow-students.

In 1668 the need to reiterate regulations concerning student behaviour was again felt, this time by the University: loitering round the College gate, speaking Scots, cursing, swearing and fighting, and playing when a student should be at lectures, were all censured, and the censors (who constituted a kind of internal spy system on student conduct) were advised to watch out for contraventions of these rules and also to keep a list of students' addresses, so that they could be sought out if they were absent from lectures.

However, before the end of the century student behaviour seems to have degenerated considerably. The performance in 1681 of a bawdy classical play within the College, by some of the students and other youngsters, presumably at least had the sanction of bearing some relation to academic studies. But worse things than that were going on. Two episodes of disorderliness which took place under Principal Alexander Monro, who was elected in 1685, are described.[13] In one, a student named Robert Brown fixed a placard on the College gates threatening to kill the regents and ordering the Principal to recant a sermon which he had preached. Despite this, no action was taken against Brown. However, when he and some friends went to the house of Sir George Lockhart, Lord President of the Court of Session, who was away from home, and frightened his wife, Monro's patience gave way: 'I confess I could no longer forbear', he relates;[14] 'I went to the class where Brown was, and called him to the Upper Gallery, and gave him all his proper names, and threatened him, if he did not immediately beg my Lady Lockhart's pardon, I would break his bones. All these big words I said to him, and the day thereafter extruded him with the usual solemnities. Upon which he frequently swore he would be revenged, and told the under Janitor that he had bought a pair of pistols to shoot me (*one* might have served)'. On another occasion a Mr Gourlay, although not a regent himself, had been employed to do the work of one of the regents, Herbert Kennedy. 'The boys found him out of his element', reports Monro, 'and drove him out of the schools with snow-balls'. After this Gourlay probably ceased to teach, but continued to live in the College until the students, learning that he had been licensed to preach by the Presbyterians (who were at that time nonconformists), 'beat up his chamber door and windows with stones; and pulling off his hat, cloak and periwig, and reproaching him with "Fanatic", forced him to remove from the chamber which he had possessed peaceably before'. Following on this further outrage Gourlay very sensibly removed himself from the College. However, Monro was inclined to take a lenient view of these escapades, since the students were displaying sympathies with the Episcopalian cause, which he himself supported. His comment was that 'they are as obedient and regular as so many youths in any part of the world'. Around this time concern was also expressed at the custom of throwing a football into the first year class, which was evidently being used by some students as a pretext for political demonstrations.

It would be altogether too easy to see in the unruliness of that period a reflection of the state of the country, which was intermittently disturbed between the signing of the National Covenant in 1638 and the Revolution in 1689, for it is far from clear that students had been much more orderly during the long years of peace which preceded the Covenant. At the same time, the College was no ivory tower, detached from current events. In 1638 the magistrand class were privately graduated because their regent, John Brown, was dismissed for refusing to subscribe the Covenant. A student notebook of the years 1652–4 contains this tag:[15]

> Vivat Carolus rex dei gratia
> Pereant hostes, inimica cedant
> tela

– a sentiment hostile to the existing government of Oliver Cromwell, which was excluding Charles II from his throne. In 1665 and again in 1677, after the King had been restored, an oath of allegiance was imposed on students before degrees could be conferred, but this may not have been universally acceptable either. In the 1680s obstreperous students were undoubtedly ready to join in the resentment felt by the people of Edinburgh, and indeed of Scotland, against the Roman Catholic policy of James VII. On Christmas Day 1680, when James, then Duke of York, had been sent to Scotland as commissioner for his brother, Charles II, the students publicly burned an effigy of the Pope, in spite of the combined resistance of the College authorities, the town guard and the regular troops – an action quite properly regarded as a reflection on the Duke, then in residence at Holyroodhouse. The punishment – it seems odd – was the temporary closing of the College, and students and their parents were ordered to give bonds for their good behaviour, but some thought such treatment was harsh for 'bairns'. The students were also blamed for having a hand in the destruction by fire on 11 January 1681 of Prestonfield, the seat of Sir James Dick, Lord Provost of Edinburgh, but this was never proved. English students were held responsible for instigating the Christmas Day fracas and subsequent trouble, and this probably explains why the retaliation was relatively mild. The Englishmen were expelled and the rest of the students allowed to return to their work. In 1686, after James had become King, Thomas Burnet, who had previously taught at Marischal College, was appointed a regent in Edinburgh. The summer before he had published theses in which he asserted the King's absolute power and as a result many parents tried to get their sons into another regent's class. Burnet was supported by a Visitation Committee, which recommended to the University that in their dictates on ethics regents should instruct the youth in the unlawfulness of defensive arms and resistance to the King, but the University rejected this. It is perhaps not surprising that at the end of 1688, when the arrival of William of Orange in England heralded James's overthrow, the students joined the Edinburgh mob which ransacked the Roman Catholic chapel which the King had established at Holyrood.[16]

Yet there was not much improvement in student conduct when the Revolution brought a new, Presbyterian, Principal, Dr Gilbert Rule, in 1690. A fresh parliamentary Commission made recommendations to ensure loyalty to the new regime in church and state, aimed mainly at the regents but concerned also that there should be higher academic and moral standards among the students, and bursars came in for particular censure. In response to a request by delegates from the universities 'that some expedients may be fallen upon for making bursars more obsequious and tractable, or for retrenching their numbers, which increasing proves burdensome and inconvenient', the Commissioners decreed 'that all bursars be strictly examined every year, and that such as do not duly attend and make sufficient proficiency in their studies be turned out of their bursaries'. It was, of course, a simple matter to apply sanctions to bursars, but it is not clear that the good intentions had much effect on the student body in general. The Faculty records contain a statement dated 1691 prepared by Andrew Massie, one of the regents, to be signed by all students: 'We underscryvers, students of the Colledge of Edinburgh, being sensible of the evill of many bad customes which have crept into this society, Do hereby declare our abhorency of them and particullarly of the barbarous practise of boxing at the Colledge gate or any where else, and that of throwing in the ball into the Bajane Class or fortifieing the Class against that attempt, and breaking and demolishing the Classes or any pairt of the Colledge fabrick, and do by these bind and obleadge our selves to forbear and abstaine from all these disorders for the future and to have no accessions to any of them directly or indirectly, wherein if we failzie we do declare our selves unworthy of this society and shall consent to our being expelled the society. Moreover we do hereby promise all due honor and reverence to the Provost, Magistrats and others, patrons of the Edinburgh Colledge, and all due respect and obedience to the Reverend primare and other masters and professors of this society. And that under the same penaltie in caise we failzie'.[17]

How much effect this good resolution had is questionable. A Faculty decree of 1695 deplored the failure of the students to pay fines which had been imposed on them for causing 'tumults and disorders contrary to the good government and peace of the College'. Other ordinances of the same year set fines for cursing and swearing, which was becoming increasingly common among students, and for drunkenness and frequenting alehouses. Any assumption that students were more guilty of such irregularities than the rest of society is checked by reference to the acts of the General Assembly, which in 1694 and again in 1697 took into serious consideration 'the impiety and profaneness that aboundeth in this nation, in profane and idle swearing, cursing, Sabbath-breaking, neglect and contempt of Gospel ordinances, mocking of piety and of religious exercises'.[18]

In 1701 a revised version of the Town Council's rules of the 1620s appeared. The main changes consisted in tightening up restrictions on bad behaviour, imposing a regular system of fines on miscreants and an attempt to maintain the office of student censor. Anyone who stirred up rebellion or sedition was to be expelled; this decree, possibly reflecting the continued threat of Jacobitism, was due to the intervention of the Privy Council. In addition to the earlier strictures against offences like swearing and drinking, students were prohibited from throwing things at glass windows, spoiling or abusing the walls, seats, desks etc., throwing stones or snowballs and playing at dice (this last said to be a vice which had lately entered the College). Again it is doubtful whether this restatement of the rules had much effect. In 1704 the Town Council lodged a complaint and delivered it to the Principal: 'The Counsell taking to ther considderatione that of late the good order and discipline of the Colledge is much decayed and the power and authoritie of the regents is by many of the schollars not deuly regairded, wherby severall disorders are committed which does exceedingly reflect upon the government of the Colledge. In considderatione wherof the Counsell appoynts the magistrats to meitt with the ministers of Edinburgh and the principall of the Colledge, being now in the beginning of his office, to consult and advyse what proper methods may be agreed towards the re-establishing of order and discipline in the said Colledge'.

This decline has been attributed, in part at least,[19] to a change in the type of regent. Earlier in the century regents had been young men anxious to secure a patron who would provide them with a parish. In the last quarter of the century they were often sons of landed families or wealthy merchants who had no considerations of career to inhibit unruly behaviour.

Most of the information given so far has been gleaned from official records, but perhaps the most intimate glimpses of what studying was like in the seventeenth century come from the student notebooks of 'dictates', consisting of notes taken down from the lecturers or regents, who spoke at dictation speed and in Latin. Each notebook generally contains several sets of lecture notes which frequently correspond to a year's course. Many of the sets of notes tail off, either because the student did not attend the final lectures or because the regent did not manage to complete his lectures before the end of the year.

The early notebooks are much longer than those of the second half of the century, and are often commentaries on Aristotle, in a very stereotyped form which shows clearly the influence of disputation as a method of teaching. Usually the master begins with a summary of the book or section he is about to discuss, and then proposes a series of questions, each of which is answered in turn. The answers consist of carefully numbered points which are subdivided and, before moving on to the next point, the master lists objections, each with replies. Even when notebooks cease to be commentaries on Aristotle and the content of the lectures changes, the form in which they are delivered lingers on, and is still to be seen in the notebooks of the 1690s.

This method of teaching was of course extremely slow and tedious. Moreover, the increasing availability of printed texts in the seventeenth century meant that it was no longer true, as it had been in earlier times, that students could become acquainted with Aristotle and other authors only through the master summarising and commenting on the texts. Frequent attempts were made by the various Commissions appointed to visit the Universities during the seventeenth century to stop the practice of dictating lectures, but they were unsuccessful, and dictation continued until the end of the regenting system in 1708 and indeed beyond.

The notebooks suggest that, despite the regulations, students were fairly adept at avoiding tedious dictation sessions, for they show that sets of notes were frequently passed on from one generation of students to the next. In several of them names of owners other than the student who actually wrote down the notes appear on the fly leaves or endpapers. For instance, in the dictates on physics by John Wishart, 1680,[20] the names Jacobus Cranston and Robert Rutherford appear on the endpapers. Cranston was the student who wrote the lectures down in 1680, but there is no record of a Robert Rutherford in the Matriculation Rolls until 1688, so presumably the notes were used by Rutherford eight years after Cranston had written them. Another set of dictates by John Wishart, also dated 1680,[21] bears on the endpaper the name of Adam Scott, who graduated in 1691. Dictates by Andrew Massie which were taken down by James Hamilton in the period from 1684 to 1687[22] contain a note to say that they were owned by Patrick Russell in 1694, while dictates on ethics from the lectures of William Law which were taken down by John Smith in 1696 were subsequently the property of Andrew Berry in 1700.[23]

It is possible that notes may even have been sold. Certainly this was the practice at St Andrews, for Alexander and Kenneth Mackenzie, who were there from 1711 to 1716 are on record as having purchased sets of lecture notes,[24] and the casual way in which their transactions are recorded suggests that the selling of dictates was more or less normal. The student would be fairly safe in acquiring sets of notes by gift or sale, because regents did little in the way of bringing their lectures up to date. Quite frequently a set of lecture notes from a particular regent is exactly duplicated a few years later. Thus the lectures by Thomas Craufurd on Aristotle's *Physics*, given in 1653,[25] were repeated in 1661,[26] and those of Andrew Massie on the Cartesian system of philosophy appeared in 1682[27] and 1690.[28] It is hard to believe that a set of notes taken down by Robert Colt in 1639[29] would still be useful in 1683, yet there are scribblings and doodles at the end bearing that date.

The Town Council, watchful as always concerning possible misconduct by students, from time to time inspected students' notebooks; there is an act of the council for February 1626, ordaining two visitations to the college by the council yearly in December and June, when the scholars' books were to be examined.

Those students who did attend lectures had various ways of relieving the tedium. Many of the notebooks contain doodles, some of them quite elaborate. Large decorated initial capitals, rather as in medieval manuscripts, are a frequent occurrence. In one particular set of dictates, taken down by Archibald Flint in 1672 and 1673,[30] there are illustrations of student games, a regent lecturing (possibly the student's own regent, James Pillans), and a man firing a gun.[31] The games illustrated are billiards, tennis, football and archery, and we have evidence that all of these were played by seventeenth-century students, although at times the Town Council tried to restrict such activities, either because they were taking up too much time or because they resulted in damage to University property.

However, on the whole the aims of Scottish university education – to produce pious and useful members of society – probably made a serious impact on the students. Several of the lecture notes contain sermon jottings interspersed with the lectures: for instance, the notes taken down by

Edward Lewis in 1686 and 1689[32] and those taken down by Robert Kirk in 1660.[33] As well as bits of sermons, Kirk's dictates have at the end a list of moral maxims under the heading 'Advices to my self 1671'.

A good summing up of the ideals of the seventeenth-century Scottish university education can be found in a set of lecture notes taken down in 1699 in Glasgow,[34] which could apply to any Scottish university in the period. Both teachers and students had responsibilities. The teacher should be a good man and have skill in teaching: he should have a fatherly concern for his pupils, should recognise their various abilities, have patience and wield discipline. In turn the pupil should live a Christian life, have a love of learning, show respect and obedience to his teachers and keep away from harmful books. For both teachers and pupils the primary requisite was that they should live moral, Christian lives – a clue to the priorities in seventeenth-century Scottish university education, which are stressed again and again both in the various Commission and University records and in the repeated claims made by the regents that the most important part of philosophy is ethics and that man's highest aim is to love God.

The order of the answers to the question, 'How is one to discern a pupil's ability?' is revealing, showing what the regents were striving most to cultivate. The list is as follows: (1) The main sign of ability is *memoria*, followed by (2) *imitatio*, (3) an enquiring mind, (4) modesty, (5) a desire for learning, (6) a thorough assimilation of knowledge. Clearly memory was the most important because the system was based on the dictation of notes, whose arguments the students had to be able to master for the examination by disputation, and various aids were recommended to the student in committing things to memory. Among other recommendations the student was advised to meditate on what he had read, to avoid all haste in reading and to study between breakfast and lunch (which was considered the best time for concentration). *Imitatio* probably came into its own more in the disputations, when pupils used the syllogistic method or argument they had been taught in the logic course.

Religion was thought to be the foundation of success in all studies, while diligence and hard work were also necessary. Finally, the aims of disputation were to reveal truth, strengthen memory, give confidence and enable Christians to argue against enemies of their faith: a fair assessment of what Edinburgh set out to achieve in the seventeenth century. And, although the various exploits of the students which have been described would perhaps seem to suggest that the University was not entirely successful in achieving the aims of its education, we must remember that only the aberrations from the norm were considered worthy of comment in contemporary records. It is probable that, in the case of the majority of students, Edinburgh's education aims were realised.

REFERENCES

1. In addition to the sources mentioned in the following notes, attention is drawn to these MSS in EUL: Extracts from the City Records relating to the University of Edinburgh 1563–1779 (EUL – Dc.5.5) and Collection of Papers illustrative of the History and Constitution of the University of Edinburgh 1611–1742, 2 vols. (EUL – Dc.1.4); and to the following printed works: *Evidence oral and documentary taken and received by the Commissioners appointed by His Majesty George IV, July 23, 1826 ... for visiting the Universities of Scotland*, vol. 1: Edinburgh (London 1837); Andrew Dalzel, *History of the University of Edinburgh*, 2 vols. (Edinburgh 1862); Alexander Morgan (ed.), *Charters, Statutes and Acts of the Town Council and the Senatus 1583–1858* (Edinburgh 1937).

2. Grant, ii, 471.

3. Morgan (op. cit., 58), thinks this a report on practice rather than an innovation.

4. cf. Professor Forbes's article, pp.31, 34.

5. Craufurd, 57 sqq.

6. Horn, 30.

7. Craufurd, 116.

8. cf. Henrietta Tayler, *The Seven Sons of the Provost* (Edinburgh 1949).

9. W. Croft Dickinson, *Two Students at St Andrews 1711–1716* (Edinburgh and London 1952).

10. Craufurd, 33–4, 42, 55.

11. ibid., 31, 37, 42, 128.

12. Bower, i, 122.

13. Grant, op. cit., ii, 478.

14. Alexander Monro, *Presbyterian Inquisition as was lately practised against the Professors of the Colledge of Edinburgh 1690* (London 1691).

15. EUL MS Dc.5.122.

16. *Extracts from the Records of the Burgh of Edinburgh 1681–89*, xl–xli, 5, 250; *Book of the Old Edinburgh Club*, xvi, 106, 172–3.

17. 8 October 1691, in Collection of papers illustrative of the history and constitution of the University, EUL MS Dc.1.4.

18. *Acts of the General Assembly of the Church of Scotland 1638–1842* (Church Law Society, Edinburgh 1843) 241, 261.

19. Horn, 32.

20. EUL MS Dk.5.27.

21. EUL MS Gen. 690D.

22. EUL MS La.III.725.

23. EUL MS Dc.8.53

24. W. Croft Dickinson, op. cit.

25. EUL MS Dc.5.122.

26. EUL MS Dc.5.55.

27. EUL MS Dc.6.23; Dc.5.115.
28. EUL MS Dc.7.92.
29. EUL MS Dc.6.53.
30. EUL MS Dc.6.4–5.
31. These are discussed in Charles P. Finlayson, 'Illustrations of Games by a seventeenth-century Edinburgh Student', *Scot. Hist. Rev.*, xxxvii (1958), 1–10.
32. EUL MS 2075.
33. EUL MS Dc.8.114.
34. GUL MS Gen. 69.

Seventeenth-Century Students and their Books

JONQUIL BEVAN

Readers of Dr Shepherd's essay may wonder if seventeenth-century Edinburgh students had books at all, for she has shown that most students arrived at University at an age when they might be expected to be more interested in footballs than in books. They were then taught by an already antiquated system which had originally been expressly designed to do away with any need for individual students to have printed books. Armed with a set of dictates and a good memory a student had little need of more. Yet increasingly, as the century progressed, some at least of the students showed a determination to own or at least have access to books for themselves.

Edinburgh University had been fortunate in the possession of a library from its foundation. Clement Litill had left several hundred theological books to the Kirk and Town of Edinburgh in 1580 and this collection was subsequently passed by the Town to its new College. In the early days this University Library was not open to students. It was 'kept in a private chamber by the Principal' until, as a result of donations, it grew too big. It was then transferred to 'the higher public hall' where it remained the Principal's responsibility; in 1626 the Principal 'had alloted to him 180 merks a-year for the charges of an servant, and for buying of coals, to give dry air for the preservation of the volumes.'[1] In 1635, however, the Library's administration was completely changed. The records of the Town Council tell us that in that year the first University Librarian was appointed and it was decided that the Library 'may be verie proffitable to all students' and that it should be 'patent [open] to all students who salbe immatriculat.'[2] As the new Librarian was obliged to maintain a fire in the Library from October to February there must have been more reasons than one for rejoicing in this newly ácquired privilege. At first, however, few students seem to have taken advantage of it. From 1636 all readers had to be formally admitted, swearing to keep the Library's new rules and signing their names in the register, from which it appears that few if any of the readers were students until the last quarter of the century.[3] It is hard to tell how rigid (or conscientious)

Librarians were about enforcing the admission rule; from 1650 to 1662 there is a gap in the register (explained largely by the Cromwellian occupation of Scotland, which the Librarian's note of 1662 describes as *tempore belli* [in time of war]) and there is another gap 1664–7. But during the 1670s it became common for some students to sign the register shortly after graduating (presumably these new M.A.s were continuing their studies, probably most of them as Divinity students) and from 1682 onwards a steady number of undergraduate students was admitted to the Library each year. These undergraduates were a minority; some were young noblemen but others were obviously particularly promising scholars. There was, for example, John Horsley, later to write *Britannia Romana* (1732), a work which Professor Stuart Piggott describes as 'magisterial'.[4] Horsley matriculated in 1699, having gone straight into second-year in 1698 aged thirteen. He signed the Library register on 7 May 1700 and graduated in April 1701. Throughout the seventeenth century no reader was allowed to borrow from the Library but clearly by the end of the century at least this rule was disregarded. On 16 June 1704 a memoir was presented to the Town Council 'conteaning severall complaints against the masters and students of the Colledge', among them the complaint that 'a great many bookes are lent out and kept out of the Liberarie contrar to the Lawes of the Liberarie', a situation not regularised until 1708, when borrowing was restricted to masters of the college and 'to such students as shall procure warrands under their own Masters hands for such books as they are to borrow'.[5]

By this time the Library had moved into a new building, usually referred to as the 1642 building although it was not completed until 1646. This building ran east and west; there was one storey to the south but as seen from the north it had 'an arched sunk storey and principal floor with a leaden roof.'[6] The Library was in the upper storey and it must have looked very handsome. Thomas Morer, who visited it in 1688, mentions the 'Donors Names set over [the bookcases] in Golden Letters' and in 1689 the Provost's wife, Lady Prince, presented a number of portraits 'for the ornamentation of the library': the first five Jameses, Queen Mary, James VI, Charles I and Charles II and their queens, and Mr Ramsay, Rector of the University.[7] Unfortunately, it must also be recorded that from 1687 'the arched sunk storey' beneath the Library was occupied by the printing-presses of Mrs Anderson, the Boadicea of Scottish printing. Mrs Anderson was a notorious monopolist who defended her position by fierce litigation. Among her privileges was that of Printer to the College and in this character she successfully persuaded the Town Council that 'the most convenient place within the college wherein the said applicant desires to erect her printing presses will be below the bibliotheck'.[8] It may have been convenient for Mrs Anderson, but it can hardly have been so for readers in the Library, for the noise of the presses must have penetrated clearly to the room above.

In 1698 the theological students decided to form a separate Library of their own and opened their Donations Book[9] with the following words:

> The Students of Theology in the Coledge of Edinburgh in the year 1698 Collected amongst themselves at the desire of Mr George Campbell their Professor, the sum of three hounder seventy six pounds, fifteen shillings Scots mony, intending their by to found a Liberary for themselves and their successors; which mony was sent to Holland & London for such books as were thought needful.

The donations which follow are principally gifts of money from various ministers. But there are also donations of books from Edinburgh and London printers and booksellers (including Mrs Anderson!), from University officials, and from some students. At least two of the books presented to this Library by students before 1700 are still in the Library of the Faculty of Divinity in New College.

So much for the public provision of books. But what could students expect in the way of private supplies? At one extreme were the wealthy noblemen. James Graham, the famous fifth Earl of Montrose, went to Glasgow at the age of twelve to be prepared for the College of Glasgow; 'thither he journeyed with a valet, two pages in scarlet, a quantity of linen and plate, a selection from his father's library, and his favourite white pony. . . . He seems to have read in Xenophon and Seneca, and an English translation of Tasso; but his favourite book, then and long afterwards, was Raleigh's *History of the World*, the splendid folio of the first edition'.[10] That was in 1624. A change in family arrangements brought about his migration to St Andrews, where, as a student, he golfed, won a silver medal for archery and hunted regularly, but also studied Greek and continued the Latin classics, making notes in his copies of Caesar and Lucan. He had his copies of Buchanan and Barclay's *Argenis* specially bound, and he subscribed for the *Travels* of William Lithgow.[11] On the whole Edinburgh did not accommodate this kind of aristocratic luxury; but some of its students were aristocrats and many came from backgrounds of solid learning and were in a position (if their parents allowed!) to benefit from 'a selection from his father's library.' Robert Napier gave three books to Edinburgh University Library in 1612, one of them a book of mathematics stamped on its title-page with the *ex libris* of his father, John Napier of Merchiston, the inventor of logarithms. Henry Charteris, Principal from 1598 to 1620, was the eldest son of a renowned Edinburgh printer; as Henry chose not to follow in his father's footsteps, the family printing and bookselling business passed to the second son, Robert. Henry's son, Robert's nephew, Laurence Charteris, was Professor of Divinity 1675–82. It is hard to believe that he had not grown up in a household surrounded by books. There are other family ties between the book-trade and the University. The Regent Andrew Stevinson was the son-in-law of the bookseller James Cathkin (died 1631). Thomas Craufurd, Regent, Professor of Mathematics from 1640, and author of the first *History of the University*, was the son-in-law of the celebrated book-dealer Andrew Hart. The inventories of Edinburgh printers and booksellers of the seventeenth century in the Record of Testaments show that they had varied and large stocks of books available to their clients and the customary lists of debts owing to the dead show that the typical clients of these Edinburgh book-dealers were ministers, writers, regents, merchants, gentry and noblemen: the sort of men whose sons customarily went to the Town's College. The sons of these fathers must all have enjoyed the advantages of access to books in their own families.

Seventeenth-century Edinburgh University produced a surprising number of graduates who were to become important book-collectors; the libraries of some of them are important research collections to this day. Many of the books of William Drummond of Hawthornden (over 700) and the whole library of James Nairn (1,838 volumes) are in Edinburgh University Library; Robert Leighton's 1,363 volumes established the Bibliotheca Leightoniana at Dunblane; Robert Sibbald gave a nucleus of 100 books from his collection of 8,000 volumes to found the Library of the Royal College of Physicians; John Gray left 900 books to the Library he founded at Haddington.

The library of William Drummond of Hawthornden has been studied by R. H. MacDonald.[12] Drummond (1585–1649) was the nephew of the poet William Fowler and inherited books from his uncle, whose poetic reputation he was himself to equal, if not surpass. He was an inveterate book-buyer. MacDonald lists some 1,400 books which belonged to Drummond and finds traces in the collection of the sort of book the poet would have learned to appreciate while a student: 'Drummond's collection of Latin books is the heart of his library, and it is significant that he continued to buy and read academic books long after he left the Tounis Colledge.'[13] MacDonald asserts that 'Drummond seems to have begun his book-buying as soon as he graduated from Edinburgh'[14] and goes on to cite the list of 'Bookes red by me anno 1606', the year after Drummond's laureation in 1605. But this is far from proving, or even suggesting, that Drummond did not read or own books before this date. In 1606 the 'Bookes red by me' numbered forty-two and at least half of these were books Drummond owned (he may have owned more); in 1607 'bookes red be me' amount to nineteen, of which thirteen can be traced to his ownership; he records twenty-nine for 1608, of which sixteen can be traced; in 1609 the list goes up to forty-one and, of these, twenty-three titles can still be identified among his books, some in more than one copy; and so on to 1614. Did Drummond really plunge into a life-time's love-affair with books as a graduate of twenty with *no* previous experience of book-ownership? At least he cannot have remembered his student days as a barren intellectual wilderness, for his repeated donations of books to his old University illustrate a continuing relationship of mutual affection and respect between Drummond and the 'Tounis Colledge'.

Robert Leighton, by contrast, left his books as a single collection to found a Library after his death: the celebrated Bibliotheca Leightoniana of Dunblane. Leighton (1611 – 84) was the son of a puritan who suffered at the hands of the authorities in England and sent his son to be educated at Edinburgh University and trained up 'in the true presbyterian form'. During his first year Leighton composed a satirical comment on Provost Aikenhead, who had refused the University a holiday:

> That which his name imports is falsely said,
> That of the oaken wood his head is made;
> For why, if it had been composed so,
> His flaming nose had fired it long ago.

This was a single fall from grace, it seems; young Leighton wrote to his father that Principal Adamson and the Regents did not think it 'so heinous an offence as he himself did justly think it' and one of his Professors later wrote to his father to congratulate him 'on having a son on whom Providence had made him abundant compensation for his suffering'.[15] Leighton laureated in 1631 in Robert Ranken's class, together with James Pillans, the future Regent. After a spell of travel in France, Leighton returned to Scotland to become, successively, minister at Newbattle, Principal of Edinburgh University (1653 – 62), Bishop of Dunblane and Archbishop of Glasgow. Throughout these changes he retained the respect of his fellow-countrymen (Bishop Burnet says that during the twenty years of his ministry and principalship he lived in the highest reputation that any man had in his time in Scotland); it was clear that he believed that religion did not consist in external matters, whether of government or worship. He did not wish his Library to become a monument to himself and the fact that his nephew (at his own expense) built a special library building to house it at Dunblane, thus perpetuating the Bishop's memory, was contrary to the terms of his will. The theses of Leighton's student years are preserved at

Dunblane; W. J. Couper remarks 'there is something pathetic about the fact that Leighton preserved these ephemeral prints, and that they accompanied him in all his wanderings. The last has his name among the forty-one classmates of his year who were then "adolescentes magisterii candidati".
. . . Another relic of those student days is to be found in the *Stoieiosis*, Edinburgh, 1627, by John Adamson. The little book is a catechism of Christian instruction designed for the use of students, and its author was the Principal of the University. Leighton's copy carries his initials at the end, and bears evidence of having been in frequent use. A book he may have acquired at the same time is William Struthers's *Christian Considerations*, Edinburgh, 1629'.[16] Other students during Adamson's Principalship (1623–52) must have had their own copies of *Stoieiosis* from 1627 onwards (second edition 1637); it is prescribed on the title-page 'In usum Academiae Jacobi Regis'.

James Nairn (1629–78) matriculated in 1646 and laureated in 1650. His Regent was Thomas Craufurd and, like Leighton, his Principal was the moderate John Adamson who was acceptable to Presbyterians and Episcopalians alike. Like Leighton, too, Nairn was to be an Episcopalian clergyman, though unlike Leighton he never attained the rank of Bishop. Yet his theological library was larger even than that of his well-travelled contemporary. Nairn made no notes in his books, nor did he even inscribe them with his name or the date. This makes a study of the library of this Edinburgh University benefactor more difficult, and we are fortunate indeed that his books are now undergoing analysis by Mr Murray Simpson.

Next in the chronological order of Edinburgh bibliophiles comes Sir Robert Sibbald (1641–1722), who matriculated in 1656 and laureated in 1659. His class (as he tells us) had several Regents, but the greatest impression was made on him as a student by the Principal, then Robert Leighton. Sibbald has left us, in his *Memoirs*, his own account of his student days:

> I past the Bajon yeer under Mr James Wyseman, who dyed the vacance th[ei]rafter.
> I was Semi under Mr William Forbess, and he dyed the vacance following.
> I was Basler [Bachelor] and Magistrant under Mr William Tweedy, who laureat me July 1659.
> Mr William Tweedy, many yeers before that, had been a regent in St. Andrewes. . . . When he came to us he gave us a paraphrase upon Aristotle his text, which gave many a disgust of him.
> It was my fortune to meet w[ith] Sir Kenelm Digby his discourse of

bodies, and the immortality of the soule, and with Thomas Anglus his
dialogues de mundo, who followeth Sir Kenelm's hypothesis, which
I read with great delight, and became a student of the Atomistick
or crepuscular philosophie. Aristotell his philosophie being then
depraved by the scholastick writters.

Mr Thomas Crawfurd taught th[e]n the Mathematicks, wednesday in
the forenoon.

The Principall of the Coledge, during the five years I studied [he had
a pre-matriculation year, to improve his Latin], was Mr Robert
Lighton, who was first Bishop of Dumblane, upon the restauration of
Charles the 2d, and th[ei]rafter was made Archbishop of Glasco, a
learned and devout man, who had excellent discourses to us in the
Common Hall, sometymes in Latine, sometymes in English, which,
with the blessing of God upon th[e]m, gave me strong inclinations to a
serious and good lyfe. I shunned the playes and divertisements the
other students followed, and read much in my study, for which my
fellowes gave me the name of Diogenes in Dolio [i.e. Diogenes, the
philosopher, in his tub].... From the tyme I entered to the Coledge,
any mony I gott, I did imploy it for buying of books.[17]

From this account we can learn a number of things. Young Sibbald had the
freedom of choice to study in his room, when his classmates were playing
games, and though he was teased for his choice, it seems to have been
accepted. Nor was the book-buying Sibbald unduly out-of-the-way;
although his conversion to a branch of modern physics was the result of his
private reading of Kenelm Digby and Thomas White, he can say that 'many'
in his class of 1658 had 'a disgust' at poor William Tweedy's old-fashioned
Aristotelianism. A little later he tells us that it was due to Leighton's
influence that he did not study for the ministry, as his mother wished. He
saw that the Church was then divided by bitter strife and 'the impressions I
retained from Mr Leighton his discourses, disposed me to affect charity for
all good men of any persuasion, and I preferred a quiet lyfe, wherein I might
not be ingadged in factions of Church or State'.[18] Accordingly, instead of the
ministry, Sibbald chose medicine, a career which was to lead him to the
utmost distinction, the foundation of the Royal College of Physicians, and
the establishment of his famous library, for which he had so early laid the
foundations.

John Gray (1646–1717) was another of Leighton's admirers, though of a
different kind. He matriculated in 1660 under the regency of James Pillans
(a former classmate of Leighton's) and laureated in 1664. Leighton
demitted the Principalship halfway through Gray's time as a student, but

Gray again came under his influence when he went, in 1672, as an Episcopalian preacher to Glasgow, where Leighton was then Archbishop. In 1684 he became minister of Aberlady, but he was ejected as an Episcopalian in 1689; he retired to Haddington, although he continued for the rest of his life to describe himself as 'minister of Aberlady'. In most of his 900 volumes Gray has written 'Ex Libris Jo. Gray, Aberladie. Summa religionis imitari quem colis [the sum of religion is to imitate Him you worship].' The Latin motto is Leighton's, and is inscribed by him in some of the books in the Bibliotheca Leightoniana. It is hard to tell how soon Gray began buying books, but a few, those by Rollock, the first Principal of the University, and perhaps some by Struthers, may date from his student days, as may some of the books by Erasmus which he owned.

Together with John Gray in Regent James Pillans's 1660–4 class was John Lauder, later Lord Fountainhall. Through most of his life Lauder kept memoirs and journals of both private and public events. He also kept careful accounts, in which his considerable expenditure on books can be related to his other disbursements, and he compiled catalogues of the books he owned. Eight months after his laureation the young graduate left Edinburgh for France in order to study civil law. He kept a notebook while he was in France, writing in one end of it an account of his experiences and using the other end for accounts and for lists of the books he bought. The manuscript of this diary is in our Library.[19] Though it is not strictly to our purpose, it is perhaps permissible to mention that the diary gives brief glimpses of the Edinburgh student life Lauder had so lately left. Young Lauder was staunchly Protestant, and records his opinion of French Roman Catholicism in strong terms; he was so infuriated by an Augustinian sermon on the Virgin Mary that he was prompted to remember the salutary discipline of his old teacher: 'It will not be an unseasonable drollery whiles to counterfit our Regent Mr James [Pillans], if it be well tymed; whow when he would have sein any of his scollers playing the Rogue he would take them a syde & fall to admonish them, thus. I think ye have forgot ye are *sub ferula* under the rod, ye most know that Im your Master not only to instruct you but to chastize you; & w[ith] a ton[e] [i.e., raising his voice,] do ye ever think for to make a man Sir [?] no, I promise you, no.' Later Lauder remarks 'We must never forget ... our sports that night we studied the stars w[ith] Mr James' and he remembers with amusement his Regent's 'griveous hat'. From the lists of books at the end of this manuscript we can calculate that in the year and a half of his French travels (March 1665–? August 1666) Lauder bought about ninety-three books. He already owned books before he went abroad, although we do not know what they were. Another book-list, a long and detailed one, complete with dates, prices and notes about acquisition, is headed 'Since my returne to Scotland from travelling, which was on the 9 November 1667 [he went on from France to the Low Countries], I have got or bought the following books. As for the books I had ather before my parture or which I acquired and bought in forraine parts, I have a full and perfit Catalogue of them in my little black-skinned book'.[20] The books he bought in France were mainly law books, but he also bought some Latin classics, some history, geography, 'Machiavellus' and some French fiction; he had hired some French romances – perhaps an early example of the lending-library system – and he bought some too. Throughout his life Lauder was to remain an enthusiastic book-collector.

It can be seen that it is not easy to find examples of books which Edinburgh graduates certainly owned while they were still students, although I think there is enough evidence to show that the notably bookish – the Leightons and Sibbalds – clearly began their book-collecting while they were still at University. But the men I have described so far were all, in their ways, exceptional. What of the ordinary student? Mr Murray Simpson has drawn my attention to an unambitious little catalogue of books owned by a student right at the end of the century; I suspect it is typical of many student collections.

The little catalogue occurs on a blank page in the Dictates of Regent William Law, written by John Smith who graduated from Law's class in 1697.[21] As was usual, once he had laureated his magistrand class Law began the new bajans' class in the following year, and in the year after, 1699, a number of additional students were admitted *supervenientes anno secundo*, that is, they were allowed to go straight into second year. One of this group was the future historian, John Horsley, mentioned above, and another was Andrew Berry, who acquired John Smith's note-book and wrote in it 'And: Berry his book anno Domini 1700 July 14th'. Also scribbled in Andrew's book are the names of Patrick, John and Daniel Campbell, who were all in his class. Did the Campbell boys 'borrow' the book from Andrew or did they perhaps have joint ownership? Whether legally or not, it is Patrick Campbell who has used the note-book to write 'A Catalogue of my books Patrick Campbell'.[22] Someone else has written alongside a sarcastic parody in Latin: 'Catalogus Librorum Patricii Campbell Empt. Edinburgi Typis Georgii Mosman' (Catalogue of Books of Patrick Campbell, bought in Edinburgh and printed by George Mosman). The Latin list continues with three joke Latin titles which display a timelessly school-boyish lavatory humour. George Mosman, to whose press these invented books are credited, was an important Edinburgh printer from 1690 to 1707 or 1708 and the official printer to the Church of Scotland. Perhaps his important position caused him to be singled out by the joker, or perhaps he had attracted attention by presenting to the infant Theological Library, on 6 January 1699, a copy of every book or pamphlet he had printed. Another possibility is that he really was the printer of one of the books on Patrick Campbell's genuine list, and it may be that this is what had suggested his name.

The genuine 'Catalogue of my books Patrick Campbell' is as follows (I have supplied the numbering):

1. a gilded bible
2. pedemontanii de Se[c]retis
3. a latine plasm [psalm?] book in prose
4. Colloquia Erasmi
5. a Xenophon in greek
6. another book of Seven languages
7. an hibreu grammer
8. a whole course of philosophy viz Logicks metaphysicks Ethicks pneunatick [sic] and physicks
9. Ricenii compendium Theologie
10. also ane Ethicks in f[olio]:
11. ane Inglish bible

The first item may have been in Latin; it cannot have been in English, or else the description of No.11 would not have been appropriate. No.2 is Piemontese Alessio's edition of Hanss Jacob Wecker's *De secretis* (*The Secrets of Art and Nature*, a book of natural history and medicine). Alessio's Latin version was in print from 1559; the title-page of Edinburgh University's 1603 edition reads 'D. ALEXII/PEDEMONTANI/DE SECRETIS/. . .' and it is clearly from the second two lines of such a title-page that Patrick Campbell copied. The fourth item, the *Colloquia* of Erasmus, was a popular Latin school book which Patrick probably owned before he came to University. Nos.5, 7, 8 and 10 would have been of use to him during his University studies. The vagueness of his description of No.6 suggests that he had not made much progress with it. Item 9 is L. Rijssenius' *Summa theologiae elenticae completa,* of which George Mosman had published an edition in 1692. The title of this book means something like *A Complete Summary [or Compendium] of Theological Refutation* and it must be the book that is mentioned in the Laws Enacted by the Faculty and Senatus for 8 October 1691: 'That for exercise on the Lords day the three superior classes are to learn Ryssens compend of Theology'. No doubt 'Ryssens compend' is therefore a book, like Adamson's *Stoieiosis* earlier in the century, that all students of that generation were expected to own.

What conclusions, if any, can be drawn from such scattered evidence over so long a period? Education at Edinburgh University in the seventeenth century was not just the soulless grind it is sometimes thought to have been. There was room in the same class for Andrew Berry and the Campbell boys, hoping to scrape through with second-hand lecture notes (though none of them laureated!) and also for John Horsley, precociously admitted to read in the Library at fourteen. A bright boy could read in his study, go star-gazing with his Regent, or attend voluntary classes in mathematics. Perhaps the very fact that the official system was rigid and old-fashioned spurred the livelier-minded boys on to independent study and helped to bring about the remarkable interest in Libraries and book-collecting that seems to characterise so many seventeenth-century Edinburgh graduates.

ACKNOWLEDGMENTS

I would like to express my gratitude for the help and kindness of Miss J. M. Barrie, Professor Gordon Donaldson, Dr John Hall, Mr J. V. Howard, Miss M. H. Robertson, Dr Christine Shepherd and Mr Murray Simpson.

REFERENCES

1. Craufurd, 92, 110.
2. *Extracts from Records of Burgh of Edinburgh 1626–41*, 158–9.
3. EUL MS Da.2.1.
4. *Ruins in a Landscape* (Edinburgh 1976) 144.
5. Morgan, 154–5, 166.
6. Horn, 12.
7. C. P. Finlayson and S. M. Simpson, 'The Library of the University of Edinburgh: the Early Period 1580–1710', *Library History*, i; D. Talbot Rice and P. McIntyre, *University Portraits* (Edinburgh 1957) xi.
8. [A. R. Turnbull] *Edinburgh and its College Printers* (Edinburgh 1973).
9. EUL, New College Library, Donations Book 1698–1965.
10. John Buchan, *Montrose* (London 1928) 35–6.
11. ibid., 37–8.
12. R. H. MacDonald, ed., *The Library of Drummond of Hawthornden* (Edinburgh 1971).
13. ibid., 20.
14. ibid., 46.
15. *DNB*.
16. W. J. Couper, *Bibliotheca Leightoniana* (Glasgow 1917) 19.
17. F. P. Hett, *The Memoirs of Sir Robert Sibbald* (London 1932) 53–5.
18. ibid., 56.
19. EUL MS La.III.270.
20. *Journals of Sir John Lauder of Fountainhall* (Scot. Hist. Soc.), 283.

21. EUL MS Dc.8.53.
22. ibid., fo.5.

OTHER SOURCES
EUL, *Exhibition Catalogue no.3 : Benefactors of the Library in Five Centuries* (Edinburgh 1963).
EUL, *Library Guides 17 : Special Collections of Printed Books in Edinburgh University Library* (Edinburgh 1978).
EUL, 'Names of Persons Admitted to the Use of the Library 1636–1753', MS Da.2.1.
EUL, New College Library: Donations Book 1698–1965.
C.P.Finlayson, *Clement Litill and his Library* (Edinburgh 1980).
W.Forbes Gray, *Catalogue of the Library of John Gray of Haddington* (Haddington 1929).
John Lauder, 'Diary of Travels in France', MS La.III.270.
George Macdonald, 'John Horsley, Scholar and Gentleman', *Arch. Aeliana* 4th ser, 10 (1933) 8.
Thomas Thomson and D.Laing, 'The Wills of Thomas Bassandyne and Other Printers in Edinburgh, 1577–1687', *The Bannatyne Miscellany*, 2 (1836) 185–296.

Philosophy and Science Teaching
in the Seventeenth Century

ERIC G. FORBES

The question is too seldom asked whether the flowering of learning in Scotland in the eighteenth century could have blossomed had the soil not been well prepared in the seventeenth. Surely not all of its manifestations were imported from France or from England, as the majority of Enlightenment historians would have one believe? There is certainly no reason to suppose that what was being taught in Oxford and Cambridge[1] had any influence upon the curricula at the Scottish universities, perhaps especially during the periods of Presbyterian ascendancy before the Restoration of King Charles II in 1660 and after the accession of William of Orange in 1689. Much more significant was the close contact between Scotland and the Netherlands; for throughout the century there was a large number of Scottish students at the Dutch universities, chiefly Leiden, where they generally went to study theology, medicine and law.[2] Not surprisingly, therefore, one can detect strong affinities between Scottish and Dutch university teaching. The theses for disputation at Leiden, for example, are very similar to the Scottish graduation theses, while most of the authorities whose works were debated are the same as those quoted by the Scottish university teachers. There was also a similarity of purpose in the university teaching in the two countries, each of which required educated men for the professions. Since rules of action were then regarded as being more important than metaphysical truths, a knowledge of practical ethics was essential whereas that of metaphysics was not; which is one good reason why the latter subject did not become an established part of the university teaching curriculum in either country before the mid-seventeenth century.

The primary sources of information about seventeenth-century Scottish university teaching are dictates (that is, manuscript student notebooks), printed graduation theses, official university and commission reports, and faculty minutes. Unpublished library accession lists, diaries and correspondence are of lesser, but by no means negligible, significance in this connection.[3]

The graduation theses, produced for the annual graduation ceremony at the end of the standard four-year course, naturally relate to the subject-matter of that course. Thus they include theses on logic, metaphysics, ethics, natural philosophy, and less frequently mathematics, geometry or theoretical astronomy. Between 1640 and 1675 they often appeared as broadsheets, but before and after this period they are in book form. The advent of the professorial system of instruction in the eighteenth century,[4] under which students were free to read whichever subjects they pleased, coupled with the lack of any financial incentive to professors to encourage students to graduate, was primarily responsible for class theses ceasing in the eighteenth century.

The paucity of works by the individual regents is largely accounted for by the fact that these men were usually rather young. Later writings by some of these gentlemen cannot unfortunately be taken as evidence of what they taught their students while employed as regents. It is evident from the frequent appearance of regents' names as signatures on the accounts of how the library funds were spent, that they themselves were responsible for deciding which books were bought for their courses. For this reason, their accession lists can be of greater historical significance than mere records of donations, though in neither case is there any guarantee that books in the library were widely read.

The following table indicates the respective distribution of these sources with regard to each Scottish university, and the time-span covered:

(a) DICTATES

	Logic (1611–1723)	Metaphysics (1637–1723)	Ethics (1612–1723)	Natural Philosophy (1613–1704)
Aberdeen	16	7	11	14
Edinburgh	25	16	24	37
Glasgow	29	21	15	17
St Andrews	13	10	11	8
Total	83	54	61	76

(b) GRADUATION THESES

Aberdeen	(1616–1712)	63
Edinburgh	(1599–1705)	68
Glasgow	(1646–1708)	8
St Andrews	(1603–1703)	37
Total		176

These figures show that Edinburgh University is most strongly represented in both respects; Glasgow University is well represented by dictates but very poorly indeed by theses; Aberdeen King's College and Marischal College, St Leonard's and St Salvator's at St Andrews, are fairly equally represented in dictates, but Aberdeen predominates in theses. What is, of course, here being compared are the numbers of dictates and theses *pertaining to* each university, and not those of dictates *preserved in* archives and repositories in each of the university cities. A separate breakdown with regard to location serves to confirm that the University Library and the National Library of Scotland in Edinburgh contain between them almost as many dictates as the other three cities together; and it can be presumed that the proportion would be enhanced by other notebooks, as yet unidentified, in the archives of the Register House in Edinburgh.[5] Edinburgh's libraries are, moreover, by far the richest repositories of graduation theses.

The first major statement of educational policy for all four Scottish universities was that of the Commissioners appointed by the General Assembly of the Church of Scotland to visit these institutions from 1639 to 1643. Their specific recommendations – heavily biased in favour of Aristotelian writings – were not followed, although the courses actually taught were not so very different in their content. The university authorities seem to have resented such governmental interference in their affairs,[6] and were thus encouraged to produce their own joint course. A number of schemes were duly proposed, but apparently seldom implemented. Nevertheless, the rules laid down by commissioners and masters at the respective universities serve to reveal the differing preferences at various times. For example, detailed proposals put forward in the year 1687 to a Visitation Committee by the masters at St Andrews reveal a distinct break with the Aristotelian tradition of philosophy, although the only authority mentioned by name was Descartes.[7] Another compatible feature of this report was its much stronger emphasis on metaphysics rather than on logic. Such changes in content became more marked just before the turn of the century, yet the actual structure of the curriculum remained remarkably static; the first year being spent mainly on Greek, the second on logic, the third on ethics, and the fourth on physics, with other courses being fitted into this framework in a variety of ways.

The emphasis on logic as a basic component of a student's training was a legacy from scholasticism; thus it is not surprising that the earlier dictates in this subject took the form of commentaries on Aristotle's texts. Almost all of these refer to medieval scholastics, particularly Thomas Aquinas, Duns Scotus and William of Occam, whose own views were discussed along with more recent interpretations of their writings by renaissance Aristotelians[8] like Cardinal Cajetan, Francis Toletus, Petrus Fonseca, Antonius Ruvius, Petrus de Mendoza, Francis LeRees, Franciscus Bonae Spei (*alias* François Crespin), Martin Smiglecki and Bartholomeus Keckermann. In addition to these, however, the regents referred to other commentators whom we nowadays recognise as being more 'modern' in their approach, namely: Iacopo Zabarella, Francis Burgersdijk, Thomas Compton, Caspar Hurtado, Rodrigo de Arriaga, Francisco de Oviedo, David Derodon, Franciscus Suarez, Pontius, the Jesuits of Coimbra, Juan Luis Vives, Bernardino Telesio and Tommasso Campanella. Zabarella's *Opera logica* (Venetii, 1578) contains one of the earliest treatments of our present concept of scientific method.[9] Burgersdijk, in his *Institutionum logicarum libri duo* (Lugduni Batavorum, 1626), sought a compromise between Aristotelian and Ramist logic. The works of the Coimbra writers attempt to fuse the new humanist approach to Aristotle with the long-established scholastic tradition. Vives, a Spanish Jesuit, stressed the empirical origins of useful knowledge. Telesius, before Francis Bacon, emphasised the importance of sense experience in the study of nature. Campanella, whom the Catholic Church imprisoned for heresy, recognised before Descartes the need for developing a system of philosophy on the concept of universal doubt. The influence of Descartes' *Discourse on Method* seems to have made itself strongly felt in Scotland in the 1670s and 1680s.[10]

Notes taken from Gerschom Carmichael's lectures on logic at Glasgow in 1697[11] and 1708[12] are worthy of special mention as containing a clear, concise exposition of the views not only of Bacon and Descartes, but of even more recent philosophers like Nicolas Malebranche and John Locke. Carmichael critically discusses aspects of Locke's *Essay concerning Human Understanding* yet, significantly, has but little to say regarding the syllogism – the 'eternal monument to Aristotle's genius', as Alexander Lunan of King's College, Aberdeen, had earlier described it.[13] George Skene and James Urquhart, later regents at that same college, both praised Locke's writings; but this was not a typical trend.

One safe generalisation which can be drawn from a study of all these logic dictates is that most of the Scottish regents were well aware of the existence of the vast corpus of Aristotelian commentaries and, in the traditional scholastic manner, tried to balance the views of various authorities against each other. Religious differences with, for example, the Spanish Jesuits prevented them from giving wholehearted allegiance to the Coimbran commentators; and their philosophical opposition to the Jesuits on questions such as that of transubstantiation undoubtedly stemmed from their religious commitments. It would also appear that the extent to which discussions on method feature in the seventeenth-century Scottish dictates bears a direct relationship to the emphasis placed upon Aristotle's *Posterior Analytics* as a text in the logic courses.[14] The form and content of the later logic teaching reflect the influences of Burgersdijk and Keckermann, and the library lists of all the universities confirm that the former's works in particular were widely available for consultation.

The teaching of metaphysics was closely bound up with that of logic; as indeed with that of ethics, natural philosophy, and theology as well. Thus, as with the logic dictates and theses, Aristotle and the scholastic commentators determined both the structure and content of the metaphysics courses taught in Scottish universities from the 1640s onwards. Later, lectures came to be separated into metaphysics and pneumatology; the source of this division probably being Burgersdijk's *Institutionum Metaphysicarum libri duo* (Lugduni Batavorum, 1642). Descartes' metaphysics began to infiltrate into the Scottish dictates and theses in the 1660s and to be accepted in the 1670s and 1680s. During the next decade one can detect a movement away from the metaphysics of Descartes and his followers Johannes Clauberg and Antony Legrand, usually (but not invariably) towards Locke. In view, however, of Descartes' well-established dependency upon scholastic philosophy,[15] the significance of this is not very great. The 'cogito ergo sum' concept was criticised by Edinburgh regents such as William Law in 1699[16] on the ground that it was not a unique principle, and scholastic metaphysics with its emphasis on substance, mode and relation is defended as being fundamental to an understanding of Christian dogmas that would otherwise remain incomprehensible. Pneumatology was concerned with the acquisition of ethical knowledge about God and ourselves, through the light of Nature; it was thus opposed to atheism and therefore, in the minds of some regents, to Cartesianism. Carmichael's Glasgow lectures of 1704[17] are thoroughly anti-Cartesian, and many other regents were distrustful by this time of the implications of Descartes' method (e.g. mind-body dualism). A strong distrust of Jesuit teaching is also implicit in the relatively frequent references made to Scottish and English Protestant theologians.

As regards ethics, lectures during the first half of the seventeenth century were mainly commentaries on Aristotle's *Nicomachean Ethics*. Besides those whose names have already been mentioned, the Italian scholastic philosopher Piccolomini, the English theologians William Ames, William Twisse and Richard Baxter, and the Protestant authors William Colville, John Strang and George Mackenzie are cited in favourable terms by different regents.[18] From the 1670s onwards there was a mixed reaction to the *Enchiridion ethicum* and other writings of the Cambridge Platonist

Henry More,[19] but widespread condemnation of the doctrines in Thomas Hobbes's *Leviathan* concerning natural law and the foundations of society. What the regents were opposed to, of course, was Hobbes's materialism with its atheistic and deterministic implications. On the theme of natural law, which formed a substantial part of the ethics teaching, the views of Hugo Grotius, Samuel von Pufendorf and Richard Cumberland are most frequently cited. The main emphasis, however, was placed upon the practical nature of ethics and its usefulness as a guide to life; which probably accounts for there being fewer references to scholastic commentators whose chief concern was with problems of interpretation rather than with that of discovering a practical code of conduct.

A manuscript student notebook of Colin Maclaurin, still in private hands,[20] contains lectures on metaphysics probably dictated to him in 1713 at Glasgow University by Carmichael, and two sets of lectures on ethics. In the second of these, the regent's views regarding natural law are clearly expressed; and he concludes (translated):

> it is clear that knowledge of natural law is not innate to men's minds . . . nor is it inscribed there by nature, as some believe; nor is it to be learnt from the mere consensus of opinion of various races and ages, whether speculative or practical, as others contend; but rather it is to be derived from the nature of things and their uninterrupted course, and a proper use of reason.[21]

This statement may be interpreted to mean that a knowledge of the God-given facts of Nature, coupled to man's application of his innate ability to reason, would lead one to an understanding of moral philosophy – an attitude that would appear to have been fairly typical of what the Scottish regents were accepting around this time, and to some extent justified the practice of introducing students to natural philosophy in the final year of their philosophy course.

Viewed in the context of the overall intellectual developments of the seventeenth century, the natural philosophy dictates constitute the most significant aspect of Scottish university teaching at that time. By studying them, one can explore the impact of the Scientific Revolution on the philosophies of that time, investigate when and in what respects Cartesian science was forced to surrender to Newtonian ideas, witness the effect in practice of Bacon's advocacy of experimental science, and so on.[22] Until the 1660s, the science taught in Scotland was based largely upon scholastic textbooks like Aristotle's *Acroamatic Physics*.[23] The criticisms which the regents made probably derive in the main from the scholastic textbooks of Zabarella, Burgersdijk, Scaliger, Toletus, and the Coimbra commentators[24] – certainly not from the regents' own observations and discoveries! Cartesian physics, which first penetrated the teaching system in the 1650s, was regarded with distrust because of its mechanistic implications. The fear of atheism was also responsible for the regents' dislike of Hobbes's physical theories and of recently revived Epicurean ideas.[25] Nevertheless, by about 1680, Cartesian physics had become accepted; initially, it was taught alongside Aristotelian physics, and later alongside the newer theories of Christian Huygens and Isaac Newton.

What has hitherto escaped the notice of historians of science, and which a recent survey of the dictates and theses has made patently clear, is that there were many exponents of Newtonian science in Scotland at the end of the seventeenth century. Newton's theory of light and colour, known through his three publications in Henry Oldenburg's *Philosophical Transactions* of 1672, 1675 and 1676 and the printed correspondence to which the first of these gave rise, appears in the teaching of John Wishart, William Law, Herbert Kennedy, William Scott, Gilbert McMurdo, Alexander Cockburn, and Charles Erskine of Edinburgh; in that of Gerschom Carmichael of Glasgow; in that of John Buchan, Alexander Fraser, James Urquhart, George Peacock, and William Smith of Aberdeen; and in that of George Martin, Alexander Scrimgeour, and John Craigie of St Andrews. Most of these regents also support Newton's theory of universal gravitation, known through the publication of the first edition of the *Principia* of 1687; four of them (Scott, McMurdo, Cockburn, and Martin) even making an effort to synthesise Newtonian and Cartesian hypotheses. By the beginning of the eighteenth century, Newtonian ideas on all aspects of natural philosophy had been adopted unreservedly by most regents in Edinburgh, Aberdeen, and St Andrews – Glasgow remaining more conservative in this, as indeed in logic, metaphysics, and ethics teaching as well. If Newton's theories of movement, gravity, and light were not taught, it was because they were too difficult for the students and the regent to understand, and not because they were regarded with disfavour. The library lists reveal that the *Principia* was acquired for Edinburgh in 1690, Glasgow in 1695, Aberdeen between 1700 and 1717 and St Andrews in 1716.

Few historians would deny that one index of the state of scientific *progress* in seventeenth-century Scotland was the extent to which Copernican astronomy was accepted as a basis for the teaching of cosmology in the universities. This has been the subject of a special study by Father John L. Russell,[26] whose analysis of the relevant dictates and graduation theses for the four universities has revealed that the traditional Aristotelian-Ptolemaic astronomy was generally accepted until the 1640s. Sacrobosco's *Spheres* supplied the practical details. The Aristotelian concept of crystalline spheres was abandoned about a decade later, although the immutability of the celestial bodies was still being taught alongside the Tychonic system (with which it is incompatible) until after 1660. At this period, the rival Copernican theory was increasingly discussed but inevitably rejected. The sudden appearance of the mechanistic philosophy of Descartes and Boyle about 1670 in theses from St Andrews, Aberdeen and Edinburgh, marked a break with the old tradition, and paved the way for the espousal of Descartes' vortex theory.[27] Robert Hamilton of St Andrews, in 1668, was the first student known to have accepted the heliocentric hypothesis;[28] but twelve more years were to elapse before it became widely accepted. Nevertheless, some regents were still voicing their concern about its apparent incompatibility with the Scriptures until the turn of the century, at the same time as others who were unhappy with Cartesian mechanism were extolling Newton's cosmology (in which heliocentricity was taken for granted) because of its strong theologial implications. The last of Father Russell's conclusions is that by the beginning of the eighteenth century, scientific teaching in the Scottish univerities was 'thoroughly up to date and probably as good as was to be found anywhere in Europe.'[29]

Within the Aristotelian-Cartesian-Newtonian framework, there are numerous references to the writings and experiments of foreign natural philosophers like Torricelli, Otto von Guericke, Giovanni Alfonso Borelli; and British scientists like Seth Ward, John Wallis, Christopher Wren, Joseph Moxon, John Flamsteed, Robert Hooke, John Keill, and of course Robert Boyle. Boyle receives universal acclaim for his air pump experiments, *treatise on the origin of forms and qualities*, and *treatise on colour*; these, along with many of his major works, all feature in library lists which generally reflect the interest shown in the writings of scientists associated with the Royal Society. French scientists such as Emmanuel Maignan, Marin Mersenne, Jacques Rohault and Edme Mariotte feature prominently in the natural philosophy dictates; while a few references are also made to Claude Deschales, Claude Perrault, Jean Leclerc and others. The two Dutch scientists quoted most frequently by the regents are Christian Huygens and Anthony van Leeuwenhoeck. The general conclusion derived from an examination of all the available primary sources is therefore that the seventeenth-century Scottish regents (in particular, those in Edinburgh) were more informed about contemporary scientific developments than the nature of the teaching curriculum and reports in standard histories of the universities would suggest.

REFERENCES
1. M. L. Curtis, *Oxford and Cambridge in Transition, 1558–1642* (Oxford 1959); P. Allen, 'Scientific Studies in the English Universities of the 17th Century', *Journal of the History of Ideas*, 10 (1949) 219–53.
2. L. W. Sharp (ed.), *Early Letters of Robert Wodrow, 1698–1709* (Edinburgh 1937) contains letters from many of those students.
3. C. M. Shepherd, *Philosophy and Science in the Arts Curriculum of the Scottish Universities in the 17th Century*, Edinburgh ph.D. thesis 1974 (EUL), contains a detailed bibliography of this entire material (cf. pp. 344–424).
4. Professorial instruction began in Edinburgh in 1708, Glasgow in 1727, St Andrews in 1747 (when the Colleges of St Salvator and St Leonard were united), Marischal College Aberdeen in 1753, and King's College Aberdeen in 1799.
5. It is difficult to estimate how many notebooks there may be, since they are classified under the names of individual students and not under each university.
6. C. Innes (ed.), *Fasti Aberdonensis: selections from the records of the University and King's College of Aberdeen, 1494–1854* (Aberdeen 1854) p. iii.
7. EUL MS Dc.1.4.
8. C. B. Schmitt, 'Towards a Reassessment of Renaissance Aristotelianism', *History of Science*, 11 (1973) 159–93.
9. W. F. Edwards, 'The Logic of Jacopo Zabarella (1533–1589)', *Daedelus Amer. Acad. of Arts and Sciences*, 21 (1961) 2745.
10. J. Veitch, 'Philosophy in the Scottish Universities', *Mind*, 2 (1877) 74–91 and 207–34, argues that the Port Royal Logic was influential in the Scottish Universities in the last decades of the seventeenth century. However, unanimous opposition to it was voiced in a joint report to a Commission in 1695.
11. NLS MS 2741.
12. GUL MS Mu.67.
13. AUL MS The K.622.
14. Schmitt, op. cit., 8, has independently come to the same conclusion from a study of different sources relating to the same period.
15. E. H. Gilson, *Études sur le rôle de la pensée mediévale dans la formation du système Cartesien* (Paris 1930).
16. GUL MS Gen. 464; NLS Adv. MS 22.7.4.
17. GUL MS Gen. 222.
18. e.g. Thomas Craufurd (EUL MS Dc.5.122, Edinburgh 1653) cites at length the *De anima* of Piccolomini; William Blair (GUL MSS Gen. 369 and 379) refers to the role of English Puritanism when discussing free will; and John Wishart (EUL MS Da. Th., Edinburgh 1668), William Blair (GUL MS La.III.735, Glasgow 1674) and Herbert Kennedy (EUL MS Dc.8.118, Edinburgh 1672) all refer to the ethical thought of Scottish Protestantism.
19. R. L. Colie, *Light and Enlightenment: a Study of the Cambridge Platonists and the Dutch Armenians* (Cambridge 1957).

20. The author is grateful to Mr Paddy Doran, the National Institute for Higher Education, Limerick, Ireland for having been given temporary access to this unique source.

21. ibid., p.184. The original is, of course, in Latin.

22. A. G. Clement and R. H. S. Robertson, *Scotland's Scientific Heritage* (Edinburgh–London 1961).

23. P. Reif, 'The textbook tradition in natural philosophy, 1600–1650', *Journal of the History of Ideas*, 30 (1969) 17–32.

24. C. B. Schmitt, *A critical survey and bibliography of studies on Renaissance Aristotelianism*, 1958–1969 (Padova 1971) contains details on the textbooks of these and other renaissance authors.

25. W. Charleton, *Physiologia Epicuro-Gassendo-Charltoniana; or, a fabric of science natural upon the Hypothesis of atoms . . .* (London 1654).

26. J. L. Russell, 'Cosmological Teaching in the Seventeenth Century Scottish Universities', *Journal for the History of Astronomy*, 5 (1974) 122–32 and 145–54.

27. E. A. Aiton, *The Vortex Theory of Planetary Motions* (London 1972).

28. NLS MS Rb.s.258.

29. Russell, op. cit., 26, p. 152.

Medicine and Science in the Eighteenth Century

J.B. MORRELL

'Medicine is my wife; science is my mistress; books are my companions; study is my grave'. (Benjamin Rush while an Edinburgh student.)

One of the most conspicuous examples of improvement in eighteenth-century Scotland was the rise to international eminence of the University of Edinburgh. In the previous century it was mainly a local arts and divinity college; by at least the 1750s it had become a university of European importance in which medicine and science were particularly nurtured. During a century when some other Scottish universities, such as Aberdeen and St Andrews, were concerned primarily with survival, Edinburgh expanded through the ability of its medical school to attract not only native but also foreign students. While most faculties of Scottish universities continued to recruit local students, Edinburgh's faculty of medicine was unique in the patently international composition of its students. In order to explain that exceptional success, I shall focus on two main themes: the broad shape of the University's eighteenth-century medical and scientific development; and the attractions which drew students to Edinburgh, especially the style of its medical and scientific teaching.

The career of the University between 1700 and 1800 fell into five quite well defined phases. The first, from 1708 to 1726, began with the abolition of regenting in the arts faculty: henceforth teaching was to be done not by ephemeral regents who carried a class through all the curriculum, but by professors with life tenure who taught a particular subject. In 1726, after decades of sporadic endeavour, the medical faculty was established primarily by John Monro, a prominent Edinburgh surgeon, by the Edinburgh College of Surgeons, and by the Town Council, which until 1858 was responsible for elections to most chairs and the general supervision of the University. By 1726 lecture courses in anatomy, chemistry, theory of medicine, practice of medicine, and midwifery were being delivered by six specialist professors, five of whom had been students of Hermann Boerhaave at Leyden University. In 1725 the scientific reputation of the University had been secured by the appointment to the chair of mathematics of Colin MacLaurin, an outstanding exponent of Newtonian natural philosophy.

The second phase covered the years 1726 to c.1755, the epoch of Alexander Monro I (anatomy) and MacLaurin. Though the latter died in 1746, medical teaching expanded in 1748 when John Rutherford instigated clinical lectures in the Royal Infirmary which Monro I and George Drummond (1687–1766), who was six times Lord Provost of Edinburgh, had established in 1738. By the 1750s Monro I was the ageing lynch-pin figure of the medical faculty, even though in 1738 Charles Alston had become the first effective professor of botany and in 1747 Robert Whytt had replaced the decrepit Andrew Sinclair in the chair of theory of medicine.

This somewhat precarious situation was resolved in 1755 when the appointment of William Cullen to the chair of medicine and chemistry launched the reconstruction of the medical faculty. This third phase, which ended in the late 1760s, saw the continuation of Drummond's policy of appointing proved teachers and known scholars to chairs, as part of his wider strategy of improving the economy and stature of the city. Within the short compass of fourteen years, William Cullen (1755), Thomas Young (midwifery, 1756), John Hope (botany, 1761), John Gregory (practice of medicine, 1766), Joseph Black (medicine and chemistry, 1766), Cullen again (theory of medicine, 1766), and Francis Home (materia medica, 1768) were all appointed to chairs, the only concession to academic nepotism being the election of Alexander Monro II (anatomy, 1758). These men were mainly Edinburgh alumni, showing that the medical professoriate had become self-regenerating. Some of them had been drawn to Edinburgh from Glasgow (Cullen, Black) and Aberdeen (John Gregory), thus beginning a familiar brain-drain.

Cullen, Monro II, and Black were primarily responsible for two golden decades, the 1770s and 1780s, which constituted the fourth phase of the medical faculty's career. In these 20 years, only four chairs changed hands, namely, practice of medicine (Cullen, 1773), theory of medicine (James Gregory, 1776), midwifery (Alexander Hamilton, 1780), and botany (Daniel Rutherford, 1786). Under the enlightened direction of William Robertson (Principal, 1762–93), important changes took place in the non-medical sciences with the advent of John Robison (natural philosophy, 1774), John Playfair (mathematics, 1785), and John Walker (natural history, 1779), who replaced a sinecurist. By the early 1780s, the University attracted about 1,000 students, the most popular class being that of Monro

11. His staggering enrolment of 436 pupils in session 1783–4 was slightly greater than the total number of about 430 freshmen then admitted each session at Oxford and Cambridge together.

The fifth phase of the medical faculty's career coincided partly with the protracted period of the French wars from 1790 to 1815. In eleven years at the end of the century, six chairs changed hands: theory of medicine (Andrew Duncan I, 1790); practice of medicine (James Gregory, 1790); medicine and chemistry (Thomas Charles Hope, 1796); anatomy (Alexander Monro III, 1798); materia medica (James Home, 1798); and midwifery (James Hamilton, 1800). Five of them went to sons of former professors, an obvious concession to the nepotism exerted by academic dynasties. Yet, during this phase of professorial control of appointments, there was a doubling of student numbers by 1815 to about 2,000, of whom almost half were medical students. Of the four classes which in the 1790s attracted over 200 pupils, three (anatomy, practice of medicine, chemistry) were medical ones. The centrality of medicine to the University was indeed confirmed by the unprecedented demand for physicians and surgeons for service in the wars, and by the founding by government of three Regius chairs, in clinical surgery (1803), military surgery (1806), and medical jurisprudence (1807).

By 1800, then, Edinburgh had seven tenured specialist medical professors and had been giving clinical teaching for over 50 years. Westwards at Glasgow, student enrolment had increased considerably: by 1800 Glasgow attracted about 1,000 students, of whom about 200 were studying medicine. The Glasgow medical professoriate numbered only two men, helped by three untenured lecturers; and clinical teaching began there in 1794. It was only in the 1820s, with a medical student population of about 400, that the Glasgow medical school began to compete seriously with Edinburgh's. At Oxford and Cambridge, medical lecturing during the eighteenth century was spasmodic and clinical teaching non-existent. With regard to university medical education, Edinburgh therefore faced little effective competition from other British universities during the eighteenth century.

The conditions under which many Edinburgh professors worked were very different from those enjoyed by their successors now. In the eighteenth century each professor derived his emolument as a teacher mainly from class fees which were paid directly to him. Generally his basic salary was low: in 1800 five medical professors received no salary at all. Though each professor had total control of the content and method of his teaching, the class fee system encouraged him to keep himself in business as a teacher. Thus many professors saw teaching as their primary job. Joseph Black felt it was important not to miss lecturing; had he done so, 'the students would be dissatisfied and would have a right to complain'.[1] In his *Wealth of Nations* Adam Smith agreed with Principal Robertson that it would be undesirable to increase the salaries of the professors, a move which might 'render them less attentive to the instruction of their students, or independent of the emolument arising from a diligent performance of their duty'.[2]

The class fee system of professorial speculation in the academic market-place encouraged professors to badger the Town Council for improved teaching facilities. Problems were most acute in anatomy, for decades the largest class in the University. From 57 students in session 1720–1, the anatomy class grew to an average size of 342 in the 1780s. At particular times there was rapid expansion: in the five years to 1764, the class grew from 134 to 187. While Oxford and Cambridge were half empty, the Edinburgh anatomy class was so overcrowded that in 1764 Monro petitioned the Town Council for a new anatomy theatre. He stressed that his present theatre was badly lit and so small that he was compelled to repeat lectures and to neglect research and publication. In buttressing his case for a new theatre, Monro II cleverly pointed to the money that anatomy students brought into the town, and stirred municipal pride by referring to developments elsewhere. He even offered a loan to the Council and promised to bequeath to his successors his famous anatomical collection. Such bait was irresistible to the Town Council which appreciated that anatomy was central to the University's ability to recruit students. The new theatre of 1764, which held 300, permitted further expansion so that by 1783 students were standing in the passage at the outer door. In order to accommodate them, Monro himself paid for new seating in the gallery and extra ventilation, subsequently obtaining recompense (albeit incomplete) from the Council. The concern for adequate accommodation and equipment reached its apogee in 1789, when after some 23 years of agitation the foundation stone of the new College was laid. Always aware of the importance of student numbers, Principal Robertson was constantly concerned to replace the old buildings, 'a most miserable musty pile scarce fit for stables', with spacious accommodation which would be nationally advantageous and would promote the flourishing state of the University.[3]

The nature of his subject affected each professor financially. If he taught practice of medicine, chemistry, or anatomy, he enjoyed a large income from class fees which by skilful teaching he could hope to increase. Professors of less popular subjects, such as botany and materia medica, received considerably less. This wide disparity of remuneration from class fees spurred ambitious professors to transfer to what they hoped would be more lucrative chairs: witness Cullen's two moves (from chemistry to theory of medicine and then to practice of medicine) and James Gregory's single side-step (from theory to practice of medicine).

By the 1780s the medical professors had become quite wealthy from a mixture of teaching, lucrative private practice, and writing textbooks. Most of them lived near the University and Infirmary, and they could afford to keep carriages. Monro I had earlier shown what was possible: he provided a country house for his father, and bought an estate in Stirlingshire. Towards the end of the century some professors were enviably rich: Black left £20,000; Cullen, who gained £3,000 from one of his text-books, bought a country house near Edinburgh as a sylvan retreat; while Monro II bought 271 acres near Edinburgh for gardening and 1,200 acres in Berwickshire for farming. Teaching at Edinburgh was such good business that as the century passed professors became keener to follow the example set by Monro I of passing their own chair to a son. This nepotism reached its peak in the 1790s, a significant case being provided by Monro III. His appointment was supported by seven medical professors, five of whom were themselves sons of former professors. Though the Town Council realised that it was desirable 'to get a better choice of candidates', it succumbed to the professorial phalanx.[4]

The class fee system encouraged professorial squabbling as part of that general quarrelsomeness upon which Benjamin Franklin animadverted as characteristic of 'men of all sorts that have been bred at Edinburgh'.[5] Where professorial proprietorial interest was threatened, tempers could run high: the 1783 dispute between James Gregory and Alexander Hamilton, about the place of midwifery in the medical curriculum, culminated years later in Hamilton's son, James, gaining damages of £100 against Gregory who had beaten him with a stick. For his part, Gregory would have been willing to pay double for another opportunity of chastening his colleague. Proprietory interests also produced defensiveness when new proposals were mooted. The most significant example of academic conservatism concerned the unsuccessful attempt made in 1777 to establish a separate chair of surgery. It was widely known that Edinburgh nowhere near rivalled London for surgical anatomy, that Monro II was not an operating surgeon but a physician, that future surgeons needed to see operations on live patients, and that dead bodies for dissection were not plentiful in Edinburgh. Though the Edinburgh College of Surgeons lobbied hard for a separate chair of surgery, on the basis of the successful lectures on clinical surgery given by James Rae from 1769, the Town Council accepted the opinion of Principal

Robertson and most of the medical professors that Monro II was capable of teaching both anatomy and surgery. His proved ability to attract students enabled him to maintain his monopoly, leaving his dynastic and financial interests unimpaired. This lacuna in the University's medical teaching was filled by Rae, whose lectures on clinical surgery were approved by the Surgeons, and such private teachers as John Bell, Charles Bell, and John Barclay who taught surgical anatomy extra-murally in the 1790s. Their success was such a telling commentary on the University that the James Gregory faction succeeded in stopping John Bell's teaching in 1799 and in driving Charles Bell to London in 1804.

The steady growth of student numbers at Edinburgh showed that the University satisfied the desires of parents and of sons who had the capacity to patronise it. Unlike Oxford and Cambridge, it imposed no religious tests on students, thus making Edinburgh a medical mecca for dissenters. Again in contrast to the two old English universities, no paternalism was exercised through residence requirements. At Edinburgh students enjoyed the freedom of a relatively cheap non-residential university: even by the late eighteenth century subsistence could cost as little as £20 per session. Yet those students intent on taking several courses and on graduating had to be middling rich in order to pay the appropriate fees. The young Thomas Ismay found in 1771 that he paid £5 to travel from Yorkshire to Edinburgh, £10 per 3 months for full board, and £20 for class fees. In his case the expense of studying at Edinburgh so stretched him financially that he confined himself to his lodgings where his frugal immolation probably accelerated his death while still a student.

In order to allow professors to recruit classes which would pay well, no entrance qualifications were required or entrance examinations set. Edinburgh was a pedagogic supermarket: any male of any age and training could attend any class in whatever number and order suited his preferences and his pocket. Even in subjects like chemistry and anatomy, Black and Monro II required no previous knowledge from their students. Inevitably every class was heterogeneous in its composition. In the medical classes there were novices who intended to complete their training at London or Paris, to graduate at Edinburgh, or to go into practice immediately after leaving Edinburgh; and there were relatively experienced students such as apprentices with a surgeon or apothecary, graduates attending for refreshment, and students from other universities.

Except in medicine few students followed the prescribed degree courses. The flexible system of *lernfreiheit* enabled medical students to take the occasional non-medical course. Thus the ambitious Philadelphian, John

Morgan, in his second session attended three medical classes and Hugh Blair's on rhetoric, his action provoking a friend to exclaim 'thou won't be satisfied without being a physiologist, chemist, physician and rhetorician. Mercy upon us, where will you end?'[6] Morgan ended with an Edinburgh M.D., being one of that small minority of medical students who bothered to graduate and could afford the £20 fee. Even in the 1780s, the peak decade of medical graduation, there were no more than 28 M.D.s per year on average. Yet to be an Edinburgh medical graduate was distinctly useful because of the reputation it conferred on its possessors, particularly in the non-golden cane sections of British medicine. For foreigners especially, an Edinburgh M.D. was a tangible symptom of accomplishment which they hoped, often not vainly, would enhance their career prospects in their native land. An important part of medical graduation was the thesis. At their worst, theses were pieces of literary hack-work scissored-and-pasted in a month or so. At their best, they were significant contributions to research. It was in his dissertation that Joseph Black solved the problem of causticity by 'discovering' a gas (carbon dioxide). Similarly, Black's own pupil, Daniel Rutherford, emulated him by 'discovering' another gas (nitrogen) and by announcing it in a thesis.

The Edinburgh system of *lernfreiheit* put the onus of choice firmly on the students without any accompanying regular system of pastoral guidance. In compensation for this impersonality, students socialised informally. For favoured students, it was possible to gain an entry into Edinburgh's polite society, especially if wealth enabled them to board with professors and their relatives. The young Thomas Percival, later an important Manchester physician, lodged with the sister of Principal Robertson, dialogued with David Hume, and enjoyed the sumptuous weekly entertainments offered by the Earl of Hopetoun and by Lord Provost Drummond. The Philadelphian Benjamin Rush had decided 'to cultivate the acquaintance of men of learning and virtue wherever I go'.[7] Armed with a letter of introduction from Benjamin Franklin to Sir Alexander Dick, immediate past President of the Royal College of Physicians of Edinburgh, Rush was quickly introduced to Hume and taken up by the Earl of Leven and his family. His fellow American, John Morgan, not only became intimate with Dick and Drummond but before he graduated was made a freeman of Edinburgh. Other students were satisfied with traditional pastimes which were revealed in diaries if not in letters to parents. Sylas Neville felt he was lucky to avoid a drinking party at which about ten students drank 27 bottles of claret, 12 of port, besides punch, and were not surprisingly 'beastly drunk'. Neville did, however, join other students in a tour of Edinburgh's brothels, where he noted that dirtiness and vice were usually combined: the exception was that kept by Mrs Jap, 'a most exact old Bawd, the Mother Cole of Scotland'.[8] Of course, meeting other students could be rewarding as well as pleasurable. Benjamin Rush was converted to the theory of republicanism through a chance encounter with John Bostock, later a Liverpool physician. The future of American medicine as well as politics was also affected. As a student Rush met another American, Adam Kuhn, who was to be appointed a professor at the University of Pennsylvania just a year before Rush. In 1762 Samuel Bard first met John Morgan, an alliance of subsequent vital importance to medical education and science in north America.

For those students who were not permanently dissipated, indolent, or decaying, hard study was the norm. An ambitious American like Samuel Bard was not distracted by Edinburgh's allurements. He worked at least a twelve-hour day:

> From seven to half after ten I am . . . employed in the mathematics . . . I then dress, and am by eleven at college, attending Professor Ferguson [moral philosophy] until twelve; from that hour until one at the hospital; from one to two, with Dr Cullen; from two to three, I allow to dinner; from three to four, with Monro in Anatomy; from four to five, or half hour after, I generally spend at my flute and taking tea . . . after this I retire to my study . . . until eleven o'clock in correcting my notes, and in general reading.[9]

At the institutional level, students could take refuge and seek succour in the various student societies. One end of the spectrum of respectability was graced in 1772 by the society which met to blaspheme and laugh at everything sacred, with members representing God the Father and God the Son. At the other end of the scale of social standing were the various medical and scientific societies. During the 1790s, for example, students could savour the Agricultural Society of Edinburgh, the American Physical Society, the Chirurgo-Physical Society, the Hibernian Medical Society, the Natural History Society of Edinburgh, a Chemical Society, and the Academy of Physics. Above all, they could attend the Royal Medical and Royal Physical Societies, each of which was so well established that it owned its own premises.

Many tributes attest to the functional importance of the Royal Medical Society, established in 1737. As an adjunct to the medical course, it gave its members the responsibility of writing papers and defending opinions in discussions which were on occasion protracted. Sometimes the Society provided the opportunity for an M.D. candidate to expose an early draft of his thesis before a critical audience. The Society was an arena in which medical orthodoxies could be challenged. In the early 1740s it may have witnessed the first serious questioning in Edinburgh of the Boerhaavian medical doctrines taught by the professors. Forty years later, it was the venue of such heated debate between the rival supporters of the medical systems of John Brown and William Cullen that the Society was compelled to pass a law against duelling. In general the Society supplemented the solitary and 'frigid plodding on books', the doctrines preached by the professors in lectures, and 'the little detail of . . . empirical practice' revealed by the clinical teaching in the Infirmary. It encouraged medical clubability; and also, as Gilbert Blane (then a President and later a famous naval physician) stressed in 1775, its members realised that 'it was in society alone, by the mutual communication and reflection of the lights of reason and knowledge, that the intellectual as well as the moral powers of man are exalted and perfected'.[10] At Georgian Oxbridge the problem of the excess leisure of students was solved mainly by ephemeral eating and drinking clubs, which had little to do with scholarship, acquiring qualifications, and preparing for a career. At Edinburgh conviviality was not excluded from the Medical Society – the fastidiously elegant Joseph Black even sang at one annual meeting – but its aim was not pleasure but edification. The centrality of the Society to Edinburgh's medical school was well caught in 1835 by John Bostock, who argued that far from being a light-hearted diversion the Society was of all British institutions the one that had contributed most to the improvement of the British medical profession.

Like their societies, alumni were very varied, ranging from quacks to the founders of American university medical teaching. One of the most flamboyant of the former was James Graham, who in 1779 set up his 'Temple of Health' in London. His entrance hall was littered with crutches thrown away by his cured patients. Upstairs Graham elaborated the well-established tricks of electrical healing with highly decorated electrical machines and contrivances, including an insulated electrical throne. His pièce de resistance was an electrified celestial bed in which for £100 a childless couple could have fertility excited in them. Graham's ensemble attracted the interest of Horace Walpole who deemed it 'the most impudent puppet-show of imposition I ever saw'.[11]

If Graham hardly imitated his alleged teachers (Monro II, Cullen, Black, and Whytt), some students from North America paid Edinburgh the most sincere form of flattery: in their home country they founded and developed medical teaching institutions modelled on Edinburgh's medical school. In the colonial period, Edinburgh was the favourite Scottish university for American students. Before the Revolution approximately 100 Americans studied there, compared with about 20 at Glasgow and about 16 at the two Aberdeen colleges. Most of the Americans came to Edinburgh to study medicine, the first American graduate being John Moultrie of South Carolina in 1749. The journey from America to the University was a major enterprise. Moultrie spent 32 days crossing the Atlantic and was chased by a Spanish ship, before reaching Bristol. Like William Shippen before him, Benjamin Rush took almost two months at sea on a stormy and dangerous voyage, his perpetual sea-sickness being relieved only by laudanum; then he spent a week on the road from Liverpool to Edinburgh. Samuel Bard took even longer to reach Britain: shortly after embarking, he was captured by a French privateer and suffered imprisonment in France for five months before Franklin secured his release.

Most colonial Americans flocked to the London hospitals to learn practical medicine by acting as 'walkers' or 'dressers' or by attending anatomical and surgical lectures. But it was Edinburgh's medical school, with its emphasis on rational medicine, which enabled colonial Americans to take home an M.D., a palpable record of accomplishment which helped them to launch or consolidate their careers in their native land. Moreover, it is clear that the American alumni of Edinburgh, who founded the first two American medical schools at Philadelphia (1765) and New York (1767), were formulating plans while they were students at Edinburgh. The early medical school of the College of Philadelphia was shaped and staffed exclusively by four young Edinburgh graduates, Morgan, Shippen, Rush and Kuhn. Morgan and Shippen clearly saw themselves as Philadelphian versions of Cullen and Monro II respectively. The Pennsylvania Hospital, used for clinical teaching, was modelled on the Edinburgh Royal Infirmary, the Medical Society on the Royal Medical Society, and the medical degree regulations on those of Edinburgh. If the existing College of Philadelphia was indebted to Aberdeen, the plan of its new medical school was 'conformable to that which is followed in the so justly celebrated school of physic at Edinburgh'.[12] Benjamin Rush was as proud as he was prescient in seeing in 1766 that Philadelphia, his birth place, was due to become the Edinburgh of America. Jealous of the Philadelphians, the Medical School of King's College, New York (later Columbia University) was opened in 1767, the moving spirits being six of the town's leading doctors, Samuel Bard, John Jones, Peter Middleton, Samuel Clossy, James Smith, and John Van Brugh Tennent. All except Middleton and Clossy had attended classes in Edinburgh, but only Bard had graduated there. Less uniform in education and qualifications than their Philadelphian rivals, they also suffered from the lack of a hospital for clinical teaching until 1791. The foundation of

American medical schools was significant for Edinburgh's future: though Americans flocked in even greater numbers to Edinburgh after Independence until about 1800, the American medical schools initiated that long process by which Edinburgh in the early nineteenth century was to become the victim of her own pedagogic success, especially when the medical school of University College, London, and English provincial medical schools were founded.

In the mid and late eighteenth century, however, Edinburgh's medical school remained supreme in Britain as a cynosure of students. Except for the minority intent on graduation, students attended classes because they wanted to and not because degree regulations forced them to do so. They voted with their fees to sit at the feet of their favourite professors. Two of the most highly regarded were Joseph Black and William Cullen, whose careers were closely related. Indeed Black began his sojourn at Edinburgh in 1766 as professor of medicine and chemistry with the great advantage of succeeding Cullen in the chair. Cullen had promoted chemistry so well that in his eleven years' tenure of the chair the size of the class had risen from 17 to 145. When Black followed Cullen, he knew that his subject was established and popular, that it was useful vocationally, and that attendance at his lectures was compulsory for a small but fairly steady cohort of medical students who intended to graduate. Moreover, Black had gained eleven years useful experience as lecturer in chemistry at the University of Glasgow.

When he assumed his Edinburgh chair Black was famous for his research on fixed air (carbon dioxide) and on latent heat. Once ensconced in his chair, Black mainly abandoned research and devoted himself chiefly to his teaching. Two of its characteristics attracted students. Firstly, Black offered an elegant and genteel exposition of his subject. As his colleague John Robison recalled, Black's personal appearance and manner were those of a gentleman and peculiarly pleasing. His philosophical calmness and repose appealed to a very mixed audience. He catered not only for medical students, whose stock of chemical knowledge varied considerably, but also for those without any previous knowledge. As well as medical students, townspeople such as blacksmiths and druggists attended his class. Through Black's teaching and mien, chemistry in Edinburgh became a fashionable part of the accomplishment of gentlemen.

The second characteristic of his teaching was the neatness and success with which he demonstrated experiments and processes in his lectures. There was of course no novelty in Black's time in accompanying a lecture by experiments: that technique was the stock-in-trade of itinerant lecturers and teachers in dissenting academies. Black's contribution was extraordinary manual dexterity applied to ingeniously contrived experiments. These were performed not with the quackery of a showman but with an unparalleled fastidiousness and elegance. Like many pupils Henry Brougham was fascinated by Black's pedagogic gamesmanship which often involved highly dangerous chemicals: 'I have seen him pour boiling water or boiling acid from a vessel that had no spout into a tube, holding it at such a distance as made the stream's diameter small, and so vertical that not a drop was spilt. While he poured he would mention this adaptation of the height to the diameter as a necessary condition of success'.[13]

The result of these two distinctive features of Black's teaching was that the size of his class rose steadily to above 200, making it at least the fourth largest class in the University. His students spread his reputation as a teacher so effectively that he was variously known as the Patriarch and Nestor of late eighteenth-century chemistry even though he never wrote a text-book to publicise his course. He attracted students from abroad, not only from north America but from Germany, Switzerland, Scandinavia and Russia. Some of his British students were so inspired by him that they followed him as university teachers of chemistry, the best known being Thomas Charles Hope (Edinburgh), Thomas Thomson (Glasgow), Thomas Beddoes (Oxford), Smithson Tennant (Cambridge) and Thomas Garnett (Anderson's University, Glasgow).

The medical teacher most appreciated by students was William Cullen, who taught for 35 years from the chairs of medicine and chemistry (1755–66), theory of medicine (1766–73) and practice of medicine (1773–90). The reverence felt by Americans for Cullen was particularly striking. John Morgan called him the Boerhaave of his age. For Benjamin Rush, Cullen was unrivalled and his lectures on the nervous system and pathology worth their weight in gold. For another Philadelphian, Thomas Parke, he was 'that shining Oracle of Physic, which I have so long wished to see'.[14] The affection of his pupils and his concern for them were based on Cullen's phenomenal memory for faces and names and his generous personality. His fame was also connected with his views about rational physic. Cullen was well aware that dogmatism in medical theories encouraged certain remedies and prohibited others: it excluded the correcting effect of experience and was therefore by itself insufficient. He also realised that medical theory was the chief means of stimulating empirical enquiry. At the same time, medical theory provided that intelligibility which was so important for the rational physician: in Cullen's view mechanical philosophy and chemistry illuminated the powers that act on the body, anatomy revealed the structure of the human body, physiology explored the functions of organs, and pathology displayed deviations from health. From all these in combination it was possible, Cullen thought, to deduce the proximate cause of disease and method of cure, both of which should be checked by experience. Mere empiricism (the application to particular diseases of specific cures entirely because in the past they have been successful) was unprogressive and therefore fruitless, even pernicious, in 'Cullen's opinion. His matured conclusion was that it was necessary to teach and study rational medicine in a way that comprehended the results of empiricism, thus acknowledging the limitations of any given medical system. His own particular contributions were to view the human body not only as a 'chemical mixt' or as a 'hydraulic machine', but as an 'animated nervous frame'; and to place great emphasis on the systematic classification of diseases, not least because nosology was in his hands a powerful didactic device.[15] He intended his pupils to be skilful rational physicians because at best their cures would be not only consequences of medical theories but also corroborated by experience. For Cullen it was not enough to produce effective physicians: it was just as important to produce 'ornate' ones. Like John Gregory before him, Cullen believed that the true dignity of rational medicine, compared with mere empiricism, lay in the superior abilities and the liberal gentlemanly manners of its practitioners. In recommending a prospective colleague to the students in his class, Cullen eulogised him as 'the most learned, most ingenious and most ornate physician ever bred at this University'.[16]

The rational medicine taught at Edinburgh, so different from London hospital teaching, encouraged the separation of medicine from surgery, pharmacy, medical empiricism, and medical nihilism. Though the clinical teaching in the Infirmary was concerned with diagnosis, prognosis, and cure at the bed-side of individual patients, the lectures offered up-to-date and comprehensive medical theory. This combination of modes of teaching was a particularly effective preparation for a career in the English provinces, the army, navy, or East India Company, where the ability to improvise was desirable. Irrespective of the various theories taught, Edinburgh's medical teaching made medicine a matter of liberal learning and ornamental accomplishment as well as of professional employment. This emphasis on practicality and ornateness was indeed central to the teaching of medicine and science at Edinburgh. It helps to explain why one medical student in 1771 was so satisfied with his professors that he was rather lost for words of adulation when he wrote home: 'Dr Cullen ... is accounted very clever ... Dr Black is a very fine man ... Dr Young is very clever ... Dr Hope is a fine man ... In short, they are all fine men ...'.[17]

ACKNOWLEDGMENTS

For permission to cite and to quote from manuscripts in their care I am grateful to Edinburgh Corporation and the University of Edinburgh. For help and criticism I am indebted to Whitfield J. Bell Jr. and to Christopher Lawrence.

REFERENCES

1. Black to Archibald Cochrane, 17 February 1786, Black Correspondence, EUL, Gen. 873.
2. EU Senate minutes, 1 April 1773.
3. F. B. Dexter (ed.), *The literary diary of Ezra Stiles* (New York 1901), i, 308, entry for 1 November 1772 quoting the view of Henry Marchant.
4. Edinburgh Town Council minutes, 7 March 1798.
5. B. Franklin, *Autobiography* (London 1905), 17.
6. W. J. Bell, *John Morgan: Continental doctor* (Philadelphia 1965), 67.
7. G. W. Corner, 'Benjamin Rush's student days in Edinburgh and what came of them', *UEJ*, xv, 126–35 (127).
8. B. Cozens-Hardy, *The diary of Sylas Neville 1767–1788* (London 1950) 156, 226.
9. A. R. Rigg, 'The colonial American medical student at Edinburgh', *UEJ*, xx, 141–150 (146).
10. G. Blane, *Address to the Medical Society of students at Edinburgh, upon laying the foundation of their Hall, April 21st, 1775* (n.p., n.d.), 4, 5.
11. Walpole to Countess of Upper Ossory, 23 August 1780, in P. Toynbee (ed.), *The letters of Horace Walpole fourth Earl of Oxford* (Oxford 1904) xi, 259.
12. J. Morgan, *A discourse upon the institution of medical schools in America; delivered at a public anniversary commencement, held in the College of Philadelphia May 30 and 31, 1765. With a preface containing, amongst other things, the author's apology for attempting to introduce the regular mode of practising physic in Philadelphia* (Philadelphia 1765) 36.
13. H. Brougham, *Lives of men of letters and science, who flourished in the time of George III* (London 1845) 347.
14. W. J. Bell, 'Some American students of "that shining oracle of physic", Dr William Cullen of Edinburgh, 1755–1766', *Proceedings of the American Philosophical Society*, 1950, xciv, 275–81 (275).
15. J. Thomson (ed.), *The works of William Cullen ... containing his Physiology, Nosology, and the First Lines of the Practice of Physic: with numerous extracts from his manuscript papers, and from his Treatise of the Materia Medica* (Edinburgh and London 1827) i, 409.
16. Neville, *Diary*, 198.
17. 'Letter from Thomas Ismay, student of medicine at Edinburgh, 1771, to his father', *UEJ*, viii, 57–61 (58).

OTHER SOURCES

R. G. W. Anderson and A. D. C. Simpson (eds.), *The early years of the Edinburgh Medical School* (Edinburgh 1976).

R. G. W. Anderson, *The Playfair collection and the teaching of chemistry at the University of Edinburgh 1713–1858* (Edinburgh 1978).

J. Bostock, *Sketch of the history of medicine, from its origin to the commencement of the nineteenth century* (London 1835).

L. H. Butterfield (ed.), *Letters of Benjamin Rush* (Princeton 1951).

E. P. Cheyney, *History of the University of Pennsylvania 1740–1940* (Philadelphia 1940).

J. R. R. Christie, 'The origins and development of the Scottish scientific community, 1680–1760', *History of Science*, xii (1974) 122–41.

B. C. Corner, *William Shippen, Jr.: pioneer in American medical education* (Philadelphia 1951).

B. C. Corner and C. C. Booth (eds.), *Chain of friendship: selected letters of Dr. John Fothergill of London, 1735–1780* (Cambridge, Mass. 1971).

G. W. Corner (ed.), *The Autobiography of Benjamin Rush: his 'Travels through life' together with his Commonplace Book for 1789–1813* (Princeton 1948).

J. Gray, *History of the Royal Medical Society 1737–1937* (Edinburgh 1952).

J. Gregory, *Lectures on the duties and qualifications of a physician* (London 1772).

D. N. H. Hamilton, *The healers: a history of medicine in Scotland* (Edinburgh 1981).

A. Hook, *Scotland and America: a study of cultural relations 1750–1835* (Glasgow and London 1975).

D. C. Humphrey, *From King's College to Columbia 1746–1800* (New York 1976)

J. B. Morrell, 'Science in Manchester and the University of Edinburgh, 1760–1840', in D. S. L. Cardwell (ed.), *Artisan to graduate: essays to commemorate the foundation in 1824 of the Manchester Mechanics' Institution, now in 1974 the University of Manchester Institute of Science and Technology* (Manchester 1974) 39–54.

J. B. Morrell, 'The University of Edinburgh in the late eighteenth century: its scientific eminence and academic structure', *Isis*, lxii (1971), 158–71.

C. D. O'Malley, *The history of medical education* (Berkeley, Los Angeles, and London 1970).

L. Stone (ed.), *The university in society* (Princeton 1975).

R. E. Wright-St Clair, *Doctors Monro: a medical saga* (London 1964).

Carlyle and the University of Edinburgh

IAN CAMPBELL

Student life in Thomas Carlyle's day is a subject at once interesting and confusing; he was an undergraduate from 1809 to 1814, then studied spasmodically between 1818 and the early 1820s. In many ways he seemed the standard undergraduate product of his time; in some ways, he was exceptional. In no way was he more unusual than in the quantity and quality of the written records which survive of this period in his life. In letters and accounts from contemporaries, and in the incomparable *Reminiscences* written fifty years on, but with the unnatural clarity of an almost photographic memory, Carlyle offers us a vivid insight into student experience significantly different from that which emerges from a document such as Lockhart's *Peter's Letters* of 1819, or indeed from official histories. Resisting the temptation (meantime, at least) to assume Carlyle's to be the authentic picture, we may employ it as an introduction to a complex question.

First, Carlyle was, like most undergraduates, a local boy from a local school, product of an educational system which at parish schools of widely different standards prepared working-class youths for higher education. Carlyle's experience at Ecclefechan was worlds apart from, say, Scott's at the High School in Edinburgh. Carlyle's was the chance encounter with the parish minister (who with his son gave him what slender Latinity he built on); the local academy run by 'Tom Donaldson', himself a Divinity undergraduate; then hated years at Annan Academy under teachers whom he could respect later in life, but whose instruction gave him little pleasure at the time.[1] Professor Horn rightly stresses the 'marked cleavage between the bulk of the Scottish students, released from the school in their early teens, and the more mature students from elsewhere, many of them men of the world and much better endowed with this world's goods than the majority of the Scots'. Carlyle's is the more restricted of these kinds of preparation. He came from a very narrow intellectual background, a world of close piety and education to the rigid standards of the 'Burgher Seceder' Church of

Ecclefechan.[2] It is hard to be altogether objective about Carlyle's parents and their influence, though vital to try to be so. Carlyle's father could be master of

> a bold glowing style ... flowing free from the untutored Soul; full of metaphors (though he knew not what a metaphor was), with all manner of potent words

but he was also remembered outside his family as

> a good scholar: he could do his ain business well; and he was looked up to as a knowing bodie. He had old-fashioned words, like nobody else. He read muckle; he was a great talker, weel gifted with the tongue. It was a muckle treat to be in his house at nicht, to hear him tell stories and tales. But he was always a very strict old bodie, and could bide no contradiction.

Authoritarian yet admirable, Carlyle's father had an incalculable influence on the future student. He was *for* education, and stood out against Ecclefechan opinion which held that you 'Educate a boy, and he grows up to despise his ignorant parents'. Above all he was for education for the ministry, and that was the dearest wish held by both Carlyle's parents. On the other hand, Carlyle's father had a settled indifference to the fine arts, which his son traced back to hard times and religious conviction.

> My Father's Education was altogether of the worst and most limited. I believe he was never more than three months at any school. ... A solid knowledge of Arithmetic, a fine antique Handwriting; these, with other limited *practical* etceteras, were *all* the things he ever heard mentioned as excellent: he had no room to strive for more. Poetry, Fiction in general, he had universally seen treated as not only idle, but *false* and criminal. ...
>
> But greatly his most important culture he had gathered (and this too by his own endeavour) from the better men of the district; the Religious men. ... He was Religious with the consent of his whole faculties: without Reason he would have been nothing; indeed his habit of intellect was thoroughly free and even incredulous, and strongly enough did the daily example of this work afterwards on me.[3]

Writing to his mother with a signed copy of his translation of a novel by Goethe, Carlyle wryly noted that it is inscribed to his father 'though I know that he will not read a line of it'[4] – an admission of the narrowness of his own background; a narrowness from which he escaped as early as his school days at Annan, where the lending library of John Maconachie was a rich resource for someone who had hitherto simply not known imaginative literature. Smollett was an early discovery, and so was Shakespeare. No prohibition ever prevented him from a knowledge of oral tradition, nor from local literature. He knew of Burns (his father had seen Burns in Ecclefechan, and typically not troubled to cross the road to speak to him) and he remembered clearly being 'perched upon honest Jamie Beattie's loom' where he 'yelled forth the hymns of Blind Harry, from my small lungs, with the voice and spirit of a Sybil'.[5]

What is clear about Carlyle's view of his own youth is a sense of *fin de siècle*: he saw his own character in the same terms as his father's in their formative influences – clearly the product of the Church, and of religious men. The 'old Seceder Clergy' are paid an affectionate tribute in the *Reminiscences*, despite 'something of rigour, of severity': 'of flowerage, of free harmonious beauty, there could not well be much in this system'. Yet overall these are the positive influences on the Carlyle family, and on his prodigally gifted contemporary Edward Irving from Annan, who went on to a short-lived sensational career in London as founder of the Catholic Apostolic Church. But the system, while producing such men, was in decay.

> It began to alter just about that period, on the death of those old hoary Heads; and has gone on with increasing velocity ever since. Irving and I were probably among the last products it delivered before gliding off.

We do well to remember this rider, along with the end of the statement already quoted from Carlyle about his father being religious with his reason – with the consent of his whole faculties. 'But he was in Annandale, and it was above fifty years ago'.[6]

It is from just this clever but culturally shifting background that Carlyle emerges as an aspiring undergraduate in 1809, walking over three days from Ecclefechan to Edinburgh, and exploring the city in those first memorable hours which are recorded in the *Reminiscences* of Francis Jeffrey – hours spent finding lodgings in Simon Square, brushing himself up to city smartness, exploring the High Street, taking a first bewildered look at Parliament Hall. After the narrow experience of Ecclefechan, Annan had been a new (if hated) liberty. There was always the weekend visit back to the family home, with the strong parental bond of respect (to father) and love (to mother), even if the intellectual horizons narrowed again to theirs. Now in Edinburgh, the freedom was something quite new. It was a six months' freedom, on his own terms; the intellectual horizons of the University, to someone coming from that part of the student body to which Carlyle belonged, poor and relatively self-educated, must have seemed boundless.

The University to which Carlyle came in November 1809 was in a visible state of transition, if religious Dumfriesshire was in a less visible state of change as it produced Carlyle. The magnificent Adam-designed New College (now Old College) was begun, but since 1793 wartime restrictions had brought building virtually to a halt, though some of the new rooms were in use (five old lecture-rooms remaining against six new ones, for use by thirty-four professors). Contractors' materials disfigured the precincts, building noises were a nuisance during lectures – small wonder that Thomas Pennant dismissed the College in 1790 as 'a mean building'.[7] Senate discussions have much to say on the desirability of proper janitorial services in a half-completed building where there are 'several nuisances about the College', including 'intruders or improper persons'. Indeed a significant number of those attending classes were not matriculated students: this was not so much owing to the popularity of the professors (as it would be in the 1820s when members of the public, Carlyle included, would come to hear, for example, John Wilson lecture on moral philosophy) as to the haphazard nature of a system where students found they could obtain a professor's class ticket without going to the expense of matriculation. In 1812 it was estimated that such students accounted for at least 200 of those present at classes. Snowball throwing, 'cutting doors' and writing on walls were nuisances in 1812, and earlier (in 1794)

> there are other Students, and likewise many other persons who are not Students, who persist in playing at ball, particularly in the Evenings, after the usual hours of teaching, by which great loss is sustained by the breaking of windows.

Classrooms were broken into and damaged, and there were occasional 'outrages' where (for instance) a medical student produced a pistol in the Anatomical Theatre. In 1810, while Carlyle was a student,

> Dr Meiklejohn also complained of the interruption occasioned by the cutting of stones within the College area.[8]

These are all necessary facts in building up a picture of the student experience Carlyle would have undergone. His was no life of dreaming towers in Edinburgh, for he would experience these nuisances in the College to the full, along with some in the streets surrounding the University area. Charles Cowan recalls walking the streets of the Old Town in 1811 to be enrolled in the High School, and encountering a street fight, and ruffians 'running after the people on the pavement, and striking them with their sticks and making a great noise'.[9] In 1813, the streets of Edinburgh still merited the description of being 'infested with hordes of mendicants ... at every hour of the day and in the most open, undisguised and obtrusive manner'.[10] Carlyle, who walked alone much in these rapidly decaying streets whose wealthier inhabitants had moved North to the New Town, or South to 'George's Square', took the risk of being alone at night. On one occasion he had his hat broken by footpads, though this was his worst adventure.

> He saw three young men of this kind hanged. 'Before that I had seen a man from Liddesdale, Armstrong by name, hanged for horse-stealing. He was a strong man, grimly silent. His body spun and twitched horribly. I saw it before my eyes in the dark and in daylight for weeks. At last I drew the horrible figure on paper as exactly as I could, and thenceforth it ceased to haunt me.'

If this was the John Armstrong hanged in 1809 or 1810 for robbing a shop in Dalkeith[11] the incident can be dated to Carlyle's earliest and most impressionable years in the city. Like Dickens he was to become an inveterate walker of the night-time city streets in London, and a fearless one. In Edinburgh he would be growing rapidly to his six-foot stature (though he remained very lean throughout his life) and this, with the rapidity of his stride, probably protected him from actual assault.

Nevertheless such details underline the realities of student life for Carlyle and his contemporaries in 1810 and afterwards. Wartime, a half-built college, a rapidly decaying urban environment all contributed to an atmosphere which must have seemed strangely at variance with that of the English Universities. Small wonder that Lockhart (a graduate of both a Scottish and an English University) should have scored a point off Edinburgh's student body in *Peter's Letters* of 1819, making his fictitious Welsh tourist write home from Edinburgh as follows:

> A person whose eyes had been accustomed only to such places as the schools of Oxford ... would certainly be very much struck with the *primâ facie* mean condition of the majority of the students assembled at the praelections of these Edinburgh professors.[12]

If the students did not possess the wealth or elegance which stereotype pictures of gentleman commoners at the English Universities evoke, then with what presuppositions did they come to Edinburgh? They were in general extremely young; Carlyle was several weeks short of his fourteenth birthday on his arrival, and was by no means exceptional. They did not seek the 'M.A.' degree, for many were content to leave the University without graduation. Nor, for that matter, did they seek a professional training in the first instance. The young and in many ways ill-prepared students who shared the classrooms with Carlyle came from a variety of school backgrounds, some as chaotic and dependent on chance intervention from friends or clergy as Carlyle's own, some from the High School of Edinburgh and its much-loved Rector Dr Adam, whose funeral in mid-December (1809) was among Carlyle's earliest Edinburgh memories.[13]

What each, rich and poor, well and ill prepared, underwent was best summed up as a training of the mind. The 'Arts' course in the Scottish Universities presupposed that a general grounding in philosophy – the training of the mind, in several specialised branches such as logic, moral philosophy, natural and mathematical philosophy, and training in languages – was a necessary prerequisite to specialised training in Divinity, Law, Medicine. The candidate for the Scottish Church was a graduate in Arts before commencing his Divinity training, or had at least completed an Arts course; Carlyle, destined for the Presbyterian ministry, was naturally to undergo such training, and the youths who occupied the benches with him would share much of his study exactly till their specialised avocations took over in fifth or later years. Many would share Carlyle's poverty: a basic course once over, they would set out to earn a slender living while completing their vocational training part-time (exactly as the 'Tom Donaldson' who trained Carlyle in Ecclefechan had been doing).

The training of aspirants for the ministry was a subject of continual debate between Church and University, and a notional curriculum for the University's guidance had more than once been suggested by the Assembly, though the University took good care not to commit itself to following it. It might run thus:

> *first year* Humanity and Elements of Greek
> *second year* Higher classes of the above, and Elements of Mathematics
> *third year* Logic and Higher Greek and Mathematics
> *fourth year* Natural Philosophy
> *fifth year* Moral Philosophy

Fourth and fifth years might be reversed, and along with these new disciplines it was assumed the student would continue Latin or Greek or Mathematics 'in one or more of the Higher classes'.[14]

It will be noted that English – rhetoric and belles lettres, as the professor taught it in the 'philosophical' schema of his time – has no place in the basic curriculum. It will be noticed also that the earlier years make allowance for the very imperfect preparatory schooling which the University authorities had learned to expect. Lockhart again has a sneer at 'the merest and narrowest rudiments of classical learning ... erudition, strictly so called' displayed at Edinburgh, though Jeffrey more sympathetically was to describe the Scottish system as

> enabling relatively large numbers of people to get ... that knowledge which tends to liberalise and make intelligent that mass of our population, more than anything else.

Benjamin Constant, who drew enormous pleasure from his years as a student in Edinburgh, left this well-known description.

> La discipline universitaire était des plus relâchées; le système tutorial, inconnu. Il était dans le caractère écossais de livrer les jeunes gens à eux-mêmes, pour les apprendre à se contrôler et à se maîtriser.[15]

Put less sympathetically, the stronger students swam strongly on the basis of their own initiative and self-discipline, the weaker ones floundered.

Carlyle's choice of curriculum was little surprise to those who would have expected him to be heading for the ministry. With some Latinity behind him from Ecclefechan and Annan, he embarked on Professor Christison's Latin lectures at eleven daily, when (another student reports) 'the then dreary and unfinished college was cheered by wintry sunshine'. Perhaps there was not sunshine enough: Carlyle's pique was raised by Christison's inability to tell the difference between himself and one Irving Carlyle, 'an older, considerably bigger boy, with flaming red hair, wild buck-teeth, and scorched complexion, and the *worst* Latinist of all my acquaintance; – so "*dark*" was the good Professor's "class-room", physically and otherwise'. David Masson, whose chapter in *Edinburgh Sketches and Memories* is still the pioneering account of this period in Carlyle's life, recorded of Carlyle that 'to the end of his life ... he was a fair Latinist', and Christison was to remember Carlyle to the extent of offering him preferment to a teaching post in 1816, so we may assume that Carlyle's Latin classes at Edinburgh were successful. Visibly, they gave him a professional skill which as teacher and private tutor he was to find most useful. Intangibly, they continued the process of widening the mind. Christison was a lecturer who believed in discoursing widely.

> Whatever occurred in the course of reading in the class, whether it regarded the language or the sentiment, he illustrated in a very miscellaneous way, calling in to his aid the writings of the most celebrated critics, poets and philosophers, ancient and modern. He also made frequent allusions to the sciences and even to the arts.[16]

Anyone familiar with the conversational style attributed to the mature Carlyle will be struck by the similarity: at an impressionable age, Carlyle may have found Christison's classes useful for more than their Latinity.

The same, definitely, did not hold true for his other first-year studies, in Greek under Professor Dunbar. Listeners found Dunbar 'grave, dry, and without interest', and his eight o'clock classes were undisciplined, cold and apparently uninteresting. 'Snores, protracted yawns, and other indecorous noises, with practical jokes of diverse kinds, wore through the long hour'.[17]

Astonishingly, this is the sum of Carlyle's first academic year: elementary language classes (with professorial inquisition sessions, but without tutorials as we know them) with no individual contact, no extramural teaching, inadequate library facilities (of which more anon) and little more beyond Carlyle's own circle of friends, relieved by letters from home, letters which came by the Ecclefechan carrier and were often accompanied by welcome presents of food, clean clothes, and small luxuries. Already, if we can take his later statement to David Davidson literally, Carlyle was tutoring to make some extra money: Davidson, he was to say later, reminded him of a major 'to whom I was sent to teach him mathematics, when I was only fourteen years old, and a very apt scholar I found him'.[18]

To continue with the curriculum: Carlyle in his second year continued to study Greek (with, we may infer, success, given his ability to tutor in this language later in life) and moved on to study elementary logic under Professor Ritchie, a solid and competent Edinburgh city minister who held the chair and had to introduce his subject to a youthful class. 'I cannot say that I am sensible of any great advantage from this course', wrote one auditor, and another dismissed Ritchie as 'great at curling, no ingenious contriver of neat little partitions of the divine spirit in man'.[19] Again, Carlyle later in life showed himself able enough in logic, and in knowledge of Scottish logical history: like his Greek studies, we may assume logic gave him little trouble.

Both, however, would be receding from the forefront of his interest in this second year, as he discovered what was to be his *métier* for the next decade of his life – mathematics. John Leslie, mathematician and natural philosopher, an eccentric scholar of European reputation, befriended Carlyle who responded warmly, his response taking the form of devoted study of the subject, extra-curricular discussion of it with his mentor, and even the experiment of putting forward new geometrical solutions one of which was to be incorporated in one of Leslie's textbooks, credited warmly to 'Mr Thomas Carlyle'. Carlyle's lecture notes are close-worked and careful (they survive in the Carlyle House in Chelsea), and his class certificate concisely testified he

> applied himself with the greatest diligence and success, & that he appeared to possess talents peculiarly fitted for mathematical investigation.[20]

A pattern is doubly established. In this second year, Carlyle's studies catch fire when he finds the inspiration of a teacher whom he can relate to personally. At the same time, the 'ministry' curriculum becomes distinctly lopsided as Carlyle's interests move towards natural sciences.

The third and fourth sessions reinforced this movement. As far as personal responses are concerned, the happy contact with Leslie was to some extent reinforced by his admiration for the veteran Professor Playfair, now an internationally renowned authority in physics or natural philosophy as it was taught in Scottish Universities. The 'fine old Archimedes with his reposed demeanour' seemed attractive to visitors like Lockhart but then Lockhart did not have to sit through Playfair's lectures, every word of them read. The evidence of surviving student notes, copiously written and carefully illustrated, in Edinburgh University Library, might make us pause before accepting Carlyle's description following, but at least we are brought face to face with the difference between visiting a Grand Old Man once, and studying under him in his declining years when a daily lecture was his sole contribution to the life of the University.

> For years I attended his lectures [*sic*], in all weathers and all hours. Many and many a time, when the class was called together, it was found to consist of one individual – to wit, of him now speaking. ... I remember no instance in which these facts elicited any note or comment from that instructor. He once requested me to translate a mathematical paper, and I worked through it the whole of one Sunday, and it was laid before him, and it was received without remark or thanks.[21]

One can understand the adolescent Carlyle's wish to see another Professor respond to his enthusiasms, but one can also see Playfair's grave reserve preventing him from the easy familiarity with favourites which came naturally to Leslie. The famous class certificate Playfair gave Carlyle at the end of the year of study, with its interpolated phrase 'I have reason to know that he has made proficiency in the study of Natural Philosophy' might have seemed to Playfair reward enough, but to the eager Carlyle it must have been bitterly disappointing.

Disappointment, too, was the response he felt to the third-year course he undertook afresh, moral philosophy under Thomas Brown, who had succeeded Dugald Stewart,

> an eloquent acute little gentleman; full of enthusiasm about 'simple suggestion' and 'relative' ditto – to me unprofitable utterly & bewildering & dispiriting 'as the autumn winds, among the withered leaves'.

Quite simply, Brown's 'fine' manner, his reliance on quotations from literature to make philosophical points, and his analytical method which was ill-suited to Carlyle's impatient nature, easily repelled Carlyle from paying much attention to the subject. To do him justice he was not alone – others write of Brown's 'affected feminine delivery'[22] – but in later life his impatience with 'logic-chopping' analysis of the human intellect ties in with this early impatience with the subject. Which came first is a subject for interesting discussion – if the later habit of mind sprang from a rejection of Brown's teaching, or whether the rejection was inevitable.

Leslie's teaching was a thread which ran through his senior under-graduate years. In his second, third and fourth years he pursued mathematics relentlessly; Brown was a disappointment in the third year, and further Greek cannot have been exciting; mathematics and natural philosophy would enliven the fourth.

In his only attempt at fiction, Carlyle was to try to put into words the experience of studying at Edinburgh in these years.

> Of his progress in the learned languages he himself made little account; nor in metaphysics did he find any light, but, rather, doubt or darkness ... Mathematics and the kindred sciences, at once occupying and satisfying his logical faculty, took much deeper hold of him; nay, by degrees, as he felt his own independent progress, almost alienated him for a long season from all other studies.[23]

Perhaps this helps to explain the fate of the extra year, 1813–14, spent at University preparing himself for part-time Divinity study while teaching for a living. The three Divinity professors he encountered then leave so little record in Carlyle's correspondence and recollections, as almost to be ciphers. Carlyle could remember the vivid speech of Professor Ritchie of Divinity and parody him to William Allingham half-a-century later;[24] Church History and Meiklejohn fade in his letters to nothing; Brunton of Hebrew is interesting for student gossip –

> Brunton, I hear, has got the Hebrew chair ... aye! aye! 'Kissing goes by favour' [is] true yet, I see. –

but for little more. Compared with the excitements of mathematics and physics, Divinity Hall is very plainly a dull place to Carlyle at this time. In 1817 he wrote after one of his periodic visits to Divinity Hall which were necessary to keep his Divinity candidacy alive,

> I heard Leslie give a lecture on heat: – it displayed great ingenuity, but his experiments did not succeed. ... I intended to have enrolled in the Divinity-Hall; but their Doctor [Ritchie] was too busily engaged otherwise to attend to me. ... I have not been within its walls for many months – & I know not whether I shall ever return, but all accounts agree in representing it as one of the most melancholy & unprofitable corporations, that has appeared in these parts for a great while. If we are to judge of the kind of Professors we should get from the Edin*r* Kirk, by the sample we already possess, it is devoutly to be wished that their

visits may be short & far between. It may safely be asserted that tho'
the Drs Ritchie junior & senior, with Dr Meiklejohn, Dr Brunton &
Dr Brown were to continue in their chairs, dosing in their present
fashion, for a century, all the knowledge which they could discover,
would be an imperceptible quantity – if indeed it sign [*sic*] were not
negative.[25]

We readily dispose of the remainder of Carlyle's student years. He had
kept up desultory contact with Divinity Hall till 1818, then resigned all hope
of the ministry. He retained his library privileges, though there again he
thought them obviously of limited utility.

> I have, it is true, the privilege of appearing on the floor of the college
> library, to *ask* for any book, – to wait about an hour, and then to fi[nd it
> missing].

Professor Jameson, whose natural history lectures Carlyle attended in the
session 1818–19, was an internationally eminent historian and geologist,
but again personal response to the man behind the reputation seems to have
counted much more to Carlyle than the reputation itself.

> Destitute of accurate science, without comprehension of mind, – he
> details a chaos of facts, [which] he accounts for in a manner as slovenly
> as he selects and arranges them.

Neither did Professor Hume of Scots Law fire Carlyle's enthusiasm, despite
the glowing tributes he drew from other students, including Scott. To
Carlyle,

> His lectures on law are (still excepting Erskine's Institutes[s]) the
> dullest piece of stuff I ever saw or heard of. Long-winded, dry details
> about points not of the slightest importance to any but an attorney or a
> notary public.... By degrees I got disheartened.... I became remiss in
> my efforts to follow our lecturer thro' the vast and thorny desart he was
> traversing; till at length I abandoned him altogether.[26]

Less than a page for two years' study; it seems about the right length, judged
by the impact made on Carlyle's letters and recollections, and the traceable
impact on his reading at the time.

The academic studies are difficult to judge overall. Plainly, a general
grounding in arts for a student from such a restricted background, and the
sheer grind of a disciplined education at such an age could not but be useful.
On the other hand, only a candidate for the ministry would have seen the
utility of the course as laid out for Carlyle and his contemporaries – and
some, like Edward Irving, plainly took refuge in wide and miscellaneous
reading as a necessary change from the stifling narrowness of their training.

Reading was always a relief from study for Carlyle; a relief, too, from the faltering of direction he experienced when he left the certainties of Ecclefechan for the freedom of Edinburgh. To go home and ask his mother 'Did God Almighty come down and make wheelbarrows in a shop', or to speak openly of the Song of Solomon as symbolical rather than literally true,[27] was to move accidentally from one rôle to the other. In Ecclefechan, religion (while rational) involved acceptance of an omniscient and omnipotent God; literal acceptance of Scripture would go hand in hand with such central tenets, and would explain (and excuse) the prohibition of imaginative literature. That his parents allowed Carlyle to go to the freethinking of Edinburgh is to their credit; that they continued to welcome home a son whose mind was plainly wandering in paths abhorrent to them is still more to their credit; most of all, they must be honoured for their loyalty to him when he announced that he could not, in conscience, be a candidate for the Church. They loyally accepted his decision, and continued to make him welcome.

Edinburgh University emancipated him from Ecclefechan; Ecclefechan, narrow as it was, was wide enough in *its* vision to make room for an apostate son. Carlyle was thus able to combine Edinburgh's education with a living link with the Scottish countryside from which he came. Throughout his description of the educative years of his youth, he stresses self-achievement, self-education through reading and discipline. The earliest description of him which survives, from the early student years soon after 1810, amply bears out the shadowy picture which emerges from the catalogues of likes and dislikes, classes enjoyed and classes spurned, fairly or unfairly.

> [Carlyle] was distinguished at that time by the same peculiarities that still mark his character [in 1849] – sarcasm, irony, extravagance of sentiment, and a strong tendency to undervalue others, combined, however, with great kindness of heart and great simplicity of manner. His external figure, though then only about fifteen years of age, was similar to what it now is – tall, slender, awkward, not apparently very vigorous. His provincial intonation was then very remarkable, and it still remains so; his speech was copious and bizarre.[28]

The letters of the period, which occupy the early volumes of the Duke-Edinburgh edition, attest to the attraction Carlyle's character had for those student friends whom he valued, and allowed to come close to his prickly personality. 'That you write so seldom', said Thomas Murray (one of his confidants), 'is the only circumstance I have to regret'. Carlyle, for his part, wrote well but rarely. 'My dear Mitchell, I opened your last letter with fear and trembling. . . . My dear Mitchell, I know I should have written you a month ago'.[29] Fierce loyalty to those he liked (Edward Irving above all others from this period of his life), and fierce and sometimes unreasoning opposition to those he disliked, characterised Carlyle as it characterises many students of his age at any period. Two things distinguish Carlyle. One is the vividness of the record he left of these troubled years of change and self-discovery. The other is his quite extraordinary reading.

Reading was a perpetual resource for Carlyle, who was easily bored and felt the need of companionship keenly. In 1815, freshly arrived in Annan from University, he complained to a contemporary of the loneliness of a tutor's life 'left to *commune with himself*',

> and tho' we cannot enjoy the spirit-stirring *crack* of our jocund cronies
> – yet if we can spend the same time, with Shakespeare or Addison or
> Stewart, we are gainers by the privation.[30]

At University, his friend Thomas Murray recorded, Carlyle read through all 45 volumes of Chalmers' edition of *The British Essayists*, 'without interruption, a herculean task', and further noted some favourite authors – Shakespeare, the English poets, Burns, etc. 'He was not given to history or metaphysics'.[31]

At Edinburgh, he had the University library, open in 1814 for 'four full hours every lawful day', though the 700,000 volumes were inconveniently stored, and in some cases in deplorable condition. Carlyle read there avidly, and added the library of Divinity Hall when his candidacy of that institution gave him access to it – interestingly, reading much more widely in science and in literature than in divinity, as records show. Later still, Carlyle was to have access to the library of his friend Irving in Kirkcaldy, and then to that of the Faculty of Advocates in Edinburgh. In Craigenputtoch he longed for a library, and even once settled in London he was to find the absence of an easily consulted major collection a continual problem till the formation of the London Library, partly at his own instigation. In Edinburgh, he was simply omnivorous. He read rapidly; he was to recall his first encounter with Irving's library.

> I think I must have read it almost through; – inconceivable to me now,
> with what ardour, with what greedy *velocity*, literally above *ten times*
> the speed I can now make with any Book.[32]

A man of seventy and more can look back and exaggerate in this way, but his summing-up that 'I must have read ... a great deal during these years' is something of an understatement.

Looking back as Teufelsdröckh in *Sartor Resartus* Carlyle was to remember his college experience: he warns us against taking *Sartor* too easily as literal autobiography, but this passage rings true.

> Nay, from the chaos of that Library, I succeeded in fishing-up more

books perhaps than had been known to the very keepers thereof. The
foundation of a Literary Life was hereby laid.[33]

The same emphasis is the one he lays on the outcome of University life in his
Rectorial Address of 1866.

What the Universities have mainly done – what I have found the
University did for me, was that it taught me to read in various
languages and various sciences, so that I could go into the books that
treated of these things, and try anything I wanted to make myself
master of gradually, as I found it suit me.[34]

And that is no bad point at which to pause in our consideration of student
life in Carlyle's time. We have already noticed that Carlyle's narrow circle at
University excluded many who were better off, and with wider experience,
men who came to Edinburgh through religious exclusion from other
institutions, or through their parents' inability to pay for an Oxford
education, though an Edinburgh one was well within their means. Carlyle's
circle excluded, too, most of those companions who shared the professors'
benches with him, played their forbidden football outside, even perhaps
attended the meetings of student clubs and societies which feature so little in
Carlyle's correspondence at the time. He may mention the Philalethic and a
couple of debating clubs, and his health was even the toast in his absence at
one student meeting,[35] but Carlyle was a man with a circle of friends no
larger than five or six (one, an enigmatic Miss Merchant, we would like to
know more about), intense attachments to certain professors such as Leslie,
huge gluts of reading in his lodgings, long solitary walks by night, or on his
favourite Arthur's Seat and Salisbury Crags. Try as we may to recreate the
actual physical setting of Edinburgh University in the ten years following
Carlyle's arrival, we picture only an institution which impinged on his vision
as little as he could arrange. For the rest, his was a world of narrow friendship
and wide reading. It was a strenuous existence, and it is easy to see in it the
seeds of future nervous working habits, dyspepsia, and strain.

Yet there is something to regret in these Edinburgh years. The
memorable description in the *Reminiscences* of Princes Street in these years,
its pavements busy with a confident crowd of North Britons going about
their business, secure in the knowledge that they are living in a culture-
capital, is very much seen from the outside. 'As for me, I never could afford
to promenade or linger there; and only a few times, happened to float
leisurely thro', on my way elsewhither'.[36] Exaggeration again, no doubt;
Carlyle would have preferred his own company, or that of his books. It was a
mixture of this attitude, and general roughness of dress and manners, which
excluded him from much that could have helped him in Edinburgh during

his protracted student years. Jeffrey's circle at Craigcrook or in his town houses, Cockburn's in Bonaly, Blackwood's salon in George Street were quite alien to him. He read the reviewers (as his letters make plain) and he followed the latest publications, but he did not contribute to this Scottish activity. Instead he kept his distance and read avidly. Biding his time, he took from Edinburgh University everything he could, rejected a large part, and moulded the rest to his wishes.

Ahead lay years of loneliness and self-doubt, the dark years of *Sartor Resartus*, a gradual shift from scientific to German interests, and thence to social and historical questions. Ahead lay schoolmastering, tutoring, translation, reviewing, essay-writing. Ahead lay the short-lived romance with Margaret Gordon, and the long slow courtship of Jane Welsh in Haddington. Marriage, Comely Bank, Craigenputtoch, Chelsea were unimagined.

It is hard to see the mature Carlyle, the striking author of 'Signs of the Times' in 1829 and *Sartor Resartus* two years later, emerging from any *milieu* other than such as has been described in Edinburgh University in this period. Wartime Edinburgh, its society reinforced by those who might otherwise have gone to the continent, its reviews claiming part of the literary glory while the future author of *Waverley* effortlessly went from success to success, was an exciting place to be, however little actual contact Carlyle could have with the producers of the literary successes of his time. The intellectual excitement of a large University is plain from his letters. Major libraries were available, and he made full use of them. Among the professors were men of international reputation, men known on the European continent as well as in their own country; in Leslie, Carlyle found an inspiration which was to carry him through a period of slackening identity and purpose, to give him a burning interest (and a means of livelihood) till German literature came to engross his thoughts.

Had Carlyle been a 'hungry schoolmaster' (his own contemptuous term for place-seeking graduates) he would have been well served by his prestigious Alma Mater. Had he been preparing for Law, Medicine or the Church, he could have received a sound basic training. Edinburgh provided these services for his contemporaries. Instead, Carlyle wanted to work out for himself where his allegiances lay, and where his calling in life would be. In the large, impersonal, bookish excitement of Edinburgh University he found just the anonymity, and just the selectivity of stimulus, to make possible the emergence of Teufelsdröckh from the chrysalis of Thomas Carlyle. Neither Teufelsdröckh nor Carlyle, looking back as Rector in 1866, seemed particularly grateful. Had Edinburgh University forced itself more on Carlyle in these years, he might have settled gracefully or – worse still – happily into one of the professions. Instead, he isolated himself in his cheap lodgings for ferocious bouts of reading, and the accompanying early intimations of dyspepsia, working out his apprenticeship as Sage of Chelsea.

When he returned to Edinburgh in 1866 to give his Rectorial Address, he was of course successful beyond his wildest dreams. When he heard the students' cheers in the street afterwards, Carlyle's reaction was an interesting one.

> I waved my hand prohibitively at the door . . . and they gave but one cheer more – something in the tone of *it* which did for the first time go into my heart. Poor young men, so well affected to the poor old brother or grandfather here, and in such a black whirlpool of a world, all of us.[37]

Perhaps now we have some idea of the thoughts which must have been crowding through his head in George Street as he waved to the crowds, and wrote finis to his relations with Edinburgh University.

REFERENCES

1. In 1866 Friedrich Althaus prepared a sketch of Carlyle's life for *Unsere Zeit*, a periodical in Leipzig. Carlyle corrected Althaus' account, and the corrected copy is preserved in NLS. The best single account of Carlyle's youthful education appears in his notes to Althaus. These can best be consulted in John Clubbe's *Two Reminiscences of Thomas Carlyle* (Durham, N.C. 1974) 29–30.

2. Horn, 91; Ian Campbell, 'Carlyle and the Secession', *Records of the Scottish Church History Society*, xviii, 1 (1972) 48–64.

3. 'James Carlyle', from T. Carlyle, *Reminiscences*, ed. I. Campbell (London 1972) 3; Frederick Martin, *Biographical Magazine* (1877). Carlyle's disapproval led to the suppression of further instalments of what was to have been a biography; Carlyle, *Reminiscences*, 12, 9.

4. Carlyle – Margaret Aitken Carlyle (his mother), 2 January 1827, quoted from *The Collected Letters of Thomas and Jane Welsh Carlyle*, ed. C. R. Sanders, K. J. Fielding *et al.* (Duke-Edinburgh edition, Durham, N.C., iv [1970] 180). (Hereafter *Letters*.)

5. *Letters of Thomas Carlyle to William Graham*, ed. J. Graham Jr., (Princeton 1950) 27.

6. Carlyle, *Reminiscences*, 177, 9.

7. Grant, ii, 197–208, especially 203; Thomas Pennant, *A Tour in Scotland MDCCLXIX* (London 1790) 69.

8. *Senate Minutes*, ii, 86–7, 535; iii (1812–24) 38; ii, 535.

9. Charles Cowan, *Reminiscences* ([private printing], 1878) 23.

10. L. J. Saunders, *Scottish Democracy 1815–1840* (Edinburgh and London 1950) 226.

11. W. Allingham, *A Diary*, ed. D. Allingham and H. Radford (London

1907) 219–20; W. Forbes Gray, 'Reminiscences of a Town Clerk', *The Book of the Old Edinburgh Club*, xiv (Edinburgh 1925) 160.

12. [J. G. Lockhart], *Peter's Letters to his Kinsfolk* ('second' [first] edition, Edinburgh, London and Glasgow 1819) i, 187.

13. As told to Ruskin: see J. Ruskin, *Works* (London 1907) ii, 351.

14. *Senate Minutes*, ii, 513–8.

15. Lockhart, *Peter's Letters*, i, 151–2; Jeffrey is quoted from George Elder Davie, *The Democratic Intellect* (Edinburgh 1961) 27; G. Rudler, *La jeunesse de Benjamin Constant 1767–1794* (Paris 1908) 122.

16. R. P. Gillies, *Memoirs of a Literary Veteran* (London 1851) i, 209; Carlyle, *Reminiscences*, 185; David Masson, *Edinburgh Sketches and Memories* (Edinburgh 1892) 230; the records of the appointment are in NLS MS 2883, and Christison's letter to Carlyle in NLS MS 1764.78; Bower, iii, 300.

17. Dunbar is described in Cowan, *Reminiscences*, 26; *The Life of Sir Robert Christison, Bart, edited by his Sons* (Edinburgh and London 1885) i, 38; Gillies, *Memoirs*, i, 208.

18. D. Davidson, *Memories of a Long Life* (Edinburgh 1890) 299.

19. Cowan, *Reminiscences*, 28; A. Campbell Fraser, *Biographia Philosophica* (Edinburgh and London 1904) 246.

20. Leslie and Playfair were two of Carlyle's instructors known particularly in Switzerland, and whose private conversation may have had an important bearing on Carlyle's early attitude to Europe; J. Leslie, *Elements of Geometry* (Edinburgh, third edition, 1817) 340. For an important discussion see Carlisle Moore, 'Carlyle: Mathematics and "Mathesis"', *Carlyle Past and Present*, ed. K. J. Fielding and R. L. Tarr (London 1976) 61–95; class certificate preserved in EUL.

21. Lockhart, *Peter's Letters*, i, 183; Moncure Conway, *Autobiography* (London 1904) ii, 90.

22. Clubbe, *Two Reminiscences*, 33; *Life of Christison*, i, 45.

23. *Wotton Reinfred*, quoted from *Last Words of Thomas Carlyle* (London 1892) 22–3.

24. Allingham, *A Diary*, 232.

25. *Letters*, i, 4; i, 97–8.

26. *Letters*, i, 159–60; i, 149–50; i, 246.

27. Allingham, *A Diary*, 253, 268.

28. Thomas Murray, *Autobiographical Notes*, ed. J. A. Fairley (Dumfries 1911) 15.

29. These may be supplemented with letters *to* Carlyle, which are listed in *Letters*, i, xlv–xlix; NLS MS 1764.58; *Letters*, i, 64, 68.

30. *Letters*, i, 53.

31. Murray, *Autobiographical Notes*, 21.

32. *Senate Minutes*, iii, 77; R. Chambers, *Walks in Edinburgh* (Edinburgh 1825) 246–7; Grant, ii, 179; C. P. Finlayson, 'Thomas Carlyle's borrowings from Edinburgh University Library 1819–1820', *The Bibliotheck*, iii, 4 (1961) 138–43; Ian Campbell, 'Carlyle's borrowings from the Theological Library of Edinburgh University', *The Bibliotheck*, v, 5 (1969) 165–8; Carlyle, *Reminiscences*, 187.

33. *Sartor Resartus*, quoted from Carlyle's *Works* (Centenary Edition, London 1896–9) i, 113.
34. Carlyle, *On the Choice of Books* (London 1866) 56.
35. *Letters*, i, 87–8; NLS MS 1764.21.
36. *Reminiscences*, 367.
37. David Alec Wilson and David Wilson MacArthur, *Carlyle in Old Age (1865–1881)* (London 1934) 53.

The Symposium Academicum

C.P. FINLAYSON

Edinburgh University's Symposium Academicum, first known as the Social Convention of the College of Edinburgh, started as a fairly staid annual social meeting of members of the Senate in the late eighteenth century and finished up ninety years later as a true Symposium Academicum with lively disputations, songs, good food and drink and latterly even cigars. It was not regularly termed the Symposium until the thirty-first meeting, in 1822.[1]

The first meeting took place on Saturday 31 March 1792 at the Star and Garter Tavern in Writers' Court, 'the propriety and advantage of a Social annual convention of the professors having been suggested at an accidental conversation about College business between Dr William Robertson, Principal of the University of Edinburgh, and Dr Andrew Duncan'. Principal Robertson, who was nearing the end of his career, was not well enough to attend this meeting, but eighteen professors were present and they drew up a set of regulations giving practical effect to the scheme.

The Social Convention was to be held annually on the last Saturday of March in a local tavern, with dinner at 4 o'clock, followed by tea and coffee at 7. The Chair was to be taken by the Principal, whom failing the Professor of Divinity, the Professor of Church History or the senior professor present. There was to be a Convenor, usually known later as the Conditor, who acted as Croupier or assistant chairman, and Professor Duncan was the first to hold this office. He was to give due intimation of the meeting to every professor, to keep a record of those present and absent (with the latters' excuses) and 'of any other particulars which the meeting may think proper to direct'. To begin with, those particulars consisted of the menu or bill of fare, a detailed account of expenses, any changes in the Senatus during the year and the total number of students attending the University. A special motion was carried unanimously at the first meeting that 'considering the great reputation which Dr Robertson, Principal of the University, has obtained by his excellent writings, the dignity he has always supported as head of this Society for thirty years and particularly the great attention he has paid to the increase and flourishing state of the Library, they should take this opportunity to bestow a mark of respect on him in his absence, occasioned by want of health, by agreeing to request of him to sit to Mr Raeburn for his portrait, to be hung up in the Library'. Professors Joseph Black and Alexander Fraser Tytler were chosen to ask the Principal if he would sit for his portrait when his health allowed.

At the second meeting, which took place in the Star and Garter on 30 March 1793, Black and Tytler reported that they had commissioned Raeburn to proceed, but at the third meeting, on 29 March 1794, among the changes reported in the Senatus was the death of Robertson on 11 June 1793. The portrait had, however, been completed, at a cost of 30 guineas for Raeburn, 7 guineas for Mr Liddle, the framer, and 6s. for John Wilson, Under Janitor, who collected the painting. The 27 Professors contributed 1 gn. and 8s. each.

In the Bill of Fare for the third meeting, typical of those early gatherings at the Star and Garter, the main items were Lamb-Head Stove, Turbot, Chickens, Jellies, Turtle Soup, Salmon, Roast Pig, Blancmange, Skink Soup and Marrow Pudding. The expenses were: Dinner, £2 10s., Fruits 12s.6d., Bread and Beer for the Porter 11s.6d., 4 bottles Port and 2 bottles Sherry 17s., 3 bottles Madeira 13s.6d., 6 pints Claret, Cherry Brandy 3s., Negus and Toddy 7s.6d., 'the Cadies' 6d., the Cook for biscuits, prawns and chestnuts 7s.6d., Tea and Coffee 16s. In addition, 3s. was paid to the collector of each professor's share, 10s.6d. to the waiters, 10s.6d. to the transcriber of the minutes, making total expenses of £10 17s. The 19 professors paid 12s.6d. each, leaving a credit balance of £1 0s.6d.

At the seventh meeting, on 31 March 1798, another portrait was ordered from Raeburn, that of Lord Provost Thomas Elder, for his 'indefatigable exertions in beginning and advancing the new buildings for the College of Edinburgh'. The minutes of the eighth meeting, held as usual at the Star and Garter on 30 March 1799, show that the artist received 35 gns, the framer 6 gns and the porter 10s., paid for by the 26 professors who had supported the scheme.

The minutes of the meeting of 25 March 1815 record more symposiastic activities in addition to the usual statistical data: 'Upon the health of the Benefactors of the University being drunk, Dr Duncan, senior, moved that as the Rt. Hon. Wm. Dundas, Sir John Marjoribanks, Robert Johnston, Esq. and John Waugh, Esq., had exerted themselves very strenuously to obtain aid from Government for finishing the buildings of the College, an extraordinary Social Meeting should be held about the beginning of

November next to which these four gentlemen should be invited that the University might have an opportunity of returning them a cup of thanks for their meritorious services'. An extraordinary meeting was indeed held on 15 December, but 'in consequence of some circumstances suggested by the Principal' the idea of entertaining the four gentlemen was for the time being relinquished.

There are indications in the minutes of the meeting of 30 March 1822 of some unpleasantness. Some of the absentees had sent excuses, others were known to be ill or out of town, but 'as Dr Monro and Dr Thomson had been so impolite as to send no answer whatever for three successive years, it was agreed that no intimation should be sent to them of any future meeting, that they might not annually have this opportunity of shewing want of respect to the University'. It was also agreed to send no further notices to Professor Leslie, who had twice intimated his intention to be absent 'in very impolite terms'. Leslie atoned at the Initial Meeting for Session 1825–6, when he attended and supplied 'some excellent wine, a full bumper of which was drunk by every member present, to his health and better attendance'.

In 1806 the meeting-place had moved from the Star and Garter to the New Club Tavern in West Register Street and it remained there until 1816. Thereafter meetings were held in the Senate Hall and on 29 March 1823 it was decided that there should in future be three meetings yearly, an Initial in November, a Mid-winter in January and a Concluding Symposium in March. The Mid-winter or Christmas Meeting of 3 January 1824, however, was attended by only five members, and although the Principal found it the most pleasant and agreeable that he had ever attended, it was resolved that no future meeting should be held 'at that dissipated season of the year'. This was confirmed on 20 November following, 'as most of the Professors are very dissipated during the Christmas Holidays'.

Plenty of attention was paid to food and drink at the meeting on the last Friday in March 1824. Dr James Home agreed 'to send a dozen of excellent Rum as a provision for the Senate's catacomb upon the express condition that one bottle and no more of that Nectar should be used every year for 12 years to come'. Besides, 'the Roast Beef and Plum Pudding were both declared to be excellent and the Mirth abundantly noisy'. Alexander Brunton, Professor of Hebrew, who, as Curator of the Library, had a house in the College, 'offered to furnish the Senate with a catacomb in his cellar for preserving the surplus picnic liquors sent for promoting their cordiality, and Dr Brown (Professor of Rhetoric), and Mr Dunbar (Professor of Greek) were appointed to get it filled with excellent wine at cheap prices, out of which *Quantum sufficit* might be taken at each Symposium'.

Fluctuating levels of attendance seem to have done little to affect enjoyment. On 20 November 1824, when thirteen members were present, the minutes record that 'though not numerous it was very joyous', and when only six Symposiasts attended the Initial Meeting for 1826–7 'the Party, though not numerous, had a peculiarly pleasant social meeting, the consequence of which was that they did not separate till a late hour, having partaken of oysters and toddy after tea and coffee'. At the March Symposium which followed, when seventeen members were present, letters of apology from Baron David Hume (owing to illness) and Lord Newton (owing to business commitments) were transcribed in the minutes. Those present had 'a merry meeting, and finished with tea and coffee about 9 o'clock, with the Proverb of the Free Masons – "Happy to meet, happy to part, and not without hopes of being happy to meet again" '.

Two meetings were held in each of the Sessions 1828–9 and 1829–30 and the Initial Meeting in 1830–31, but then 'from accidental circumstances the Symposia were in abeyance from November 1830 till April 1833'; the next meeting recorded was, however, not until April 1834, when thirteen members attended under the chairmanship of Principal Baird. The next meeting was fixed for the statutory date, last Friday in November 1834, but the Senate Hall was booked that day for the Annual General Meeting of the University (when the Matriculation List was closed and above 1,100 students who attended had the Sponsio Academica read out to them and 'were suitably exhorted by the Principal'), so the Symposium was transferred to the British Hotel, 70 Queen Street, and Professor Alexander Brunton took the chair in the absence of the Principal, with an attendance of seventeen.

The British Hotel, whose landlord was J. H. Barry, was used again on 15 April 1835 and although only six members were present some almost preferred it that way. 'The Symposium was never celebrated with more harmony or in a more agreeable manner ... although those present had reason to lament the absence of too many of their brethren, even of some who had intimated formally their intention to be present. But they were in some respect consoled by Mr Barry's excellent wine, which, they felt assured, the members who had failed to attend would not grudge to those who had come with the hope of enjoying their society'. For the first time the minutes record the name of a musician at the Symposium: 'Professor [Douglas] Cheape [Civil Law] favoured the company with a song of that sober and temperate mood and measure which best befit the attention and enjoyment of learned ears. So much was this the case that the Professor, on being strongly entreated, was so obliging as to repeat it'. Now that the organisation was over forty years old it began to appreciate its history. 'Some little time was pleasantly, yet mournfully, spent in looking over the curious record of former meetings, particularly of the olden time, and the effect was a strengthening of the conviction of all present of the propriety of continuing such stated meetings of entertainment which not only help to smooth brows furrowed with learned toils, but to unite in brotherly bonds those otherwise connected in the grave and high functions of Academic tuition'. A mood was induced somewhat critical of the increasingly convivial character of recent Symposia and it was the unanimous opinion of all present that their meetings 'can only fitly and appropriately be held in the Senate Hall in the midst of the images and recollections of the illustrious dead and that no considerations connected with the quality of the repast or other trifling inconveniences ought hereafter to prevent the stated dinners from taking place in that hallowed apartment'. It was therefore resolved that the first Symposium of the next session should be held in the Senate Hall on the third Friday of November and that the dinner should consist of such dishes as might be sent there or prepared in the house of the College porter. Friday, it was agreed, was more suitable than Saturday because it permitted a later hour for dinner and enabled the servants to rearrange the apartments on the morning immediately following. Behind this decision lay a change in the Scottish dinner hour, which 'had moved slowly round the household clock from twelve to four, where a generation manfully stayed its course, but now [in the late 1850s] it bounded forward in half-hour leaps, fixing itself for a time at six o'clock'.[2] The usual time for the Symposium therefore became 7 p.m.

It turned out, however, that the Senate Hall presented difficulties. On 20 October 1835 Professor Alexander Brunton resigned from his office as Conditor: his letter, bound into the Minute Book, stated, 'I know by experience that I cannot make satisfactory arrangements for dinner in the Senate Hall without an expense which would thin our ranks considerably' and he added that the majority of the members disapproved of dining together twice in the year. The result of this was that no further Symposia were held for thirteen years.

On Friday, 23 December 1848, 23 professors met at the Douglas Hotel, St Andrew Square (familiarly known as 'Slaney's' from the proprietor, Thomas Slaney), which remained a favourite venue into the 1870s. Principal Lee was in the Chair. In a serio-comical interlude Professor Robert Christison 'was solemnly deposed from the high office of Conditor Symposii as a punishment for his negligence in having allowed these social gatherings to fall into desuetude, and Archibald Swinton, Professor of Civil

Law, was unanimously elected as his successor'. After an evening 'spent in much hilarity, the diet was adjourned at 11 o'clock to the Observatory on the Calton Hill, where Professor Piazzi Smyth enlightened his colleagues by an exhibition of the starry heavens through a powerful telescope'.

An experiment was made with the Senate Hall on 21 December 1849; this time the Principal, whose official home was in the Old College, 'surrendered the use of his kitchen for the entertainment' and so avoided the expense of outside catering, but this cannot have been entirely satisfactory, for the next Symposium was held in Archers' Hall, beside the Meadows, which the Royal Company of Archers had been forced by financial difficulties to let for use as a tavern. There were two meetings at Greliche's Hotel, 100 Princes Street, in 1853, one on 21 January and the other on Christmas Day. On the second occasion the minutes contain a note of expenses: dinner and wines, £17 11s., waiters 13s., postage of circulars 5s. and fee for the collector of payments 5s., totalling £18 14s. In 1856 the Lord Provost and two Bailies were invited as guests of sixteen professors to 'celebrate the amicable termination of a long warfare between the Senatus and the Patrons of the University', and the Provost and a Bailie were present again in January 1857. The 1859–60 Session was marked by a meeting 'of a peculiarly joyous and festive description as being the first which had taken place since the University received an independent constitution, that glorious event having occurred on the 15th October 1859, at which date by Ordinance of the University Commissioners the provisions of the Act 21–22 Victoria c.83 came into operation'.

An expansive phase followed, initiated in 1860, when two additional convivial meetings of the Senate were recorded in the Minute Book. The first, on 10 April, was in honour of Gladstone, who was installed that day as Rector, and the second, on 18 May, in honour of the installation as Chancellor of Lord Brougham, who examined the Symposium Book 'with the deepest interest'. When Gladstone was again the guest of honour at the Douglas Hotel on 10 January 1862 'the festive demonstrations usual at these Convivial Conventions were gone through with their customary hilarity' and for the first time the musical performances are detailed: they included *The Massacre of the Macpherson*[3] by Professor Aytoun and a song 'descriptive of the manufacture and varied uses of glass by Professor J. H. Bennett'. Another special rectorial Symposium Academicum was held for Thomas Carlyle in 1866,[4] and two other rectors, the Marquis of Hartington (1879) and Lord Rosebery, are mentioned in the Minutes as special guests at regular meetings.

Still greater things were to come. Prince Alfred (who was to become Duke of Edinburgh in 1866) had matriculated at the University on 29 October 1863 and resided at Holyroodhouse while he attended the classes of Professor Cosmo Innes (History), Allman (Natural History), Tait (Natural Philosophy) and Lyon Playfair (Chemistry). He was entertained at a meeting on 22 January 1864 and the proceedings occupy five pages of the Minute Book. After the healths of the members of the royal family had been drunk, 'The Prosperity of the University of Edinburgh' was proposed by the Conditor Emeritus, Mr Campbell Swinton. Professor Maclagan, in the character of Signor Mario [Count Giuseppe Mario, the famous tenor] sang *Spirto Gentil* from *La Favorita* (Donizetti), with a slight variation in the libretto which converted it into a song illustrative of the virtues of chloroform, and subsequently, at the request of the illustrious guest of the evening, sang in his own character this song commendatory of cold water:

Air – 'Love's Young Dream'
Oh! The days are gone when claret bright
　　Inspired my strain
When I sang on every festive night
　　About champagne,
Prime '44 in floods may pour
　　And glasses gaily clatter
But there's nothing half so safe to drink
　　As plain cold water.

All five stanzas are recorded in the Minute Book. 'Professor James Miller then favoured the company with the original ditty entitled *Alcohol* . . . Professor Blackie delivered a Latin lay in praise of College life, the Conditor (Professor Aytoun) recited with Celtic energy *The Massacre of the Macpherson* and Professors Christison, Bennett and Maclagan sang Bishop's glee *Meinheer van Dunk* with great taste and execution'. The Prince had to leave at 9 o'clock for the Caledonian Railway Station, as he was due next day at a shooting party at Drumlanrig, and the Symposiasts then turned to 'serious' business, including the solemn trial of Professor Miller (Surgery) for 'drunkenness' and the consumption of spirituous liquors, aggravated in the case of a 'teetotaller'. Professor Maclagan (Forensic Medicine) deponed that he had analysed four of the 'entrements' (side-dishes) of which Miller had that evening gluttonously partaken, and had found that they contained large quantities of ardent spirits. After further proceedings the accused was requested to sing a song, which he forthwith did, to the delight of the company,.

The Symposia of January 1865 and 1866 were much occupied by

investigations into a letter from a Paris hotelier, M. Duraud, alleging that a Professor of Theology, said to be from Edinburgh, had left without paying his bill. Professors from the Faculty of Law were requested to look into the matter and the enquiry quickly took the usual serio-comic turn. Crawford (Divinity) suggested that all the professors in the Faculty of Divinity should have a free trip to Paris so that the culprit could be identified, and Syme countered with the proposal that the hotelier should be brought to Edinburgh, which would be cheaper, though less pleasant for the theologians. 'As there seemed to exist some difference of opinion among the members as how best to deal with this very serious affair, the Principal suggested the propriety of endeavouring to restore harmony by song', while the prosecution of the case was left to the Dean of Law. The following pieces of music, 'all of a strictly academic character', were submitted:

The Philosophy of Bantingism – a Doleful Dietetical Ditty, by the Vice Conditor (Professor Douglas Maclagan), to the air 'A wee bird cam' to our ha' door'. William Banting was the author of *A Letter on Corpulence addressed to the Public*,[5] in which he recommended a slimming diet, and the 'Ditty' is fully transcribed in the minutes, beginning with this stanza (the first of eight):

A wee man cam' to me ae day
In sair distress and pantin',
An' a' that I could hear him say
Was, 'I've been tryin' Bantin'.
An' whan I saw him look sae ill,
Wi' sheer starvation gantin',
I drew for him a pint o' yill [ale],
For I've nae faith in Bantin'.

The next two songs were by Professor John Stuart Blackie, the first a rendering of Horace's *Integer Vitae* to the tune of 'Maggie Lauder', the second one called *The Pope*. The fourth song was *The Battle of Glen Tilt*, again from Maclagan;[6] it describes an outing in 1847 by a party of naturalists headed by Professor John Hutton Balfour. On their way through Glen Tilt to Blair Atholl they were met by the Duke of Atholl and some attendants and ordered to go back to Braemar the way they had come as they were on a private road. This they politely but firmly refused to do, as they believed that the road they were on had been used as a public one from time immemorial. They stood their ground in spite of heavy rain and eventually escaped over a wall in the direction of Blair Atholl Inn. The song's penultimate stanza describes the climax of the encounter:

The gangin' back was easier said
Than it was dune, by far, man;
The nearest place to rest their head
Was up ayont Braemar, man.
'Twas best to seek Blair Athole Inn
For they were drookit to the skin.
Sae syne they a'
Lap o'er a wa',
Wi' a guffaw,
An' left the Hielan' hills, man.

Professor Balfour, who was present, testified to the historical accuracy of the narrative. The fifth musical item, by Professor Balfour, was *The Graduation Song: A Medical Student's Lament*, 'a melancholy ditty by David Leitch to the air "O, no, we never mention her"'. The full text was asked for and transcribed into the minutes of a later Symposium (14 January 1870). The sixth and last song of the evening was the German *Alter Schweise*, from Blackie. From this point, when a clear tradition of singing had been settled, several songs established themselves as favourites, and were given again and again over the years – *Spirto Gentil, The Battle of Glentilt, Meinheer van Dunk, The Graduation Song, Integer Vitae, The Pope*, all of which had appeared by the mid-'60s, and some which were introduced later.

On 12 January 1866 the toasts included those of Sir James Young Simpson, 'the first Scotch professor created a Baronet', and three new professors, Masson, Macpherson and Oakley. In replying, Masson 'said a great deal about Aberdeen (his native city) but nothing about the Symposium, Norman Macpherson said a great deal about the Symposium but nothing about Aberdeen'. Dr Christison complained that the minutes of the last meeting, so far as they related to the Theological Faculty, 'were so devoid of all trace of fun that future generations on reading the Minute would have no difficulty in taking it *au grand serieux*'. The account of the continued enquiries into the allegations of M. Duraud (the Paris hotelier) occupy no fewer than five pages in the minutes of the present meeting, but the fact that the private investigator employed was M. Vaut Rien prevents this business, at least, from being taken seriously. The words of *The Song of the Glass*, sung by Dr Bennett, were now recorded. The chorus runs:

Come push round the flagon, each brother,
But fill bumper in ere it pass
And while you hob-nob with another
I'll sing you the song of the Glass.

In six stanzas it was explained how the Goddess of Art fashioned glass from offerings obtained from the seashore by Beauty, Pleasure and Genius:

'Tis well, said the Goddess, as smiling
Each offering she anxiously scanned,
On the altar mysteriously piling
The brine and the wrack and the sand,
Mixing up with strange spells as she brewed them
Salt, soda and flint in a mass
With the flame of the lightning she .used them
And the marvellous compound was glass.

One of the new professors, Macpherson, failed to sing when called on and was sentenced to the statutory penalty of salt and water, but by the clemency of the Chair this was commuted to mulled claret. For once the Symposiasts concerned themselves with a serious question, the correct colours of the University's coat of arms, and the Professor of Public Law (James Lorimer) was appealed to, in his capacity as Lyon Clerk, 'to utter an authentic roar on this heraldic question'. At the following meeting Professor Christison, on Lorimer's behalf, reported that the official document relating to the arms was preserved in the Library.

In 1867 the Symposium took place on the last Friday (29th) of March, in accordance with a general opinion that a date at the end of the winter session was better than one during the 'formidable festive month of January', but next year it was decided to go back to the second Friday in January. At the same time (1868) it was resolved that the Symposium should have its place in the *Calendar*, and an insertion there for 1869–70 must be one of the few contemporary printed references to the Symposium.

At the 1867 meeting there was a long programme which included the following in addition to old favourites: Thackeray's 'pathetic ballad of *Little Billee*', recited by Professor Masson; *The Cock, the Cat and the Cuddie*, a vernacular version of Ferrari's rondo *Il galetto, il gattino e l'asinello*, by a trio of Christison, Bennett and Maclagan; *The Ewie wi' the crookit Horn*, by Blackie; the Northumbrian ditty *Dog Cappie* by Robert Lee – which led to an atrocious pun about *dog*matic theology and threatened *pun*itive measures. The proceedings concluded with 'a dose' of the familiar *Spirto Gentil* – chloroform – which 'produced its due soporific effect', whereupon 'the Symposiasts retired to rest'.

The meeting on 31 March 1868 was 'unusually small' and 'it being found ... that there were vacant spaces which rendered friendly intercourse impossible, Captain Christison of the IV Company, Queen's Edinburgh Rifles Volunteer Battalion, as senior officer being in command, ordered the

Battalion to change front and take ground at right angle to its original position, the officers in the centre. This movement was executed with perfect steadiness and the corps was posted as follows: at the East centre of the table, Professor Christison, Commanding in Chief; on his right, Professors Macpherson and Muirhead; on his left, Professors Tytler, Masson and Balfour. At the West centre of the table, Conditor Maclagan, Second in Command; on his right, Professors Crawford and Turner; on his left, Professor Blackie and ex-Conditor A. C. Swinton. Professor Crawford officiated as Chaplain'. After criticisms of the French grammar of the menu, Blackie was reminded of a promise to produce one in Greek; this he did in the following year, and it was engrossed in the Minute Book. William Turner was present as the 'junior professor' and he was informed that only now was he properly inducted into his chair of Anatomy, so that all emoluments which he had already received must go to the Symposium Fund, but he stated that there were no endowments pertaining to his chair. Blackie presented a *Song of Geology*, inspired by his attendance at Professor Allman's class, where 'he had earned a certificate of very regular attendance but acknowledged that he had not presented himself for examination'. The first of twelve stanzas ran:

I'll sing you a song that needs no apology.
Attend and keep watch in the gates of your ears!
Of the famous new science which men call geology,
And gods call the story of millions of years.
Millions, millions – Did I say millions?
Billions and trillions are more like the fact.
Millions, billions, trillions, quadrillions
Make the long sum of creation exact.

And the last:

And thus was completed – miraculous wonder
The world – this mighty, mysterious thing!
I believe it is more than a beautiful blunder
And worship and pray and adore while I sing.
Wonder and miracle! God made the wonder
Come happy creatures and worship with me!
I know it is more than a beautiful blunder
And I hope Tait and Tyndall and Huxley agree.[7]

At the next meeting, on 5 February 1869, it was the turn of the new Principal, Sir Alexander Grant, to be informed that 'certain ceremonies which were gone through in the Senate Hall' did not constitute a valid induction and that not even an ordinary Professor, much less a Principal, was fully inducted until he had taken his place at a Symposium. Now he held 'the united offices of Principal and Symposiarch' and his health was proposed 'in pocula poculorum'. Blackie followed with an appropriate German number, *So nimm ihn hin Dem haupt will ich bedecken*, and 'the chorus as constituting the cheers with which the toast was received was sung enthusiastically'. The Chairman, in returning thanks, expressed 'his satisfaction at finding himself thus surrounded by his *Princy*-Pals'. Another toast was to Lyon Playfair, now the M.P. representing the University, 'the "sweet little cherub that sits up aloft" keeping watch on the interests of the University'.

On 14 January 1870 the health was drunk of the Chancellor, the Rt Hon. John Inglis, who replied that he felt 'privileged to share in so joyous a meeting, where, in common with all the other guests, he had the satisfaction of being laughed *with* and not *at*'. Professor Blackie opened the musical part of the programme with his song *Sam Sumph* to the air 'Duncan Gray'.[8] Professor Maclagan followed with the 12 stanzas of a new song, *The Leddies*, to the air 'The Ewie wi' the Crookit Horn', a comic protest against University education for women. The last stanza foretells the probable reversal of male and female roles and looks to the Symposium as the last male refuge:

> There's nocht remains that I can lairn
> For men to do, but schew and dairn,
> An' byde at hame and keep the bairn,
> Whan Madam's at her College Ha'.
> But since at least they've left us still
> Ae nicht in peace – oor glass we'll fill,
> An' just to show we've nae ill will
> We'll drink 'The Leddies, ane an' a' '.

The health of Masson, well known for his advocacy of the cause of women, was added to the toast given in the last line of the song, and in his reply he tried to treat the subject seriously but found the mirth of the meeting too much for him. Professor Balfour's *Graduation Song*, first given many years earlier, was now transcribed into the Minutes, and the first three stanzas of its sixteen show the general trend:

> You ask me, Tom, to fill my glass
> You call on me to sing;
> You know I cannot, for, alas!
> I'm going up in Spring.

My airs so volatile before
Are of the fixed sort,
My wit that roused the merry roar
Confined to a retort.

I cannot dance, my only *steps*
Are up the *stairs* to class;
I cannot laugh, save with a dose
Of nitrous oxide gas.

Apart from old favourites, Professor Maclagan gave *The Lost Star*, of which the first stanza runs:

I saw from the peak over Teneriffe's seaside
A star that in Aries most gloriously shone,
I looked through the great Equatorial on Speyside,
The Ram was still there, but the bright star was gone.

'The Symposiasts, believing that notwithstanding the extinction of this luminary by the Professor of Practical Astronomy (Charles Piazzi Smyth) they would find as many stars as usual to light them on their way home tonight, adjourned after spending, according to their wont, a hilarious evening'.

On 13 January 1871, with 24 members present, Professor Blackie gave a new song, *Sow not in Sorrow*. Then 'an animated discussion arose as to a place called in maps and geographical works, the island of Eig. Some professed not to believe in its existence and Professor Masson suggested that an expedition should be sent. Professor Norman Macpherson, however, told them that he knew the place. It had plenty of comfortable caves where all the Faculties of the University could be accommodated separately. Nevertheless a two-man team consisting of Professors Blackie and Lorimer was appointed to enquire into and report on the place, Blackie to concentrate on the language spoken on Eig and Lorimer to study its social conditions and customs.' The Conditor was 'instructed to note that this Eig was one to be duly hatched'. The Conditor sang *The Bacco Box* and Professor Blackie a translation of *Was blazen die Trumpeten*.

On 5 January 1872 the Principal, Sir Alexander Grant, noted that the choice of Professor Wyville T. C. Thomson to lead the *Challenger* expedition showed that the University was maintaining its reputation. Lorimer intimated that Blackie and he had found the island of Eig, but that its social customs were not in accordance with natural law inasmuch as while there certainly was a chief on the island there was no chieftainess; however, there was every probability of this being reformed by the present chief and everybody was pleased with the intention and example of the chief except the Catholic priest, who saw a laudable example he could not follow. Professor Fleeming Jenkin (Engineering) said that he would not be content with anything short of an engineering survey which would bring out the yolk of the egg (Eig) and was asked by Sanders (Pathology) if he referred to a matrimonial yoke (yolk). The Conditor stated that 'if there were any reason to believe that upon the hypothetical island called Eig there could be supposed to grow anything approaching to the nature of a tree, he would have said that the Symposiasts were beating about the bush'. He then boldly proposed the Chief of Eig and the future Mrs Norman Macpherson, thus revealing Professor Macpherson as the laird of Eig.

The meeting of 24 January 1873 was at a new venue, the Palace Hotel, 1 Castle Street. There was an unusual item on the menu, namely 'a dish of excellent bananas from the Royal Botanic Garden, for which the Symposiasts recorded their thanks to their flowery colleague, the Regius Keeper of the Garden, Professor J. H. Balfour'. The special guest was the Lord Provost, who declared himself 'prepared if necessary to give a special licence to the hotel when the Symposium was held to keep the bar open after 11 p.m.' This was minuted, on the understanding that 'the extension of convivial hours was to hold good during the whole three years of the Lord Provost's term of office'. One new musical item was a song by the Master of the Merchant Company called *A Thousand a Year*, which may well have been based on J. S. Blackie's rhyme:

A thousand a year in my pocket
And six months to do as I please.

In the course of returning thanks for the toast to him, the Conditor remarked that the University, alone among those of Scotland, had its own 'cook' [John Cook, Factor to the University] and its own 'cellar' [W. J. Sellar, Professor of Humanity].

On 20 February 1874 the Symposium returned to the Senate Hall, where the dinner was provided by Mr Dickie, Officer of the Royal College of Surgeons, and the wine by Messrs Weir and Rolland. Among the toasts was one for Prince Alfred, now Duke of Edinburgh, on the occasion of his recent marriage to Princess Marie Alexandrovna. Later on there was a momentary flurry about the disappearance of the Conditor's silver snuff-box, which he had passed up the table for the use of ex-Conditor Swinton. After a strict search, however, during which there was a dispute as to whether Conveying and Conveyancing were synonymous – a suggestion hotly denied by the Professor of Conveyancing, J. S. Fraser Tytler – the box was found in the Conditor's own pocket, and he felt calm enough to join Sir Robert

Christison in the duet *Could a man be secure*. The Master of the Merchant Company sang *The Lass that Loves a Sailor* and Professor Blackie followed with his *Song of Toasts* to the tune 'Leipsig soll leben', nine stanzas in all, the first being:

Fill a glass, fill to the brim, fill, hurrah ho!
'Tis not every day that we do what we please,
So unbuckle your waistcoats and drink at your ease
ἐν συμποσίῳ, ἐν συμποσίῳ.

With the meeting on Friday, 2 April 1875 the Symposium moved to the Balmoral Hotel, 91 Princes Street, which remained its venue for the rest of its recorded existence. The Lord Provost sang *The Bonnie House o' Airlie*, and Blackie, after mystifying his fellows with a Gaelic song, *Mairi Laghach*, gave his own *Jenny Geddes* to the tune of 'The British Grenadiers', beginning:

Some praise the fair Queen Mary, and some the good Queen Bess,
And some the wise Aspasia, beloved by Pericles,
But o'er all the world's brave women, there's one that bears the rule,
The valiant Jenny Geddes that flung the three-legged stool,
With a row-dow-at them now! Jenny fling the stool!

'The song gave rise to an animated discussion as to whether the stool hurled at the head of the Dean in St Giles had three or four feet'. Professor Wallace even doubted the historical existence of such a person as Jenny Geddes, but found no one to back up his theory. 'There being likely to be no agreement among the respective supporters of the quadruple and tripedal theories of Jenny's missile, Sir Robert Christison remarked that as the Symposium had by a committee been the means of settling the difficult geographical question as to the existence of the island of Eig, there was good hope that by the same agency the historical question as to Jenny Geddes might be definitely settled'. Blackie, Wallace, Jenkin and Mackay, with John Small, the Librarian, as convenor, were appointed to report. Rutherford sang *The Pibroch of Domnhuil Dhu*. The Conditor was praised for his exertions on the occasion of a recent fire in the Southminster Theatre (situated between Nicolson Square and South College Street), which 'threatened to invade the University buildings', and Masson 'expressed his ease of mind as to the safety of his property in the University, which consisted of his gown, hood and cap'.

The committee appointed to investigate the Jenny Geddes question reported on 31 March 1876. The stool said to have been hers had been inspected in the Antiquarian Museum. It had four legs and was so heavy that the Dean would not have survived a blow on the head from it. The

Committee was inclined to favour a statement by Robert Mein in his pamphlet *The Cross removed, prelacy and patronage disproved* (1756) that it was his grandmother, Barbara Hamilton, who had led the disturbance in St Giles. Masson begged leave, as a minority of one, to present a separate report: the main report 'concedes too much to the wretched spirit of scepticism prevalent in this day. Jenny Geddes and her stool are precious articles of our national belief not to be given up without danger of sapping the foundations of society in our beloved Scotland'. Masson's 'evidence' goes on for three pages of the Minute Book. Music followed, with an unusual number of fresh items: *The Chough* (Crow), a trio by the Conditor, Mr Small and Professor Rutherford, the last-mentioned supplying the novelty of a piano accompaniment; Blackie gave Alexander Ross's *Wooed an' married an' a'*; a new member, Eggeling, sang *In kühlen Keller*; Rutherford, Small and the Conditor gave Joseph Mazzinghi's *Ye Shepherds tell me* and King's glee *The Witches*, again with Rutherford at the piano.

At the 1877 Symposium 'the beef which formed one of the *pièces de résistance* was stated by Mr Thien, the Maître d'Hotel, to be American and was universally voted to be excellent, whilst the rest of the viands and the wines were held to be of the same quality.' The Principal, Sir Alexander Grant, in giving the toast of the Symposium, said that it 'lives on moisture as a plant in the tropics lives on rain drops. A Symposiast looks for this Festival as an Indian herb does for the monsoon. It is not, however, for rain that he looks but for a certain ether which pervades the Symposium and animates its members during the whole year. It had been thought that the Symposium was a sort of Secret Association, but the Universities Commission would clear away all such nonsensical ideas and would show that the Symposium was the real foundation of the prosperity of the University. . . . He coupled the toast of the Symposium with the name of the greatest friend of the University, and truest Symposiast THE CHANCELLOR (John Inglis), who, he rejoiced to think, had declined to be called to the High Court of Appeal in London and had remained true to Scotland, the Court of Session and the Symposium'. In a rich musical programme Blackie sang *The Quaker's Wife* but the other items were mainly by a quartet – Professor Rutherford, the Conditor, Mr Small and Mr John Christison, W.S., son of Sir Robert and Secretary of the University Court – who gave *When winds blow cold, Warum bist du so ferne, Was ist das ein durstig Jahr* and Heinrich August Marschner's *In autumn we should drink, boys*. The Conditor sang *Chancellor Inglis* to the tune 'Kate Dalrymple',[8] which was included in the programme in each of the following five years. The Conditor closed the meeting with *The Silver Tassie*.

At the 1878 Symposium the quartet sang Bishop's glee, *Come thou monarch of the vine* and two German lieder. The Conditor proposed the toast of Sir Wyville Thomson, home from the long and successful *Challenger* expedition, and Thomson 'gave the old naval toast "Sweethearts and wives", coupled with the healths of Professors Simpson and Rutherford. Simpson said something very eloquent in reply regarding woman in her right place, and this was held to be an obstetrician's view of the toast'; Rutherford, replying to the 'Sweethearts' part of the toast, said 'he had not yet found that individual but was prepared to search in hill and dale even in mines and would, when he found her, convey the sympathetic expressions of the Symposiasts to her.'

The Minutes for the Symposium held on 31 January 1879 are unique in that only the number, not the names, of those present, is recorded. The Conditor had 'accidentally left on the table the list of Symposiasts along with a favourite screw pencil with which he was wont to record the events' and although he had called at the hotel next morning he found neither list nor pencil. The special guest of honour was the Marquis of Hartington, Lord Rector, and the Chairman, Sir Alexander Grant, in referring to the Rectorial Address given earlier that day, said 'the way it had been received, even through showers of peas, showed the respect of the students for their Rector, who might return home with the satisfactory feeling that he had achieved "peas with honour" '.[9] Later there followed 'a great innovation introduced by the Rector, who asked and obtained permission to light a cigar. This proceeding seemed to be approved by a majority of Symposiasts, who speedily followed the example of the Rector and it was probably in the cloud in which he was enveloped but to which he did not contribute that the Conditor lost his list of Symposiasts and his pet pencil'. The Chancellor 'proposed the health of the Conditor in terms so forcible that that functionary fell into a state of transient coma and was unable to record what the Rt Hon. Gentleman said' but on being roused to consciousness by Professor Masson seizing his pencil to make some notes, was able to return thanks and after a short interval joined the Christisons in singing Ferrari's rondo of the *Cock, Cat and Cuddie*. Professor Sellar thanked the Rector for introducing cigars so early in the evening and Professor Eggeling sang *Nur ihr Bergen*. The Conditor said that he had found one of the Symposiasts using a special large glass capable of containing eight fluid ounces, that he had clearly traced it to Professor Calderwood but that on analysing what remained in it found it to be 'not generous claret but only weak Crawley water'.

In 1880 'for some mysterious reason occult in the Balmoral Hotel's

kitchen, dinner was not served till half past seven'. The twenty-five
Symposiasts who had arrived, with Sir Daniel Macnee as guest, at the usual
hour of 7 p.m., were ravenous, and voted the dinner excellent, 'it being well
spiced with Lacedaemonian sauce'.[10] Sir Alexander Grant, in proposing the
toast of the University, remarked that 'there were old people who had
praised the Symposium when the number present was that of the Muses, but
their number had increased to three times that of the Muses and was
increasing'. The Conditor (Maclagan) sang *Muirland Willie*. In inducting
two new professors, Dickson and Chrystal, the Chairman remarked that
they had had the audacity to give lectures without having been duly
inducted, but for that offence they had now made *amende honorable* by
appearing at a Symposium'. 'Benton's chronograph', a pendulum device for
recording periods of time, had been introduced to measure the length of
speeches: Dickson's reply took 35 seconds, Chrystal's 45, and 'they were
received, especially the former, with great applause'. Blackie sang *Sow not in
Sorrow*, saying it was an old one but never before sung at a Symposium,
forgetting that he had in fact given it in 1871. Rutherford sang *Tom Bowling*.
Sir Robert Christison, 'the oldest in years but youngest in spirit of the
Symposiasts', was toasted with three cheers and one cheer more, and 'spoke
of the old times when Symposiasts were wont to adjourn to the Observatory
to see more double stars than exist in the Catalogue, and were so confused in
their reckonings as to wander up and down closes in their endeavour to find
their way home'. Rutherford then sang *Braw, braw lads*. Mr Small, the
Librarian, presented a document which 'showed that the Symposium was
an old institution'. This was an extract from a work by the nonconformist
Edmund Calamy, *An historical account of my own life with some reflections on
the times I have lived in (1671–1731)*. In 1709 he visited Edinburgh to
receive a D.D. and wrote: 'I was invited by the masters of the College to go to
Leith with them to take a fish dinner with which they were to entertain their
Principal Carstares, according to annual custom. . . . One thing that gave a
peculiar relish was the entire freedom and harmony between the Principal
and masters of the College, they expressing a veneration for him as a
common father and he tenderness for them as if they had all been his
children. Were it so in all societies of that sort they would be much more
likely to answer the end of their institution than by running into wrangles
and contentions and harbouring mutual jealousies and suspicions'. The
toast of the Principal was received with hearty cheers and a general chorus of
' He's a jolly good fellow', and Professor Eggeling sang *Ein Wandernder
Musikanter*.

On 31 January 1881 the new Rector, Lord Rosebery, was a guest, and when he replied to the drinking of his health he confessed that he had been 'somewhat anxious as to the costume to be worn at a Symposium, being afraid that the Symposiasts were expected to appear in their *togae*, but as he had not seen any gentlemen in fancy dress pass the doors of the New Club he had been relieved on that score. He was however troubled as to his Rectorial address when he thought of the many learned men from all countries who might be here [for the Tercentenary] in 1883, as he could not undertake to speak in any other than his own language. He hoped that as one means of helping it would be well to have the Professor of Celtic literature appointed and inducted before that time'. Blackie sang his *Song of Toasts* with an additional verse:

Fill a glass to the Rector, Hurrah ho!
A rara-avis, a wise young Lord
With a tongue well drilled and a brain well stored
And a face fair to show here
ἐν συμποσίῳ, ἐν συμποσίῳ.

When the healths were drunk of three new Professors – Shield Nicholson (Political Economy), Baldwin Brown (Fine Art) and Laird Adams (Hebrew), their replies were timed: Nicholson 64 seconds, Brown (who 'confined himself to returning thanks being afraid of the Conditor'), 62·5 seconds; Adams (who showed no fear of the Conditor) within one minute. The Conditor sang *The Bacco Box* and Eggeling sang a new song which was to be a favourite for the remaining life of the Symposium – *The Scotch Professor* [Blackie] *on the Nile*, to the tune 'Ein lustiger Musikante'.[11]

In 1882, after the Conditor had sung Alexander Rose's *Woo'd an' Married an' a'*, 'a waiter distributed among the Symposiasts a series of small boxes, the purpose of which, at first unintelligible to the Conditor, became obvious from clouds of fragrant incense arising all along both sides of the table, a practice which showed itself on the occasion of the Rectoris-Symposiastical appearance of the Marquis of Hartington'. Rutherford sang *O'er Nelson's Tomb* and the Conditor once more sang *Chancellor Inglis*, the concluding verse of which was received with three cheers:

Now long may he
Our Chancellor be;
Now let the glasses clatter
To his health and the fame
Of the ancient dame
That is our Alma Mater.

The last Symposium recorded in the Minute Book took place at the Balmoral Hotel on 22 December 1882, with an attendance of 27, including

Rosebery, Lord Provost Harrison and the Master of the Merchant
Company. The Rector had now gone through 'a wonderful experience in
delivering his address including a strong demonstration of free trade in
peas'.[12] Professors Ewart, Chiene and Geikie returned thanks in 57 seconds,
30 seconds and 47 seconds respectively. 'The Rector proposed the health of
ex-Professor Blackie on the filling up of the Celtic chair this day.[13] The
Rector thought that this would relieve the University from the danger of
a serious invasion because he had daily seen a crowd of persons in kilts
crowding towards the portals whom he supposed to be candidates for the
chair'. Alongside the old favourite *The Scotch Professor* there were novelties
– Hogg's *McLean's Welcome to Charlie* (Rutherford), *Hame cam' our
Gudeman* (Geikie), *Jock o' Hazeldean* (Blackie) and *Neeps* (the Conditor), a
new item, of which the first three stanzas, to the tune 'When Jeanie wi' her
seam by the fire', are as follows:

> There's an auld frien' o' mine, a neebourly chiel
> Wha likes a day's shooting uncommonly weel,
> But he'll tell, gin he meets you, he dreams when he sleeps
> O' a terrible day in the Muirlee neeps.

> On heather he'll walk just as weel as you can
> On stubble or hay fields he'll march like a man,
> But the half o' the pleasure awa frae him sweeps
> The prospect o' crossing the Muirlee neeps.

> He says that whenever he ventures to stir
> Frae the croon o' the rig to the howe o' the fur,
> He's just like a boat in a storm on the deeps
> When he's pitchin' aboot in the wide sea o' neeps.

Professor Fraser, proposing the toast of the 3340 students of the University,
'felt sure that it was an influence emanating from the Symposium which had
done so much to promote genial feeling among the students as evidenced by
the admirable social meetings of the Students' Club and by the Students'
Ball, mildly suggesting that some time or other there might be a call for the
establishment of a Chair of Dancing'.

No further minutes seem to have survived. Certainly the existing volume
is itself practically full, so if the Symposium continued after session 1882–3
there must have been a second volume at least. It may be that the
Tercentenary, which followed the last recorded meeting, proved too much
even for the seasoned Symposiasts and that the Symposium went
underground or ceased to exist thereafter.

REFERENCES

1. The record of the Symposium is preserved in a Minute Book of 500 pages, measuring $10\frac{1}{2} \times \frac{1}{4}$ inches, written in fine calligraphic hands, bound in grey vellum and with two red decorative bands across the spine (EUL MS Dc.2.75)

2. Anna Stoddart, *John Stuart Blackie* (1895), i, 331.

3. In the *Scottish Students' Song Book.*

4. This is not recorded in the Minutes, but is mentioned in D. A. Wilson and D. W. Macarthur, *Carlyle in Old Age* (London 1934) 55–8. We are indebted to Professor K. J. Fielding for this reference.

5. 3rd edn. 1864.

6. Printed in Maclagan's *Nugae Canorae Medicae, Lays by the Poet Laureate of the New Town Dispensary*, 1850, 1873.

7. Tyndall was John Tyndall, F.R.S., 1820–93.

8. In the *Scottish Students' Song Book.*

9. Dried pease were a favourite Rectorial missile at that time, mentioned again in the Minute of the last meeting, in 1882.

10. That is, hunger.

11. In the *Scottish Students' Song Book.*

12. cf. note 9.

13. Blackie had actively canvassed for funds to found a Celtic Chair.

An Early African Graduate

GEORGE SHEPPERSON

In 1768, Benjamin Rush of Philadelphia received his doctor's degree at Edinburgh and returned home to become surgeon-general of the Continental Army, a member of the Continental Congress and of the Pennsylvania convention which ratified the Constitution of the United States of America, and founder of the first American anti-slavery society. After that time, Edinburgh increasingly attracted from British possessions overseas students who were drawn towards movements for political reform and national independence. They came to Edinburgh more because of its reputation as a medical centre than for any political atmosphere about the place. But that a certain air of freedom may have been among the attractions for the colonial student is suggested by an observation by William Wells Brown, an escaped American slave and a leading black abolitionist who, while on an anti-slavery tour, visited Edinburgh in 1851, and was pleased to see at the Medical School 'among the two or three hundred students, three coloured young men, seated upon the same benches with those of a fairer complexion, and yet there appeared no feeling on the part of the whites towards their coloured associates, except of companionship and respect'.[1]

In the mid-nineteenth century, these 'coloured young men' at Edinburgh would have been blacks from the British West Indies[2] and occasionally from the United States. By the end of the century, when the Scramble for Africa had almost run its course and Britain had acquired a new lion's share of empire, their numbers were augmented by increasing numbers of Africans.[3] One of these Africans was James Africanus Beale Horton, now a famous figure in the history of African nationalism.[4]

Horton was born in 1835 at Gloucester village, near Freetown, Sierra Leone. He belonged to the Ibo people of West Africa. His father, a liberated slave who became a carpenter, was not related to the original African settlers, the Nova Scotians and Maroons, whom the British had brought across the Atlantic to the new colony of Sierra Leone in 1787. Horton, therefore, had some social leeway to make up – a fact which may explain part, at least, of his subsequent development.

The mid-nineteenth century, in spite of all its confident progress, was the period of the 'white man's grave' in West Africa. The death-rate among European doctors determined the War Office to train suitable Africans as Medical Officers to serve with Imperial Garrisons in West Africa. Horton, a promising youth, was sent to the Church Missionary Society's Fourah Bay College.[5] On completing his studies in 1853, he was one of the first two to be chosen for the War Office scheme.

After taking his M.R.C.S. in London, he came to Edinburgh. It was then his fourth year of study of medicine. He matriculated on 19 October 1858 and lived at 50 Rankeillor Street.[6] While he was in Edinburgh, Horton became president of the Pathological Society. He graduated M.D. on 1 August 1859. His thesis, *The Medical Topography of the West Coast of Africa, with sketches of its botany*, was published in the same year.[7] It shows something of the spirit which, during the next decade and a half, was to produce the group of Horton's writings that enables him to be called one of the fathers of African nationalism. This is clear from the preface which expresses the following hope: 'that this Publication may be the means of exciting some interest ... on behalf of Africa is the sincere wish of AFRICANUS HORTON.' An Africanist note is sounded here not only in the general sentiments but also in the dropping of his European-sounding first and third names.

Horton's nationalism was not of the tribal variety. His thesis provides evidence of this when he writes, 'Iboes, Yorubas, Mandingoes, Soosoos, Joloofs, or Yoloohs, Timnehs, Krew, and Dahomians ... by their intermarriages are destined to produce the finest race in Africa'.[8] The comparative approach, which was to provide the perspective for his nationalist *magnum opus* of 1868, is in evidence in his thesis when he uses a passage from Tacitus on the Germans to illustrate the development of African houses in Sierra Leone.[9] Furthermore, his doctoral dissertation displays something of that criticism of European ways which has provided African nationalism with much of its *élan* when, in his health hints to foreigners in Sierra Leone, Horton suggests that they should take an annual holiday, 'instead of toiling in the pursuit of wealth all the year round'.[10]

After he had received his M.D., Horton was commissioned in Britain with the rank of Staff-Assistant Surgeon in the Army and sent to the Gold Coast, the setting for much of his career and a centre of nascent nationalism to which he contributed, although it probably influenced him as much as he influenced it. During his twenty years with the Army, he served not only in the Gold Coast but in most parts of British West Africa from Senegal to the Bight of Benin. He thus became not only one of the first African doctors but also one of the first African regular Army officers – a singular distinction, for Britain was to commission very few Africans indeed during the next eighty years. He continued his associations with Edinburgh, as a Foreign Fellow of its Botanical Society. His interests, however, became increasingly political.

Between 1865 and 1870 Horton published two pamphlets and one book which constitute his main claim to a position in the history of ideas of African nationalism. Their titles indicate both his sentiments and his tactics. The first pamphlet is called *Political Economy of British Western Africa; with the requirements of the several colonies and settlements (the African view of the Negro's place in nature). Being an address to the African-Aid Society* (London, 1865). In it Horton attempts to 'prove the capability of the African for possessing a real political government and national independence'. The second is called *Letters on the Political Condition of the Gold Coast since the exchange of territory between the English and Dutch Governments, on January 1, 1868; together with a short account of the Ashantee War, 1862–4, and the Awoonah War, 1866; Addressed to the Right Hon. E. Cardwell, D.C.L., Secretary of State for War, and the Right Hon. Earl Granville, K.G., D.C.L., Secretary of State for the Colonies* (London, 1870). The title of Horton's book is even more evocative than those of the pamphlets: *West African Countries and Peoples, British and Native. With the Requirements necessary for establishing that self government recommended by the Committee of the House of Commons, 1865; and a Vindication of the African Race* (London, 1868).

It is understandable that Horton, in the 1860s, should have considered necessary a 'Vindication of the African Race'. The trend of some contemporary thinking is evidenced by Carlyle's well-known racialist reactions to the abolition of slavery in the British colonies and the United States. Carlyle represented those British thinkers who interpreted society in fixed racial categories and eschewed the developmental ideas of a Darwin. Outstanding among these was Robert Knox, the Edinburgh anatomist. Knox was no longer in Edinburgh when Horton came to Britain, but it is at least possible that he met him in England. Certainly, Horton knew Knox's *The Races of Men* (London, 1850), particularly its sixth chapter on 'The Dark Races of Men' in which the controversial anatomist stressed that 'the true black or negro race seems to have attained his ultimatum centuries ago'. Horton devoted a whole chapter of his *West African Countries* to attacking 'false theories of modern anthropologists' – among which he included Hume's essay 'On Natural Character' – in particular those of Knox's correspondent and friend in the Anthropological and Ethnological Society of London, Dr James Hunt, whose essay about white supremacy, *On the Negro's Place in Nature* (London, 1863), had already supplied an indignant sub-title for Horton's pamphlet of 1865.[11]

Horton's book is significant for the history of nationalist thinking in Africa not only for its exposure of contemporary racialism and for its continual assertion of the spirit of independence. Horton refuses to be bound to the simple dichotomy of 'nation' and 'tribe' which hypnotises so many modern politicians and thinkers, black and white. His careful analysis of African societies on the west coast has, of course, its limitations today. But he has no hesitation in applying the description 'nationality' to an African group when it seems justified, and his book reveals the inadequacy of the term 'tribe' for every kind of African society. It seems to show that, however true it may be to say that national*ism* in Africa today results from the influence of political ideas of nineteenth-century European origin, there were nations in Africa before ever the white man set foot there.

No account of Horton's contributions to African nationalism can conclude without a reference to the letter which he wrote in 1873 to a Sierra Leone newspaper, *The Negro*,[12] on the necessity for a West African university. It is a document which deserves favourable comparison with Edward Blyden's justly famous Presidential address to the Liberia College in 1881.[13] In it, Horton showed that he had been working for a West African university since 1862; that he stood for a curriculum in which both the humanities and the sciences would be represented; and that, as always, his aim in pressing for a centre of African higher education was 'the vital regeneration of the Negro race'. He gave practical expression to his beliefs in his work for the affiliation of Fourah Bay College with a British University and when he left part of his estate for the promotion of scientific education in Sierra Leone.[14]

James Africanus Beale Horton retired from the Army in 1880 with the rank of Surgeon-Major. Three years later he died at the early age of forty-eight.

It is regrettable that this lively and intelligent man, like so many others of his kind, left few records of his association with Edinburgh. In the main, one can only speculate on what the democratic intellect of the mid-nineteenth century Scottish universities may have meant for him. In addition to his negative reactions to racialist thinkers, with their fixed categories, an occasional trace of the typically Scottish developmental social thinking is to be observed in his writing.[15] Perhaps, however, what he took away most from Edinburgh in the 1850s was his conviction of the importance of

Science, and the presence of no other feeling among the white students in the
Medical School towards the occasional coloured student in their midst than
that, in the words of a contemporary, 'of companionship and respect'.[16]

ACKNOWLEDGMENTS

I am indebted to Mr Christopher Fyfe, former Sierra Leone Government Archivist
and now Reader in African History, Edinburgh University, and to Mr C.P.
Finlayson, former Keeper of Manuscripts, Edinburgh University, for help with this
essay.

REFERENCES

1. William Wells Brown, *Three Years in Europe* (London 1852) p.310.
   Further praise of Edinburgh's lack of racial feeling is provided in a Negro
   American church periodical by a Liberian living in Edinburgh (Archibald
   Johnson, 'The Ubiquity of the Negro', *African Methodist Episcopal
   Church Review*, Philadelphia, 1892, pp.266–7) who was delighted to see
   at 'Portobello, a coloured man in full Scotch costume, *à la* Rob Roy...
   dancing with some innocent-looking ruddy-cheeked Scotch lassie'.
2. Edinburgh-educated West Indians of a nationalist persuasion include
   Barbadian Dr Albert Thorne, who, in the belief that 'Africa is the only
   quarter of the world where we will be respected as a race', organised in
   Britain and America from the 1890s to the 1920s movements to take New
   World blacks back to Africa. Thorne collected donations for one of his
   early schemes in 1895–7 from members of the University. (*See Appeal
   addressed to Friends of the African Race* and *The African Colonization
   Scheme*, pamphlets, in Church of Scotland Papers, Miscellaneous Bundle,
   Pamphlets No.1, National Library of Scotland; and cutting from *New
   York Age*, 12 August 1922, in James Weldon Johnson Collection, X,
   scrapbooks, Yale University Library.) Two delegates from the 'Afro-
   West Indian Literary Society, Edinburgh' attended the first Pan-African
   Conference in London in 1900: Dr R. A. K. Savage, M.B., ch.B., and a Mr
   Meyer (Alexander Walters, *My Life and Work*, New York, 1917, p.254;
   The Times, London, 25 July 1900, p.150).
3. Examples of Edinburgh-educated Africans who made some mark on early
   African nationalist movements include Bandele Omoniyi, a Yoruba from
   Ife, who matriculated in 1906 and 1907 in the Faculty of Medicine.
   Omoniyi wrote *A Defence of the Ethiopian Movement* (Edinburgh 1908)
   and published three articles criticising British rule in West Africa in *The
   Edinburgh Magazine*, VII, 1907, pp.1435, 1453 and 1476 respectively.
   Another Nigerian was 'Brazilian' Moses da Rocha whose correspondence
   with a black American nationalist shows that, if he was interested in
   developing the ideology of the 'African personality' or *négritude*, he was
   not altogether sure that life in Edinburgh was helping him, for he speaks of
   'various troubles with beastly landladies', 'jealous Black Traitors and

Conspirators in Edinburgh', 'callous Bureaucrats', and 'a dour professor
who talks much of the power of the devil' (John Edward Bruce Papers,
Schomburg Collection, New York Public Library, MSS 211, 1585, and
MSS 212–13, 1587; also 1902. B. Misc. 13–17, 1426). Among other
notable African students at Edinburgh were H. R. Bankole Bright,
L.R.C.P. & S.(EDIN.), 1910, a founder of the National Congress of British
West Africa and a pioneer Sierra Leone nationalist (M. C. F. Easmon,
'Sierra Leone Doctors', *Sierra Leone Studies, Freetown*, 6, 1956, p.82);
Hastings Kamazu Banda of the Malawi Congress Party, Nyasaland,
L.R.C.P.(EDIN.), L.R.C.S.(EDIN.), L.R.F.P.S.(GLAS.), 1941; and Dr Julius
Kambarage Nyerere, for whom see George Shepperson, 'Edinburgh
University's First African Prime Minister' and 'The University of East
Africa' in *University of Edinburgh Gazette*, No.28, October 1960, pp.22–6
and No.37, October 1963, pp. 37–40, respectively.

4. Since the original article (*University of Edinburgh Gazette*, No.32,
   January 1962, pp.23–6), on which the present essay is based, was
   published, the growth of Horton's fame, *pari passu* with the development
   of independent African states in the 1960s, has been reflected in the
   increase of publications about him. These include Davidson Nicol, editor,
   *Africanus Horton: The Dawn of Nationalism in Modern Africa. Extracts
   from the political, scientific and medical writings of J. A. B. Horton, M.D.
   1835–1883* (London 1969); James Africanus Horton, *West African
   Countries and Peoples* (Edinburgh 1969; reprint of the original edition of
   1868, with an introduction by George Shepperson); *Letters on the
   Political Condition of the Gold Coast* (London 1970; reprint of the original
   edition of 1870, with an introduction by E. A. Ayandele); E. A. Ayandele,
   'James Africanus Beale Horton, 1835–1883: Prophet of Modernization
   in West Africa', *African Historical Studies* (Boston, Mass.), IV, 3, 1971,.
   pp.691–708; Christopher Fyfe, *Africanus Horton; West African Scientist
   and Patriot* (Oxford 1972).

5. T. J. Thompson, *The Jubilee and Centenary Volume of Fourah Bay College,
   Freetown, Sierra Leone* (Freetown 1930), Appendix, List of Students . . .,
   p.ii.

6. *Edinburgh University*. 1859. *Medical Examinations*.

7. London, 1859. The manuscript thesis was submitted in March 1859. On
   the title-page, 'Native of West Africa' follows Horton's name.

8. ibid., p.11.

9. ibid., p.13.

10. ibid., p.29.

11. Further details of Knox's racialist thinking and his relationship with Hunt
    are to be found in Henry Lonsdale, *A Sketch of the Life and Writings of
    Robert Knox* (London 1870), especially pp.285–330, 381 and 384–5.

12. Thompson, op. cit., pp.54–6.

13. 'The Aims and Methods of a Liberal Education for Africans', in Edward
    Blyden, *Christianity, Islam and the Negro Race* (London 1887)
    pp.82–107.

14. Among Horton's writings which reveal his scientific interests are his
    contributions to tropical medicine: *Physical and medical climate and*

meteorology of the West Coast of Africa (London 1867), the title page of which states that Horton was a 'Fellow of the Noelic Society of Edinburgh'; *The diseases of tropical climates and their treatment* (London 1874); and *Guinea worm, or drancunculus, its symptoms and progress, causes, pathological anatomy, results and radical cure* (London 1868).

15. cf. Horton, *West African Countries*, pp.67–8.
16. William Wells Brown, op. cit., p.310.

The First Generations of University Women
1869–1930

SHEILA HAMILTON

Why should women merit a separate study in this volume when there is no equivalent chapter on men? Why indeed should consideration be given to their history at all? By the 1920s and 1930s it was taken for granted that university education should be co-educational in one form or another. Yet over the three centuries and more before 1892 a woman student had only very rarely been seen at the University. There are scattered references to some ladies attending one or two lectures in the late eighteenth century, and the University had one minor controversy to deal with in the first half of the nineteenth century with the case of Dr James Barry, who graduated M.D. from Edinburgh in 1812 and from 1813 to 1859 was a medical officer in the British Army. Scandal arose when Dr Barry was discovered on death to be a woman.[1]

The second half of the nineteenth century was a period which saw the flourishing of the campaign to promote the provision of higher education for women. It was part of the larger 'women's movement' which witnessed demands for the 'vote for women' and for changes in the legal position of women in marriage and divorce, and which altered the economic position of women. The University, under extreme pressure, was at the centre of the higher education campaign from the 1860s onwards. It had an association with the women's movement in which long-term achievement and progress stood alongside short-term controversy and debate, legal recriminations and nationwide publicity. The first phase in the campaign was one of struggle and conflict from the early 1860s to 1892 and the second was one in which integration and acceptance within the University were countered by demands for just recognition of the new status of women graduates.

Elizabeth Garrett was the first woman to try to gain admission to both Edinburgh and St Andrews Universities as a matriculated medical student, in 1862. However, the most renowned period is that of the later 1860s and 1870s when Sophia Jex-Blake arrived in Edinburgh to campaign vigorously for the medical education of women.[2] The issue of medical education of women as opposed to general higher educational provision was the controversial spark which highlighted the nationwide demands of Victorian women to be offered the same educational opportunities as men, whether in general arts or medical subjects.

Miss Jex-Blake campaigned energetically in Edinburgh on behalf of the medical women and she gained the sympathetic ear of many of the Professors in the University. With her small band of followers who also hoped to study medicine, Miss Jex-Blake won the first round in the struggle when women were permitted to matriculate and to attend classes in 1869, separate at first and then in the Extra-Mural School. The University even went as far as printing the regulations governing women students in the *Calendar*. There then occurred the famous Surgeon's Hall riot in 1870, when men students hustled and impeded the women from attending an Anatomy lecture. The men medical students revealed quite clearly their prejudices and opposition, reflecting to a certain extent the professorial attitudes. It was one thing to attend extra-mural classes on the fringes and another to study seriously to prove their academic ability.[3] The medical faction opposed the admission of women to the Royal Infirmary, thus preventing them from receiving clinical instruction. The riot itself became a legendary incident in the medical campaign and did much to arouse indignation at the way the women were treated. There were others who felt that if women were set on a medical career then they should cope with all the unpleasantness which arose. Press coverage, especially in *The Scotsman*, tended to favour the women's cause, and indeed funds soon poured in to aid the newly set up Committee for the Medical Education of Women. Bitter legal battles ensued, yet even then it seemed the women medicals were near to their aim, which was to continue their studies at the University in order to graduate. The opposition of people like Professor Robert Christison in the Medical Faculty reflected the attitude of many in the medical profession that the next step after graduation would be for women to practise medicine and this threat to the men's professional status aroused much fear and opposition.

In 1872 an action of Declarator against the Senatus was raised in the Court of Session by the women students after it became impossible for the women to go any further with their studies without admission to classes in the Faculty as opposed to the Extra-Mural School. In the Outer House, Lord Gifford confirmed that the women had the right to complete their studies and to graduate. The Senatus appealed to the Inner House in 1873 and the decision this time went against the women medicals, stating that it had been an illegal act to admit women as matriculated students in 1869. This was in spite of the women paying fees which were double the normal payment, in order to receive instruction.

The women medicals conceded defeat in Edinburgh and reluctantly moved on elsewhere to await legislation. It was an Enabling Bill introduced by Russell Gurney and applied to all Universities in the United Kingdom, passed in 1876, which gave permissive legislation to universities to act on the medical women's claim. The women knocked hard at all university doors. It was the Irish College of Physicians and Queen's University of Dublin which proved prepared to open their examinations and diplomas to women. Sophia Jex-Blake, who had already taken the M.D. of Berne University, presented herself for examination in Dublin and succeeded in having her name added to the Register of the General Medical Council in 1877. Miss Jex-Blake had also been instrumental in creating the London School of Medicine for Women and later returned to Edinburgh, where she set up a Medical School for Women in 1886. In that same year the Royal College of Physicians and Surgeons in Edinburgh opened its licentiate to women.[4] The medical campaign, while a major chapter in the women's education campaign, was only part of the story.

The developments have to be seen against the background of improvements in secondary education as a preparation for university admission. The introduction of the local examination scheme of the Scottish universities offered both boys and girls the chance to obtain certificates which would give some indication of their level of education. In 1865 Edinburgh University set up its Local Examinations scheme, run by a committee of Professors. By 1883, 891 candidates were coming forward to the forty-seven centres for examination. Of these 746 were girls, and it was their response which maintained the success of the scheme until the authorities introduced the Leaving Certificate in 1888.[5] The University had therefore made a substantial contribution to girls' education by offering a means to measure their educational attainment, no matter whether they were educated privately by governesses, in ladies' seminary or in local school.

The University also found itself involved in the *higher* education movement. The Edinburgh Ladies Education Association (E.L.E.A.), the first of its kind in Scotland, started in 1868 in an atmosphere of great controversy and debate over the medical campaign. There is little evidence in the Association's papers of any hysterical outbursts or frontal attacks on the University and little reference to the medical campaign where fiery activists like Sophia Jex-Blake reigned. There was an almost conscious attempt to steer clear of any controversy whatsoever and to make steady, if less spectacular, progress. The purpose of the Association was stated thus:

> It is not the aim of the Association to train for the professions; but its promoters desire in the education of women to give them the advantages of a system acknowledged to be well suited for the mental training of the other sex.[6]

The emphasis is significant. It was making quite clear that it did not aim to threaten any professional status. It aimed at the general cultivation and improvement of the mind through its lectures. The Association ran its organisation and classes along the lines of the Arts Faculty.

The E.L.E.A. had been set up by some pioneering women from the Edinburgh Essay Society, a small élite ladies' society. Mrs Mary Crudelius, the wife of a Leith merchant, was the guiding force in the foundation of the Association, with the help of Sarah Siddons Mair from the Essay Society and Mrs Daniell, Mrs Ranken and others.[7] These women were in the correct circle of Edinburgh Society to use their influence, especially to obtain the guidance and advice of David Masson, Professor of Rhetoric and English Literature, a prominent supporter of the women's cause, who in 1867 outlined his view in the *MacMillan's Magazine*:

> The women of this country ought to be educated or to have the option of being educated at the same institutions as the men, up to the very highest, with the same gradation, by the same teachers, and in a manner as thorough, continuous and systematic. Till this is done our nation is unjust to half its members and exists spiritually, intellectually and in every other respect at but half its possible strength.[8]

In the first year, 265 women attended Masson's classes in English literature. By 1873, 335 women were enrolled in the classes of the Association. They studied such subjects as Mathematics, Moral Philosophy, Chemistry, Physiology, Botany and Biblical Criticism. All were taught by the University Professors and lecturers. In 1874, the links with the University were further strengthened by the introduction of a University Certificate in Arts for women, providing they had sat the Local Examinations and attended three of the Association's classes. It was offered at both higher and ordinary level, and the Association itself gave a Diploma to students who had passed at least seven of the Association examinations.

By 1877 the Rules and Calendar of the Association were being printed within the *University Calendar*, and again therefore Edinburgh University had forged its links with the cause of women's education. In that year also the closer links with the University were reinforced by a change in the Association's constitution and name. The ex-officio position of Professors on the executive was confirmed, and one of them was appointed Vice-President. A more significant reminder of the direction which the

Association was taking was its new name, the Edinburgh Association for the University Education of Women. The Association continued to attract students to its classes and carried on its campaign to obtain a university education for women. It was also active in promoting scholarships and bursaries and sending petitions to Parliament and it sent a memorial to the Scottish Universities Commission. The women of the E.L.E.A. had shown that they were capable intellectually, physically and emotionally of studying to University standards.

The outcome of the women's campaigns and the continual discussion and public debate on the matter eventually produced the Universities (Scotland) Act 1889, which appointed Commissioners to draw up Ordinances relating to various aspects of the University system. Their Ordinance No.18 (Regulations for the Graduation of Women and for their instruction in the Universities) was passed in 1892. In 1893 the first eight ladies were capped at Edinburgh University.[9] As they were all Association students who had previously received the University Certificates and sat the required exams, they were able to graduate soon after the Ordinance was passed.

The position of the medical women at Edinburgh was still a matter of dispute. For years they continued to attend most classes in the Extra-Mural Schools, though they graduated from the University, and it was only in 1916 that they were allowed to become full members of the University. It is clear that the Jex-Blake issue had introduced an element of conservatism and suspicion into the ranks of the medical faculty. The episode had been an aggressive and courageous attack on a reactionary, exclusive, male-orientated institution. Yet a closer examination reveals that only some individuals within the University stood in opposition. Many members of the Senatus, including Professor Christison, favoured the general education of women. It was mutterings among the medical men about mixed classes, graduation and the threat to their professional status which provoked the antagonism to women medical students.

Alongside this stormy interlude had occurred the foundation of an association which did not threaten to enter educational fields like Law, Divinity and Medicine, where practising one's profession would follow. The Rules of the Edinburgh Association for the University Education of Women were after all printed in the *University Calendar*, and many members of the University Senatus, including the Principal, David Brewster, actively supported the Association and promoted its activities. The Association acted as a pressure group to change opinion and achieve recognition of its demands. Professors who favoured the women's cause had also been prepared to speak out in their favour in the press, in the University and to the Scottish University Commission. Parallel events took place in a similar fashion at the other Scottish Universities. The first phase had ended with the 1889 Act and the Ordinance of 1892 which gave women access to university instruction and graduation. Classes at Edinburgh were mixed from the start, with the exception of the medical ones: in Glasgow separate instruction continued for some time at the Queen Margaret College, which had been incorporated in 1893 but still remained distinct.

The second phase covers the period from 1893 to the end of the First World War. It was a period of adjustment and integration, with the watershed of the War followed by two decades when general developments in student life and welfare were more significant than the division of the sexes. The impact of women in this second phase can be looked at in two ways: the social activities of students as indicative of the integration of the new female arrivals, and secondly the quantitative data.

There were first of all some aspects of continuity from the pre-1893 period. The E.A.U.E.W., now that its main objective had been achieved, turned to providing facilities and amenities for the new women students. The first concern was to provide a meeting-place for the women and the second was a hall of residence. The Association therefore closed its common room and library in Shandwick Place and opened a flat in 8 Hope Park Square, which was closer to the University. This was not thought of as a permanent arrangement but the flat was nonetheless a significant focal point and place of union, with forty-two members in its first year. It was the predecessor of the Women's Union which was founded in 1905.[10]

The second concern was to provide accommodation for women students whose homes were outwith the Edinburgh area. The Association acted in 1894 by opening Crudelius Hall at 457 Lawnmarket, named after the founder of the Association. In 1897, a second residence was opened at 6 Archibald Place and this was called Crudelius House, the first residence being renamed Burns' House. In the meantime two prominent members and activists of the Association, Miss Houldsworth and Miss Louisa Stevenson, had put forward the suggestion that a proper hall of residence should be opened as a necessary provision for women students. As a result Masson Hall Incorporated was set up under the terms of the Companies Act 1862, with a Committee of Management. Funds were raised in the three-year period 1894–7. Miss Louisa Stevenson herself subscribed £1,000 and other contributions came from some national figures in the women's movement like Mrs Garrett Anderson, Miss Emily Davies and Louisa Lumsden, other ladies of Edinburgh society, Professors and educationalists who had supported the Association. Louisa Stevenson became Honorary Secretary of Masson Hall Inc., and Sarah E. S. Mair Honorary Treasurer. Professor Masson, who had consented to the use of his name in honour of his tremendous contribution to the women's campaign, was one of the Vice-Presidents. It was the pioneers of the 1860s and 1870s who were once again involved in this new venture. The Hall opened on 24 November 1897 at 31 George Square. The head of the hall was to be a lady graduate who would understand Scottish University life. Who better than Frances H. Simson, one of the first eight ladies in 1893?

With the opening of Masson Hall the experiments in Lawnmarket and Archibald Place came to an end. Masson Hall served as a central meeting place for non-residents, who for a small fee could use its facilities and dine there. The Association closed its premises in Hope Park Square and the reading room and library were relocated in Masson Hall. The E.A.U.E.W. continued its links with Masson Hall by making some of its scholarships conditional on residence in the Hall. The rôle of the Association was thereafter an administrative one, its main objective having been achieved.

So by the end of the first decade amenities for women students had been provided by the heroines of the day, namely the women pioneers in the Association (with professorial help). It was now up to the women students to use these facilities, to expand them and to carve a niche for themselves in the University. At the same time they had to integrate into the academic community and gain acceptance.

One of the first concerns of women students was representation. They required a body to voice their grievances and in 1895 a Women's Representative Committee was formed. Miss A. C. Sutherland was its first Chairman and Miss Frances H. Melville was Secretary. It appears to have remained in existence until 1899, when a Women's Committee of the S.R.C. was organised, with the sanction of the Senatus. The Women's Representative Committee Minutes[11] reveal that their concerns were varied. They discussed issues as diverse as the nails on seats in the Reading Room causing damage to clothing and the campaign to open all scholarships in the University to women. Other women's societies were able to send their representatives to the Women's S.R.C. Committee when it was set up.

The facilities in Hope Park Square and Masson Hall were inadequate as numbers increased. In 1892 about seventy women had matriculated, with the addition of fifty non-matriculated music students, but in 1905 over 400 women were matriculated students. Therefore in 1905 a separate union was opened at 55 Lothian Street with a reading room, dining room, small committee room and kitchen. The 7s.6d. annual subscription soon rose to a half guinea. This increase may account for the fact that in 1906 only 130 out of the 500 women were members. The wife of Professor Baldwin Brown and Dr Elsie Inglis were influential in its foundation. The Union aimed to give women the 'advantages of a corporate life' and to act as a centre for 'intellectual and social intercourse'.[12] The Union moved its premises to George Square in 1920. Women graduates were prominent in its organisation, with the wives of Professors offering a supportive, even supervisory, rôle.

The Students Representative Council received statutory recognition in the 1889 Act. It was representative of students' interests and a channel of communication. The University Union, *The Student* magazine and *Student Handbook* were all outcomes of the development of the S.R.C.[13] Women students integrated themselves quickly into these new developments. Social activities and a corporate identity were both part of the new image of university life which emerged at the turn of the century. Some credit must also be given to the arrival of women students as a stimulus to fostering these new social activities in the University.

The effect of university life on women students and in turn their effect on the institution itself, can be assessed from their social pursuits. University societies for both men and women students were a vehicle for social interaction, a means to achieving a corporate life; they helped to make students feel involved in academic life and they also softened the impact of a timetable devoted exclusively to study. They were secondly an outlet for political expression. Finally, societies reflected new attitudes and trends within the changing university tradition. One trend was the expression and discussion of women's topics, which reflected past struggles and reinforced the fact that total integration was not immediate. Thus these three aspects – social interaction, political expression, independent female expression – were present to a lesser or greater extent in many facets of the University societies.

The societies were of three types, namely mixed, male and female. The mixed societies encompassed the social and political aspects, with consideration occasionally given to certain women's issues like the franchise. The Musical Society was one of the first to open its membership to women. Religious societies like the United Presbyterian Society and the Free Church Society appear also to have admitted women to their ranks and indeed to have held debates on 'the admission of women to the professions' and on 'female suffrage'. Women also joined societies such as the Caithness Society and the Dumfries and Galloway Society. The arrival of women at the University and their propensity to take Arts subjects led to the formation of French, German and Education Societies.

The Associated Societies – the Celtic, Diagnostic, Dialectic, Philomathic and Scots Law – were long-established bodies, independent of the S.R.C. and viewed as the aristocracy of the student bodies. They tended to reflect their restricted membership in their debates. While the Philomathic society was prepared to discuss the issue that 'chivalry is dying out' (21 January 1898) and that 'adult suffrage is desirable' (11 February 1898) and even to hold joint debates, the Dialectic showed its true colours in its debate on 13 December 1900 when it put forward the motion that 'women will be the last thing civilised by man'.[14] The male societies tended to pursue political issues before anything else.

However, women students also struck out on their own paths. If they did not form a totally independent university society they would at least start a women's branch or committee. Examples are the Arts Students' Christian Association (women's branch), Conservative Association (women's branch) and Women's Liberal Association. The membership fee for the second and third was one shilling. Other female societies like the Women's Christian Union, the Women's Cycling Club and the Women Students' Athletic Club, were separate bodies. The Women's Physical Society and the Women's Celtic Society emerged after 1918. Most of these women's societies were exclusive to women in that they concerned themselves with female topics. They occasionally veered to the political and held joint debates with the men's societies. A dance or 'at home' day also soon became part of a society's syllabus, thus emphasising the social element. In setting up these separate women's organisations, the women students imitated the types of society in which the men were involved. There appears to have been no concerted campaign to demand entrance to the male societies as of right. With admission and graduation won, the women were content to avoid antagonism.

The women's societies deserve consideration in more detail. The first is the Edinburgh University Women's Debating Society (W.D.S.). It was the first university society for women, and it held its first meeting on 22 November 1893.[15] It existed until about 1923, when the Talking Women Society took over as the new female debating society in the University.[16] In the varied syllabi of the W.D.S. over the years the flippant vied on occasion with the serious, and debates touched concerns which reflected the 'new woman' image of the 1890s. Two of the early questions asked were 'Should women smoke?' and 'Is dancing right?' The motion was carried 'That girls should have equal advantages with men in athletics and gymnastics'.

Consideration was also given to the issue of whether the 'freedom enjoyed by women in the present day tends to raise their standard of morality'. The franchise was a recurring topic, reflecting the women students' awareness of the activities of their pioneering predecessors and of contemporary issues. The topics for debate on education were many. For example, they debated that 'girls should be taught only by women' (1896) and in 1897 'that the higher education of women tends to unfit them for their domestic duties' and later 'that a woman's university with full powers of granting degrees to women only would be a distinctly retrograde step in women's higher education'.[17] The women were aware of the division of thought on the higher education issue, where the separatist view that women should be taught separately conflicted with the attitude that separate education was second-best and that mixed education to exactly the same standard as men was the only solution. *The Student* tended to mock the efforts of the society in its initial stages. In 1893 it announced the spurious motion for debate by the W.D.S. – 'Should potatoes be boiled in their skins?'[18] The comments in the paper did cause some offence to the society's committee who suggested that all notices of their activities should cease to be sent to *The Student*.

The W.D.S. held inter-university debates with Glasgow and St Andrews Universities. Contact was made with the Queen Margaret Debating Society at Glasgow in 1896 and with the St Andrews society in 1902. These were important links to make, continuing the earlier connections made by the various educational associations and drawing on the new common identity as university students. The inaugural address in the W.D.S. at the beginning of each academic year was usually given by one of the Professors, an educationalist or one of the women pioneers. For example, Louisa Lumsden spoke in October 1896 on the early days of the higher education movement. The extent to which the women students were reminded of their inheritance and the debt they owed to their predecessors was a constant theme of this period and is thus a significant part to emphasise.

In the Minutes of the W.D.S. there were two main concerns, business procedures and membership figures. The first item continually took the form of fining latecomers and those who failed to observe the correct procedures in debates. There was an eagerness to ensure that their conduct at all times was proper and correct. The second item, membership, was a continual cause for concern. While the membership figure never exceeded fifty, the peak year being 1906–7, the average attendance in each year was substantially less, though At Homes, dances and drama activities attracted more support. The entrance fee was one shilling and the annual subscription 2s.6d., which was no more than in many of the other societies. The society aimed to educate women students in public life. As it said in a *Student Handbook* entry:

> If you wish in after life to be able to head an insurrection, give a public lecture, conduct the business of a sewing meeting, or dismiss cook with perfect ease – here you may learn the act.[19]

The syllabi were always topical and concerned very much with female interests. It therefore must be accepted that low membership figures in themselves did not imply failure. The fact that the society continued in existence for nearly thirty years is evidence enough of its utility and success.

The medical women's position was problematical with regard to the W.D.S. The Senatus would recognise the W.D.S. only if membership was restricted to matriculated and music students. The medical women were classed as non-matriculated students. As the W.D.S. had therefore to admit the medical women as visitors, the latter tended to maintain a separate identity in their own societies. They had their own debating society, which held joint meetings with the W.D.S. and merged with the society in 1910. They started the Edinburgh University Women's Medical Society and Women's Medical College Christian Union. The isolation of the medical women tended to give the impression that the Arts women were a group unto themselves.

The second women's society which is worthy of consideration is the Edinburgh University Women's Suffrage Society. Founded in 1909, its aim was to educate opinion on the franchise issue. It held meetings and debates, distributed literature and corresponded with the press. The emphasis was placed on these methods being non-militant, to avoid any association with suffragette activities. The society was also affiliated to the Scottish Universities' Women's Suffrage Union. The information on the society is somewhat sparse, only one copy of the society's magazine *The Only Way* now being available. In fact it appears that the magazine was published only twice, in 1909 and 1913. It was therefore a reflective piece rather than one of immediate propaganda value and consisted of short articles and stories. In the 1913 edition Frances H. Simson reminded students of the day when the early pioneers had cared about the franchise in addition to their work for higher education and appealed to students to continue the battle on their behalf.[20] This appeal was aimed at both sexes for by 1911 entry to the society was open to both men and women.

The foundation of this suffrage society followed on from one of the last battles which University women had with the university authorities. The names of Frances H. Simson, Chrystal MacMillan, Frances H. Melville, Elsie Inglis and Margaret Nairn appear as the main participants. All were

Edinburgh graduates. In February 1906 the first general election arose in which the university seat of Edinburgh and St Andrews was contested. The women graduates applied to the Registrar for voting papers and were refused. The women believed that as members of the General Council they had the right to vote as university members under the terms of three Acts of Parliament.[21] This view was put to the test when an action was brought by Margaret Nairn against the Universities of Edinburgh and St Andrews in the Court of Session.[22] The women took issue on two accounts. First, they believed that voting papers should not have been denied. Secondly, they had an unshakeable belief in their right to vote. The first stage of action resulted in the ruling by the Lord Ordinary, Salvesen, that in the interpretation of the various Acts and Ordinances, the main conclusion was that 'person' in the 1868 Franchise Act did not include women and they therefore did not have any voting right. The women's response was to appeal to the Inner House, where Lords McLaren, Pearson and Ardwell considered the rather complicated interpretation of the law and confirmed on 16 November 1907 that the initial judgement had been the correct one. The last stage of the fight took Frances Melville, Frances Simson and Chrystal MacMillan to the House of Lords, where they made a last dramatic appeal. The case was dismissed in 1908 and the women had to pay costs. A committee had been set up in anticipation of raising funds for this eventuality. The women's fight was as much against the legislation as the University authorities but it nonetheless marked another milestone in the series of confrontations with Edinburgh University.

This legal conflict was part of the wider suffrage issue. In a nationwide campaign the Suffragettes had undertaken a militant programme of action in which women chained themselves to railings, disrupted meetings and went to prison. Emily Davison lost her life under the hooves of the King's horse in 1913.[23] In spite of and in contrast to these events, when one woman student who attended from 1908 to 1912 was asked whether she had been aware of the suffrage campaign she said:

> Was that when I was at University? . . . It didn't enter into our life very much. . . . It didn't make a great deal of impact on me or any of my friends really. We were too busy with our own affairs and having any freedom we wanted. I mean I don't think the vote mattered to us at that age very much. . . . We followed the news about them and all those awful things that went on in London and everywhere else, the demonstrations. . . . One read about them all the time. My friends and I somehow didn't get caught up in it in any way. It was outside our lives. . . .[24]

Her comments were echoed by other informants who were not aware of the controversies of the time. The battle with the authorities on this issue may also explain in some part the somewhat undynamic image of the Suffrage Society. The controversy had already raged. Yet while it appears that the society, like the W.D.S., had a low membership and was not very articulate, it did not necessarily mean that women students as individuals would not have taken part in outside suffrage organisation. During the First World War, the war efforts of women students in the University and their activities in the war itself, which produced heroines like Dr Elsie Inglis at the Serbian front, finally introduced an element of acceptance which had been tinged in the pre-1914 era with a hint of toleration. The general war work of women in Britain did much to confirm changes in attitude and the culmination of this was the Act giving the vote to women over thirty in 1918.

One of the notable aspects of the women's societies was their homage to their pioneering predecessors. Frequently people like Louisa Stevenson, Frances Simson and others were made honorary Presidents or Vice-Presidents. It is not insignificant therefore to find that the honorary Vice-Presidents of the Edinburgh University Women's Suffrage Society were Chrystal MacMillan and Frances Simson. Frances Melville and Chrystal MacMillan were both prominent figures in the Women's Debating Society, an activity which was to stand them in good stead.

The women students had their representative bodies in the Women's Committee of the S.R.C. and a share in the new university tradition of corporate lifestyle within the Women's Union. They had maintained some individuality but not at the expense of cutting themselves off from mixed social affairs. Women went to S.R.C. dances under the scrutiny of their chaperones, the wives of Professors. Informal dances or 'hops' were not generally chaperoned. The social connections are emphasised in this recollection:

> 'I used to go to University dances and you'd get to know the men there, you see, and then you'd be bound to meet them just round about the University quarters all the time. . . . I think they rather vied in how many girl students they knew. . . . I remember there were always chaperones at the dances, usually Professors' wives and they sat in a row on a raised desk and you were introduced to them when you went in . . .'.[25]

Many women did not confine their activities to university functions. Students who stayed at home still remained within the family social circle. The trend was soon to develop, and was predominant by the 1920s, of students attending other functions, especially the new fashionable Palais de

Danse, a public dance hall in Edinburgh. One woman graduate recalled attending sixty-three dances in one winter session, although not all these functions were university ones. Some of the women students used to miss classes to attend the afternoon session in the 'Palais'. Attendance there became an extended form of social interaction, showing that women students were part of society and not living in isolation in the academic community. Thus there were two main strands to social activities throughout the period. A separate identity was maintained by the women alongside steps being taken towards a more integrated university life.

While an assessment of social activities reveals the informal impact of women on the university, it is the quantitative evaluation over the longer term which shows the steady progress women were able to make. The following graph shows the male and female matriculation figures from 1892

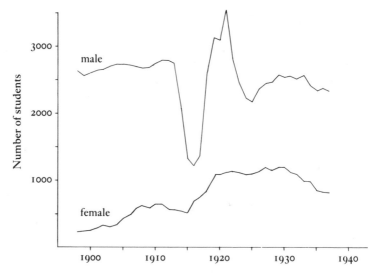

to 1939.[26] Before 1914 the gap between men and women is considerable, although the female matriculation figures do show steady progress, more noticeably from 1904/5. Women were a small minority in a male-dominated institution but it was by no means oppressive to women students. There is little evidence in the 'memories' of informants to suggest that this quantitative gulf affected the university atmosphere to any great extent. 'There was a sort of homely feeling about it'.[27] The dramatic impact of the First World War is evident by the sharp plunge in male matriculations. While statistical equality between the number of men and women students was never quite achieved, in the individual faculties new trends were appearing. In the Arts Faculty, women for the first time outnumbered men, a trend which was to re-appear in the 1920s. In the Medical Faculty in 1914, the number of women in the School of Medicine for Women was 106, but by 1918, two years after women were admitted to full university instruction, their number was 372. Mrs Chalmers Watson[28] and Sarah E. S. Mair offered to pay £4,000 within a year to defray whatever financial outlay would be involved to facilitate the introduction of medical classes on the condition that women were admitted to professional teaching, had equal privileges and that instruction was provided at an early date. The influence of women within the University had grown considerably. The last vestige of opposition to medical women had finally been removed.

There was a period of recovery by men students after the war, but it soon balanced out, while at the same time women made steady gains. The 1930s area of the graph shows the impact of economic depression, where both male and female matriculation trends are downward. The atmosphere after the First World War in the University reflects the general trends of the 1920s to gaiety and renewal. In the University it was not a period beset with struggle between the sexes despite the obvious numerical superiority which men students had. The only adverse comments on university life are found in Jennie Lee's autobiography, in which her aggression or outrage against the authorities is based on her political beliefs and the 1926 General Strike issue and not on any inequality of the sexes.[29]

By 1914 more than one thousand women had been capped at Edinburgh University.[30] This marked the culmination of a long but successful campaign by women to gain admission to the Scottish universities, the fulfilment of the ambitions of the nineteenth-century pioneers. In 1868 Professor Masson had stated that until the needs of women's education were fully recognised and fulfilled, '... we persevere in the guilt of a great injustice, and we dawdle on as a nation at but half our possible nobleness and strength'.[31] The Ordinance of 1892 and the achievements made thereafter by women in higher education reversed Professor Masson's statement of injustice.

REFERENCES
1. June Rose, *The Perfect Gentleman* (London 1977).
2. There is further information in Margaret Todd, *The Life of Sophia Jex-Blake* (1918); E. Moberly Bell, *Storming the Citadel* (London 1953); Sophia Jex-Blake, *Medical Women* (Edinburgh 1886).

3. One of the other students, Miss Edith Pechey, came out top in the Chemistry examination at the end of the 1869–70 session. The Hope Scholarship was an annual award to the best student in this examination, but Miss Pechey was awarded a bronze medal while the scholarship went to the man below her in the examination list. Professor Hope himself reluctantly decided this on the grounds that the women, who were taught separately, could not be considered as true class members. The decision aroused much bad feeling and damaged the University's reputation, making the women's campaign in Edinburgh a national issue.

4. Moberly Bell, op. cit.

5. James Scotland, *History of Scottish Education*, ii, 67.

6. 1st Report, E.L.E.A., 1867. See also Elspeth J. Boog Watson, *The Association for the University Education of Women 1867–1967* (pamphlet).

7. Katherine Burton, *A Memoir of Mrs Crudelius* (Edinburgh 1879). The first meeting was held on 15 October 1867 and marked the foundation of the E.L.E.A. The Edinburgh Essay Society became the Ladies' Edinburgh Debating Society. See Lettice Milne Rae, *Ladies in Debate 1865–1935*. Sarah Elizabeth Siddons Mair, D.B.E., LL.D. (1846–1941), was a lifelong supporter of women's rights, an ardent campaigner for women's education and a keen suffragist.

8. David Masson, 'London University and London Colleges and Schools of Sciences', *MacMillan's Magazine*, xvi (1867) 432.

9. W. N. Boog Watson, 'The First Eight Ladies', *UEJ*, 23 (1967–8).

10. W. N. Boog Watson 'The Story of the Women Students' Union', *UEJ*, 24 (1970) 188.

11. Women's Representative Committee, Minute Book 1895–1899, EUL, Masson Hall papers, unclassified.

12. *Atlanta's Garland, being the Book of the Edinburgh University Women's Union* (1926).

13. A. Logan Turner (ed.), *History of the University of Edinburgh, 1883–1933*, 338.

14. *Edinburgh University Student Handbooks*, 1897–1914.

15. Edinburgh University Women's Debating Society, Minutes 1893–1914, EUL MSS Gen. 160–3.

16. Margaret Laurence, 'Anecdotage (1927–1931)', *UEJ*, 28 (1977).

17. W. D. S. Minutes, 19 November 1897. A majority voted for the motion.

18. *The Student*, 8 (1894) 300.

19. *Edinburgh University Student Handbook*, 19 (1914–15) 258.

20. *The Only Way* (Edinburgh University Women's Suffrage Society), 1913.

21. The three acts were as follows: (1) Representation of the People (Scotland) Act, 1868; (2) Universities Elections Amendment (Scotland) Act, 1881; (3) Universities (Scotland) Act, 1889.

22. Nairn v. Universities of St Andrews and Edinburgh, 1908 S.C. 113, 1909 A.C. 147.

23. Antonia Raeburn, *The Militant Suffragettes* (London 1973) 201.

24. Author's tape no. 18, side A.

25. ibid., side A.

26. Based on figures from Annual Statistical Returns and Statistics in the *University Calendars*.

27. op. cit., Tape no.18

28. Mrs Chalmers Watson, M.B., M.D., C.B.E., 1873–1936 (née Alexandra Mary Campbell Geddes). She was the first woman medical graduate at Edinburgh in 1896. She was a prominent figure in the medical field.

29. Jennie Lee, *This Great Journey, A volume of autobiography 1904–45* (London 1963).

30. See footnote 26 above.

31. David Masson's inaugural address to the first E.L.E.A. class in a reprint from *The Scotsman* (17 January 1868).

Of Chambers and Communities:
Student Residence at the University of Edinburgh, 1583–1983

ROY M. PINKERTON

'There is a strong and widespread feeling that the full advantages of a university education are not attainable by a student who does not spend at least a part of his university career under conditions of community life.'[1] Such a feeling, voiced by the University Grants Committee in 1948 at the start of the post-war expansion of halls of residence, stems from the conviction that where students live and what kind of accommodation they have are matters of some importance, a conviction that has not always been strongly felt in Edinburgh.

It would, however, have been shared by the Town Council of the 1580s. In planning the 'Tounis College' of 1583, the Council had as models the medieval Scottish universities in St Andrews, Glasgow and Aberdeen, all of which had to some extent imitated their predecessors at Oxford and Cambridge and on the continent. These were primarily residential colleges, with students eating, sleeping and studying in the same building. This was to be Edinburgh's pattern also, and the Town Council resolved on 8 November 1583 'that all the students of the townis college sall nichtlie ly and remayne in their chalmeris within the sam'. The college's first premises were a cluster of buildings on the site of the present Old College, one of which, Hamilton House, was adapted to provide classrooms, a large hall and three 'chambers' or sleeping apartments. A further fourteen chambers were built nearby: these were provided out of a substantial bequest and were still unfinished at the beginning of the first session, in both respects foreshadowing developments of more recent years. These rooms were shared, students sleeping two to a bed and paying £2 rent per person; anyone who wanted a bed to himself was charged £4. Burgesses' sons paid no rent, but were expected to provide their own furniture; for the others the basic necessities were supplied.

These early arrangements displayed a true collegiate spirit, but soon became impossible to carry out in practice. Although the number of chambers slowly increased, often as a result of individual benefactions, they simply could not keep pace with a steadily growing student population. In the 1620s, for example, when student numbers had risen to over 300, there were only twenty-three sleeping apartments, and it is clear that long before then the college had ceased to be, if indeed it ever had been, fully residential. This failure to develop as planned was the result not only of shortage of accommodation, but of the absence of any 'common table', an essential prerequisite for a properly residential college. It thus became a matter of convenience as well as necessity to reside outwith the college, and although a tiny proportion of students continued to occupy chambers for many years this was generally because they were too poor to go elsewhere or because they came from abroad: of the three residents left in 1773, all were poor and lived rent-free, and one came from Poland.

If the bulk of the students no longer lived in, they at least lived close by. College Wynd, Bristo Street, and the surrounding areas became a veritable 'university quarter', students lodging either with private householders, a practice that was to play a major part in Edinburgh student life, or in some cases with their professors. This latter arrangement benefited both sides: professorial salaries were supplemented (Principal Robertson appealed in 1768 for funds to build houses for professors sufficiently commodious that they 'could then more readily ... receive young gentlemen under their immediate care'), while the students were able to further their academic studies, were protected from unscrupulous landladies who might not always air beds properly or provide adequate meals, and were under a degree of supervision, shielded from contact with the seamier side of Edinburgh life. This question of supervision was an important element in the dilemma which faced the potential student of the eighteenth century: was the excellence of the academic education provided at Edinburgh worth the dangers, both moral and material, of unsupervised life in lodgings? Likewise, if the university was to maintain its reputation and attract good students, could it afford to ignore their extra-curricular welfare?

Precisely this issue was responsible for an early attempt to set up in Edinburgh what might later have been called a hall of residence. At the end of the seventeenth century English students from a dissenting background, barred by their religion from entering Oxford or Cambridge, began to come north in increasing numbers. Intense rivalry developed between the Universities of Glasgow and Edinburgh, each determining to attract as many of these southern dissenters as possible. Accordingly, in 1709 a number of those who championed Edinburgh's cause put forward a scheme[2] to enhance her public image, and proposed that a 'convenient lodging for a competent number of students' be provided, if possible within the college precincts. Supervision was to be the responsibility of 'persons of approved learning, prudence, and religion', who would oversee their charges' academic progress and also 'direct their diversions and inspect their manners'. The English dissenters were envisaged as the principal beneficiaries, but since access to 'the publick Boarding House' was also to be permitted to 'such of the students as shall happen to lodge and eat in private houses' it is clear that the scheme was seen as having a much wider potential, and it is a matter of regret that lack of active encouragement from the university authorities doomed it to failure. Its merits were, however, recognised by the Town Council, who encouraged one of the principal architects of the scheme, local preacher James McEwan, to experiment on his own. The Council leased a house in Niddry's Wynd to him and gave financial support. Unfortunately nothing is heard of this venture after 1712, and nothing is known of its success.

It was to be another 150 years before anything similar was tried. The Edinburgh landlady reigned supreme, her rod of iron not infrequently tempered with feelings of genuine affection for her charges. They in turn regarded these custodians of their freedom with mingled fear and respect. Oliver Goldsmith, who studied medicine at Edinburgh from 1752 to 1754, remembered his first landlady (he soon found another) in College Wynd chiefly for 'the mutations of the culinary art through which in a week a single loin of mutton passed: a brandered chop, a fried steak, collops with mutton sauce, and so on until . . . finally a dish of broth was manufactured from the bones on the seventh day and the landlady rested from her labours'. Charles Darwin's landlady of 1825, a Mrs Mackay, was by contrast, 'a nice, clean, old body, exceedingly civil and attentive'. Foreign visitors expressed surprise that students were allowed to reside where they wished, growing numbers of overseas students experienced difficulty in finding suitable lodgings, but by and large the eighteenth and early nineteenth centuries passed without any significant developments. One lone voice may be noted, that of a contributor to *The Cheilead*, a curiously named and ephemeral student publication of 1826:[3] 'if a proper place were provided,' he argues, 'and students not forced, but recommended, to live in it, and where the holders would be honest and moral, we have little doubt but that it would tend not only to the prosperity of the College, but to the ultimate good of the Metropolis'. Prophetic words, but still sixty years ahead of their time.

It is apparent that, with the possible exception of the very early years of the Town's College, the university authorities saw no reason to concern themselves with where a student lived, let alone assume any responsibility for accommodating him. Like so much else in the modern university, this became a proper subject for debate only after the Universities (Scotland) Act of 1858 began to breathe new life into what had become an increasingly moribund set of institutions. Even then, the question of residential accommodation was not high on the agenda: greater priority had to be given to new chairs, better teaching facilities and more adequate equipment. St Andrews had a brief flirtation with an English-type 'College Hall' in the 1860s, but it was too exotic a flower to blossom on Scottish soil. A similar seed in Edinburgh hardly broke ground: in 1863, on the initiative of the Senatus, The Edinburgh University College Hall Company Limited was floated, with the object of establishing 'a Collegiate Hall ... in which students at the University may have board and lodging ... and an opportunity of associating together under suitable superintendence'. Support from both university and city was mildly enthusiastic, but the necessary finance was not forthcoming and the company was wound up.

Among those who were quick to realise the benefits which such an establishment might bring to the university was Principal Grant. From his outburst of 1869 against the misplaced generosity of educational benefactors who in founding their schools had 'half surrounded this city with a ring of palaces' instead of providing 'colleges for the residence of University students' to his invitation at the tercentenary celebrations of 1883 to 'some pious millionaire' to 'buy up the whole of George Square and turn it into sets of chambers for students' he remained a staunch supporter of the advantages of a residential system. So too was his successor, Sir William Muir, but these far-sighted men found themselves pitted against an entrenched opposition to anything that would diminish the traditional independence of the Scottish student. 'The whole conception (sc. of a College Hall),' wrote Grant despairingly in 1883, 'seems to be at variance with the genius of a Scottish University', a view that was to linger on for some years yet.

Where officialdom was frustrated, private enterprise was to succeed. Within four years of Grant's remarks a hall of residence was established, the first successful foundation in Scotland. The person responsible was the colourful and avant-garde educationalist, Patrick Geddes. In a career that ranged from an assistantship in Botany at Edinburgh to the chair of Sociology in Bombay, he threw himself energetically into a wide variety of pursuits, including the development of a new concept of community residence. As a young lecturer at Edinburgh, his concern at the conditions in which his students were living led him to lease three flats in Mound Place, which he refurbished and opened in May 1887 as 'University Hall': the building in question is still a hall of residence, renamed in his honour Patrick

Geddes Hall in 1978. That University Hall was much more than the 'public boarding house' envisaged by earlier enthusiasts is clear from Geddes' philosophy. Not only would a resident benefit from the close association with his fellows from other faculties, but to prevent the students from becoming too introspective a small proportion of places was made available to young professional men in the city. To those critics who saw in a communal residence the erosion of 'that independence which rightly is an old and cherished tradition in Scotland' Geddes was reassuring: there were to be no wardens and no supervisory committee; the students would 'assume full control of the internal management', deciding what rules should be imposed and how they should be enforced, supervising the domestic staff, choosing new residents, and so on. This principle of self-government lay at the very heart of Geddes' thinking: residence in hall was not to be a comfortable escape from the real world, but a preparation for it, an educational experience in itself.

University Hall was an immediate success. Further property in the Old Town was rented, and Ramsay Lodge, adjoining the Castle Esplanade, was built, enabling numbers to rise to 120 by 1894. The student body was enthusiastic, social activities flourished, and ex-residents look nostalgically back to 'that mêlée of heterogeneous but congenial spirits which was one of the charms of University Hall'. In 1896, when Geddes' energies in extending his various enterprises outran his business capabilities, a limited company, The Town and Gown Association, was formed to manage the Hall's affairs. For fifty years University Hall continued to bear witness to the clarity of Geddes' vision, until financial difficulties in the 1930s spelt its end. By then, however, the spark that Geddes had ignited had taken firm hold and was quite unquenchable: halls of residence had come of age.

The initial growth of University Hall coincided with the opening up of university education to women. It was unthinkable that they should be exposed to the unsupervised life of lodgings, and the 1890s saw the opening of a number of women's halls and the formation of limited companies to run them.[4] Some were short-lived, but two halls which opened in George Square in 1897 survive to the present day: Masson Hall, founded by The Edinburgh Association for the University Education of Women, and Muir Hall, intended specifically for female medical students. Further places for women became available in 1916, when The Edinburgh Association for the Provision of Hostels for Women Students opened three purpose-built halls at East Suffolk Road: this association was a composite one on which the various educational institutions in the city were represented, and students from all of these were eligible for residence. These halls have since expanded, and continue to provide much-needed places for women students.

Initially, however, these new developments failed to bring about any change in the university's official position. Professors served in a private capacity on the various associations and their wives managed the women's halls, university publications advertised the residences, but otherwise the university remained aloof. The first real initiative on the part of the University Court came in 1917, prompted by a request from the Carnegie Trust to consider how best the Trust's substantial surplus might be spent. It was noted that the absence of suitable accommodation was losing Edinburgh potential students: Scottish parents were coming to prefer Oxford or Cambridge, where residence was compulsory, while candidates for the Indian Civil Service were permitted to attend only those universities offering residential facilities. It was also remembered that Cecil Rhodes had deprived Edinburgh of a share in his scholarships because of its official indifference to Geddes' efforts to establish halls. Acknowledging that 'the absence of corporate life is likely to prove increasingly . . . a serious danger to the reputation and usefulness of the University', the University Court adopted a twofold response. The companies running Muir and Masson Halls were in financial difficulties, and these halls were taken over in 1918 and 1919 respectively. The decision was also taken to build halls for men: four possible sites were considered, but no money was immediately available, the Carnegie Trust surplus having been used for other purposes, and the scheme hung fire.

Support came from a totally unexpected source. During the General Strike in 1926, student volunteers helped to keep essential services going. Many of them were assigned to Leith Docks, where their activities provoked the expected cynical jibes:

> Four and twenty blacklegs, working night and day,
> Fed on eggs and bacon, getting double pay;
> Helmets on their thick heads, bayonets gleaming bright,
> If someone burst a sugar-bag, the lot would die of fright.[5]

These same students, however, so impressed the General Manager of the Docks, Thomas Cowan, that he donated £10,000 to the university in appreciation of those who had 'demonstrated afresh the grit and pluck of our university youths'. On hearing the University Court's decision to use this benefaction to convert five houses in George Square into a men's hall, Cowan promptly gave a further £20,000 and set up a scholarship fund for residents.

In October 1929 Cowan House opened its doors to ninety-two student

residents, six junior members of staff, and a warden. The Cowan
Scholarships were intended to benefit 'young men who in respect of
intellectual force or other personal characteristics are likely to have a useful
influence on their fellow-students and to become a credit to their university',
and it was clear from the start that the university hoped that all residents
would be of this calibre, or if not that they would attain to it by virtue of
residing in Cowan House. The warden's annual reports of these early years
show that there was a conscious attempt 'to institute a vigorous community
life, to think in wider perspective through the interchange of ideas, and to
encourage a less effeminate type of social life than what is common in the
university'. A library was established, a dramatic club made a successful
debut, the tennis courts proved popular, but emphasis remained firmly on
intellectual ability, and students whose work failed to reach 'the standard
required in the House' were condemned to a term's residence in lodgings.
Reports that complain of 'a regrettable introspectiveness and parochialism'
or 'restiveness and misdirection of interest' might suggest that the
university was countering its long years of neglect with a too eager
assumption of its new paternal role, but the residents were happy and
applications for places far outstripped the number of rooms available.

It would, of course, be churlish to suggest that part of the attraction of
Cowan House lay in its proximity to Masson Hall. The two stood side by side
in George Square, but it was not expected that their respective residents
should dare to do likewise. Indeed, the arrival of men next door had called a
halt to some of Masson's more unusual activities: 'the joy of sleeping out on
summer nights,' the warden noted, 'was reluctantly abandoned'. It had
been hoped that George Square Gardens would provide 'a common and
natural meeting-ground' for the sexes, but the proprietors refused to allow
access to the men. Ladies, whether from Masson or from anywhere else,
were admitted to Cowan House on Sunday afternoons, a ruling that was
relaxed – to every afternoon – in 1961; Masson was even stricter with male
visitors. Like much else, this artificial separation between the two ended on
the outbreak of the Second World War, when it transpired that they had to
share the same air-raid shelter!

The steady growth of halls in the years following 1887 must not obscure
the fact that the vast majority of students not living at home had still to find
accommodation in lodgings. As student numbers increased, these were the
golden years of the landladies of Marchmont and kindred districts, whose
legendary devotion to duty, 'even to the point of holding their own credit
involved in their lodgers' examination results', earns them a worthy
mention in an official U.G.C. report.[6] Lodgings, and landladies, come in all

shapes and sizes, and the need to ensure minimum standards of cleanliness and comfort had long given the university authorities cause for concern. As early as 1866, Principal Brewster offered to compile a register 'of all the Boarding and Lodging Houses in Edinburgh, with the names of Clergymen or other persons who vouch for the respectability of those who keep them', but he died before the committee to which this suggestion was remitted could give it its blessing. Principal Muir introduced a 'Directory of Lodgings' in 1885, but not until 1928 was the essential step taken of inspecting lodgings before recommending them to students: an 'Official Register of Lodgings and Private Hostels' was then compiled and made available for consultation.

By the 1930s the university was clearly taking much more than a passing interest in the problem of accommodating its students. Any incipient feelings of complacency, however, were cruelly banished by the war. When it ended, the accommodation situation was much worse, with a large increase expected in the student population and fewer householders willing to take in students. In 1945 the only residences for men were Cowan House and a small hall for divinity students established in the post-Geddes expansion of the 1890s: these provided places for 119 men out of a total of 1,669. Women fared slightly better: 316 female students out of a total of 1,333 had rooms in Masson and Muir Halls and in the university's share of the Craigmillar Park complex.

A number of remedies were sought, most of them temporary. Appeals to the citizens of Edinburgh to accept more student lodgers produced little response. Ramsay Lodge was rented from the almost defunct Town and Gown Association as a possible prelude to buying it, but the asking price was too high and it was occupied by students for only one term. A large house in Inverleith Place was gifted to the university and run as a hostel under the name of Norway House for some years, while another in Mortonhall Road, Blackford Mount, was used for a brief period as a residence for Indian students, whose particular problems had been exercising the authorities for some time. In both these cases, the residences had been established without sufficient preliminary consideration: they were too small to be economical, Norway House was too far from the university, and the segregation of students of one nationality in Blackford Mount proved to be fraught with problems. The only long-term development was the appointment of a Superintendent of Student Accommodation and Welfare, whose principal function was to find accommodation for the vast numbers of new students.

These remedies could not penetrate to the heart of the problem, whose solution, wrote Principal Fraser in 1946, 'can be found only in the greatly extended provision of university students' residences'. He was careful to point out that the university's official policy was still 'to accept no responsibility for the provision of residential accommodation', but acknowledged that 'various changes in social and economic conditions' in recent years had created a new situation which the university could no longer ignore; it now accepted that the educational and material advantages of community life ought to be more readily available. In thus affirming Edinburgh's position, the Principal was identifying with the views of the U.G.C., whose periodic reports from 1921 onwards had stressed the value of residence in halls and had strongly urged Britain's universities to increase their stock of such accommodation.

It takes more than wise advice and good intentions, however, to build a hall of residence. Patrick Geddes had visionary zeal, Thomas Cowan a generous purse; Edinburgh's next benefactor, Sir Donald Pollock, had both. Born in 1868, the son of a Galashiels minister, he studied medicine at Edinburgh and after practising for a number of years embarked on a second career in industry, where his eventual chairmanship of the British Oxygen Company and a number of other directorships brought him rich financial rewards and a baronetcy. A notable public figure whose support of good causes was unstinted, he formed in 1936 the Pollock Trust, largely for the benefit of the University of Edinburgh. He also bought up property in the city, with the intention of providing 'a Great Students' Union, Residential Halls for Students, Residences . . . for the Principal, Professors, and other members of the educational staff . . ., gymnasiums and athletic grounds', the whole benefaction to be in memory of his parents. His plan was to restore and adapt the various properties himself, and present the university with 'a complete unit ready for immediate occupancy', but in 1943, during his rectorship of the university, tax laws forced him to modify his plans and he donated most of his purchases undeveloped. Intended for student residential use were the two mansions of St Leonard's and Salisbury Green, with extensive grounds in their splendid setting adjoining Holyrood Park. Before the war St Leonard's had housed a girls' school of independent views, St Trinnean's, the original of its better known and more simply spelt comic namesake, and Sir Donald's intention to open this as a women's hall was duly carried out in 1946. Salisbury Green opened as a men's hall in the following year. Like Geddes, Sir Donald disapproved of wardens, and these two small halls had only a resident housekeeper, Sir Donald himself exercising general oversight and taking an active interest even in such mundane matters as visiting hours until well into his eighties.

The surrounding ground, then under cultivation as a market-garden, was a prime site for further residential development, and all seemed set fair for expansion. Unfortunately it became apparent that Sir Donald's views on development did not coincide with those of the university, and as the main benefactor he could not be altogether ignored. He wanted to build a group of women's halls around St Leonard's and a group of men's halls around Salisbury Green, the open space between preserving the spectacular outlook towards Duddingston Loch: the university's priority was for men's halls, not women's, and a different part of the site was preferred. Despite the increasing urgency of the university's accommodation problems, this impasse continued for several years and only in 1954, when there was some danger of the site being taken over for corporation housing, was a compromise reached.

Six halls were to be built, four for men and two for women, housing 150 students each; these were to be grouped in pairs, each pair having its own central refectory. The first block went ahead more or less as planned, Holland House opening in 1960 and Fraser House in 1964, the slight differences between them testifying already to a growing need for economy. In 1961 the whole programme of development on the site was radically altered: a drastic cut in the U.G.C.'s budget for new building, a dramatic rise in the number of student places required, strong student pressure for more self-catering accommodation, and the realisation that individual refectories were highly uneconomic were all contributory factors. Accordingly, the present layout was adopted: six halls, of different and cheaper design, grouped around a central block containing a refectory, common rooms, and other facilities. The halls were duly completed, two providing self-catering accommodation and all in operation by 1967, but the central block fell a victim to further U.G.C. cuts and the Holland/Fraser dining-hall had to soldier on alone, coping with vastly increased numbers, until 1970. In that year, the present refectory was at last erected, largely because the halls were being used as the Games Village for the Commonwealth Games and adequate facilities were absolutely essential. Finally, a new Cowan House was opened in 1973, the name continuing the traditions of the earlier hall which had had to close ten years previously to allow for re-development in George Square. St Leonard's was converted to staff and office accommodation in 1965, but Salisbury Green continues to house students. The whole site thus contains ten halls, with accommodation for 1,800 students, one of the largest residential communities to be developed in any British university.

That so large a complex, expanding in so piece-meal a fashion, should have acquired such character as it undoubtedly has is a tribute to the foresight of those responsible for its growth, in particular its first Principal Warden, Very Rev. Professor John McIntyre. Sir Donald's strictures on the presence of members of staff could not possibly be maintained – in so large a community wardens have an administrative rôle, let alone a supervisory one – and from the start staff and students have been in general agreement on most important matters of policy. The Pollock Halls Committee, which is responsible for the day-to-day running of the site, was from the beginning composed of staff and students in equal numbers, a commonplace now but a bold departure in the 1960s. Any community of 1,800 individuals is, of course, bound to have its problems, and it would be senseless to pretend that the inhabitants of the Pollock Halls are simply one big happy family: the economies of design forced on the university have in some cases led to conditions which do not meet with universal approval and in others have given the stamp of institutionalism to the site, while the sheer numbers involved tend both to submerge the individual and to render impossible any true fostering of the kind of community spirit found in University Hall or Cowan House. On the whole, however, students are appreciative of the facilities provided, and the benefits that the halls have brought to the university are considerable.

While the Pollock Halls tend to dominate any discussion of student accommodation over the past thirty years, it must not be forgotten that the university has responded in other ways, both traditional and experimental, to the residential needs of its ever-growing student population. Masson and Muir Halls had, like Cowan House, to move from George Square, but were almost immediately relocated, in South Lauder Road and Drumsheugh Gardens respectively. An imaginative and highly successful venture of the 1960s was the conversion of a group of near-derelict tenements at Mylne's Court in the Lawnmarket; these historic properties, dating back to 1690, underwent a massive programme of restoration and renovation made possible by two generous benefactions commemorated in the names of Edward Salvesen Hall and Philip Henman Hall. The latter is the university's only hall specifically for postgraduates (who are, of course, eligible for places at the Pollock Halls and elsewhere), and as such it meets a long-felt need: several attempts were made in the 1940s to found a postgraduate hall, but too many other projects claimed a higher priority. Associated with Mylne's Court is Patrick Geddes Hall, part of which, after being relinquished by the Town and Gown Association, served for many years first as a women's hostel and then as a residence for divinity students. In being able to provide for their residents a more intimate and homely atmosphere than is possible in the larger houses at Pollock, these smaller halls have a valuable rôle to play.

One type of accommodation which originated in Edinburgh is the Student House. In 1959 the university acquired a house in Drummond Place which had been divided into single-room flatlets for business women. Students were installed as an experiment, and this proved immediately successful. Kitchen facilities are provided, but students have to do their own cooking and basic cleaning; each house has a resident warden, but in general students are expected to be as independent as possible and personally responsible for their own comfort. This type of accommodation, combining some of a hall's advantages with a greater degree of independence than it normally allows, proved so popular that other universities soon followed suit, while in Edinburgh the number of Student Houses has risen to the present total of twenty-nine, housing over 600 students.

This significant increase in the provision of halls and related types of accommodation ensures that 26·7 per cent of the student population can now be given places, a great improvement on the immediate post-war figure of 7·1 per cent. Equally significant have been the steps taken to assist those who either do not wish to apply for a place in halls or are unlucky in obtaining one. Earlier in the century, such moves as the establishment of an official register of lodgings showed that the university was gradually taking an interest in such matters, although it was slow to admit publicly any responsibility for them. Policy statements of the 1970s, however, clearly acknowledge that the university now recognises its responsibility (shared, admittedly, with the local authority and with the individual student) 'for assessing the housing needs of its students, for meeting a proportion of that need itself, and for satisfying itself that the needs of the remainder are being met.' To this end, the University Accommodation Committee was strengthened and the Student Accommodation Service reorganised in 1973, with specific remits both to cope with present problems and to look to the future and gauge possible requirements. In the past, students may have paraded their independence; now they are content to depend on the expertise of the Accommodation Service, and have even been known to protest – something their predecessors would never have dreamt of doing – if they considered that that Service was not responding to their needs with sufficient alacrity.

The practical steps implementing this new policy are of various kinds. Lodgings with board still exist, although in less plentiful supply than before. The decline of the traditional landlady and the attractions of other kinds of accommodation are responsible for a drop in the percentage of students in lodgings from 37·7 per cent in 1945 to 12·7 per cent in 1981. In a successful attempt to keep this percentage from dropping any further, a Guaranteed Lodgings Scheme was introduced in 1976, making it more attractive for householders to open their homes to student lodgers.

There have always been students who have ventured into the private sector and endeavoured to rent flats on their own account. The independence which such an arrangement permits matched the student mood of the 1960s, but in an increasingly competitive market supply soon fell far short of demand. The appointment of a Flats Officer in 1968 removed from the students some of the burden of finding suitable accommodation and coping with the legal problems involved, and in 1973 a comprehensive housing management service was introduced by the Accommodation Service, another area in which Edinburgh has been one of the pioneer universities. Properties are leased by the university and let to students, who thus have no dealings with private landlords. This scheme has proved particularly popular, and in addition to flats and houses scattered throughout the city a number of larger blocks, newly renovated by property developers, have been taken over, such as those at Cowgatehead, in James Court, and in the Crown Commissioners' development in Nicolson Street. Other attempts to increase the stock of private sector accommodation through involvement with Housing Associations and with local authorities at Wester Hailes and at Livingston have not been notably successful. Another type of assistance for those wishing to be slightly more independent is provided by the Accommodation Service's agency scheme, whereby students are put in touch with the owners of vacant property and left to complete negotiations themselves.

In meeting the needs of today's students, there is thus a considerable dependence on the private sector. While this is welcomed, it is also appreciated that it would be folly to rely too heavily on it: leases terminate and are not renewed, new Rent Acts give rise to changing conditions of tenancy, and in general the university is at the mercy of others. The only certain way of countering such problems is for the university to increase its own stock of accommodation, and this is now regarded as a major priority. The principal obstacle is lack of finance, whether it be for buying a vacant site and erecting a new building or for converting an existing property. In 1968 the U.G.C.'s financial policy changed yet again and universities are now virtually obliged to rely on benefactions or to develop a system of loan-financing. Edinburgh has been fortunate on both counts: substantial gifts and bequests have been received, and after some initial reluctance on the part of student officials to sanction loan-financing a Residential Development Fund was set up in 1977, into which residents in university-provided accommodation pay a small sum each year. New university property provided by such means can, of course, be of any type, but apart from an extension to Salisbury Green and a distant possibility of utilising vacant ground on the Pollock site, further full-board halls of residence are not envisaged. Rather is it intended that the increasing demand for flats should be met, and accordingly a sizeable block is being converted in South College Street – a traditional area for lodgings in the seventeenth and eighteenth centuries – while land at Blacket Place and in the Pleasance is earmarked for further purpose-built development.

All this is a far cry from the seventeen chambers of 1583. A modern university the size of Edinburgh cannot hope to be fully residential, in the sense in which the founding fathers would have understood the word. What it can do is to take practical steps to show that it shares their conviction that the conditions in which students live are of supreme importance. Edinburgh's record in this respect may not always have been one to be proud of, progress may at times have been reluctant and due more to expediency than to careful planning, but as the university moves into its fifth century it may fairly claim that it is facing up to its responsibilities in the matter of student residence with much greater vigour and vitality than ever before.

ACKNOWLEDGMENTS

For permission to consult records, for helpful discussions and for general assistance, I am happy to record my gratitude to the Secretary to the University of Edinburgh, to the Senior Wardens, past and present, and their staff, and to staff in the Buildings Office, the Old College Filing Room, the Student Accommodation Service, and the Special Collections Department of the University Library; to the Librarian of the University of Glasgow; and to a number of friends, especially W. J. Windram, from whose advice, criticism, and sound common sense I have considerably benefited.

REFERENCES

Many of the quotations in this essay are from minutes of committee meetings or similar records. As these are not generally accessible, I have not provided precise references, but have usually indicated in general terms in the text the source of the extract.

1. *Report of the University Grants Committee for the years 1935–1947* (HMSO 1948) 54.
2. This scheme is explained in detail in a letter of 21 November 1709 from James McEwan to Principal Stirling of the University of Glasgow, preserved in the library of that university (David Murray Transcripts).

3. The collected issues are in EUL. The name seems initially to have been derived from 'cheil' or 'chiel', which may conceivably have been a nickname of the compiler, and the title-page contained the phrase, 'I am a queer and quizzy Cheil', but in the second issue, when some had 'said it was the thousandth part', the secretary of the group of students which produced it declared the true derivation to be 'from χείλευς, *labri*, "and they were all of one lip", as the Septuagint renders the Hebrew in the chapter of the tower of Babel.'

4. There is information about them in Mrs Hamilton's essay.

5. Published originally in *Student*; quoted in J. H. Burns and D. Sutherland-Graeme, *Scottish University* (1944) 135.

6. *University Grants Committee: Report of the Sub-Committee on Halls of Residence* (HMSO 1957) 6.

Manuscript Sources in the Library
on the Life of the University

MARJORIE ROBERTSON

The collection of manuscript material relating to the University of
Edinburgh is one of the special interests of the University Library. The
following list outlines the principal sources available in the Library's
Department of Special Collections for the history of life in the University.
Since the list specifically concerns the social aspect of the University's
history, the official university archives, also housed in the department, have
not been included, although material such as court and senate papers,
matriculation and library records and class lists is of course basic to most
studies of university history.

Much of the most valuable source material concerning the life of a
university is ephemeral in nature and thus rarely survives for later
generations of scholars. For this reason, in anticipation of the Quatercentenary of the University, the University Library in 1980, the year of its own
Quatercentenary, launched an appeal to all Edinburgh graduates and staff
for documents and other material relating to the life and history of the
University. The generous response to this appeal has produced a wealth of
material, including many personal reminiscences. This collection, once
sorted and added to the Library's stock, will present to future scholars a
much fuller picture of life in the University of Edinburgh in the twentieth
century.

I am grateful to Dr J. T. D. Hall, Keeper of Special Collections, for his
advice and for drawing my attention to certain items.

Papers illustrative of the history and constitution of the University of
Edinburgh (2 vols.), 1611–1742. (Dc.1.4)
'Injunctions for the Janitor of the Colledge,' 14 November 1639. With
signatures of janitors, 1639–1732. *And* 'Leges Bibliothecae.' With
signatures of persons admitted to the use of the Library, 12 December
1636–14 November 1753. (Da.2.1)
'Register of the Universitie of Edinburgh, 1644.' Including injunctions

for the janitor of the College and 'the Discipline of the Colledge of Edinburgh, wherein is contained the offices and duties of the professors, masters, scholars, bursars and servants as it hes been observed many years ago.' (Da.4.1)

Thomas Craufurd, professor of mathematics. History of the University of Edinburgh, 1580–1646. Original manuscript. (La.III.232)

Transcript of same by William Henderson, librarian, 1673. (Dc.4.3)

Transcript of same by John Paul, man-servant to Professor Andrew Duncan, Sen., 1791. (Dc.5.8)

Signatures of graduates of Edinburgh University to the renewed Solemn League and Covenant, 11 April 1649. (La.III.229/2)

Sir John Lauder, Lord Fountainhall. Narrative (incomplete) of his travels in France, 1665–7. Containing references to his student days at Edinburgh, 1660–4, his regent, James Pillans, and fellow students.

(La.III.270)

Transcript of same, 19th cent. (La.III.273)

Dictates by James Pillans taken down at Edinburgh University by Archibald Flint, 1672–3. Illustrated by Flint with sketches of regents lecturing, students playing games, etc. (Dc.6.4–5)

An advertisement. These are to give notice to all noblemen, gentlemen ... that we, the students in the Royal University of Edinburgh ... do resolve to burn the effigies of Antichrist the Pope of Rome, at the Mercat-Cross of Edinburgh, the 25 of December instant, etc. (Edinburgh, 1680.) *Printed*. This incident gave rise to a number of published pamphlets.

(Da.)

Notice of a performance of Terence's *Eunuchus* in the University by the students, with some pupils of Kelso High School, 1681. *Printed*. (Da.)

David Gregory, professor of mathematics. Memorial to the Committee of Parliament for visiting schools and colleges, n.d. (1687). (Gregory Papers, Folio C.) (*In* Dc.1.61)

Also notes by Gregory on his dispute with the Town Council at the time of the visitation of the University in 1690, including 'Ane account of the tumults in E^{dr} Colledge in the spring 1691.' (Gregory Papers, Folio B.)

(*In* Dk.1.2²)

'The humble petition of the gentle-men of the Colledge to Her Grace the Dutchess of Buckleugh,' 1706. Concerning the students' vengeance on the postilion of the Duchess and its consequences. (*In* La.II.90/2)

Draft petition of the professors of the University of Edinburgh to Her Majesty's High Commissioner about a desired increase of salaries, 1707.

(*In* La.II.63)

'Considerations and proposealls for encourageing of parents in sending their sones to the universitie of Edinburgh,' 1709. (La.II.407/6)

Letters (2) from Christopher Taylor and Benjamin Bennet to Principal William Carstares about the design to attract English dissenters to the University, 19 September 1709 and 21 February 1710.

(La.II.407/9–10)

Correspondence of Charles Mackie, professor of history, 1710–65. University news especially in letters from J. Stevenson, J. Pringle, J. Gordon, W. Wallace, J. Mitchell and A. Murray. (La.II.91)

Senatus Academicus. Minutes, 1733– . (Da.)

Part of a merchant's account for clothing material bought by Oliver Goldsmith while a student at Edinburgh University, 1753. (La.II.195)

Letters (5) from Joseph Black to his father, John Black, describing his studies at Edinburgh University, 1753–5.

(Gen. 874/V/6–11, Dc.2.76^8, Gen. 873/I/1–2)

Benjamin Rush, M.D. Journal, 1766–8. *Microfilm* and *typed transcript.* (Original manuscript in Indiana University Library.) Rush studied medicine at Edinburgh, 1766–8. (Mic. M 28, Dk.2.18)

Letter from Thomas Ismay to his father, Rev. Joseph Ismay, describing life as an Edinburgh medical student, 23 November 1771. *Transcript, 1935.* (*In* Gen. 530)

Sylas Neville, M.D. Part of a diary written during his stay as a medical student in Edinburgh, 1771–6 and also 1781. *Microfilm.* (Manuscript of the Norwich and Norfolk Historical Society.) (Mic. M 29)

Discourse on truth, written for the Speculative Society by A. F. Tytler, Lord Woodhouselee, 14 December 1772. (La.II.433/5)

Chirurgo-Medical Society. Laws and regulations, 1774, dissertations, 1781–2. (Da. *Deposit*)

Physico-Chirurgical Society. Dissertations (4 vols.), 1775–85 (with gaps). (Da. *Deposit*)

Royal Physical Society. Dissertations (29 vols.), c.1777–1827 (with gaps), library borrowing ledger, c.1795, minute book, 1878–1911, cash book, 1895–1907. (Da. *Deposit*)

Natural History Society of Edinburgh. Dissertations (12 vols.), 1782–1806 (with gaps). (Da. *Deposit*)

Copy of a communication to the Natural History Society by the Earl of Buchan on 'the order of the leafing of trees and shrubs at Melvil . . . anno 1779,' sent in a letter to William Thomson, 27 June 1782. (*In* La.II.588)

Letter from Ignace Luzuriaga to Joseph Black, professor of chemistry, proposing the physician to the King of Spain and the professor of anatomy at Madrid for honorary membership of the Royal Medical Society, n.d. (? November 1787), with Black's draft reply.

(Gen. 873/III/44–5, 48)

Minutes of meetings of the Committee of Associated Students held in the Library of the Royal Medical Society, 11 and 12 November 1789. Concerning a dispute with the Senatus over the presence of students in the procession for the laying of the foundation stone of the new college. (Da.)

Draft report by Joseph Black to the trustees for building the new college about the provision of houses for professors and the needs of the professor of chemistry, 30 December 1789. *Also* a draft letter to Robert Adam, the architect. (Gen. 875/III/174–5F)

Chirurgo-Physical Society. Dissertations, 1789–91. (Da. *Deposit*)

Robert Heron. 'Journal of my conduct, begun August 14, 1789,' 1789–98 (with gaps). Containing references to attendance at classes and the Natural History Society. (La.III.272)

Letter from John Robison, professor of natural philosophy, to Joseph Ewart giving news of the University, 30 December 1790. *Xerox.* (Ewart Papers.) (Phot. 1727)

Papers illustrative of Edinburgh and the university life of the time, 1790–1830. Chiefly letters to Dr James Brown of St Andrews from Thomas Chalmers, Sir James Ivory, Sir John Leslie, etc. (Dc.2.57)

Dialectic Society. Records, 1791–   . (Da. *Deposit*)

Symposium Club. Minutes of the Social Convention of the College of Edinburgh, 31 March 1792–22 December 1882. (Dc.2.75)

American Physical Society. Dissertations, 1794–7. (Da. *Deposit*)

Hibernian Medical Society. Dissertations, c.1798. (Da. *Deposit*)

List of questions for discussion in the Speculative Society, n.d. (watermark 1801). (Dc.6.111/163–4)

Diagnostic Society. Records, 1816–   . (Da. *Deposit*)

Case and queries by the Principal and certain professors of the University as to College houses, 15 February 1817. *With* a letter from Professor Alexander Irving to Principal Baird giving an opinion on the claim, 10 March 1817. *And* Statement by the Principal ... as to his claim for an official house in the new buildings, 31 October 1825. *Printed.* (J.H.Balfour Papers.) (Da.)

Pencil sketch of the civil law class, 1819, by James Hall, youngest son of Sir James Hall of Dunglass. (Dc.1.100⁸, f.9)

Letter from Thomas Carlyle to James Johnstone describing Hume's lectures on law, 6 May 1820. (*In* Dc.4.94²)

Letters from Prince Adam Constantine Czartoryski written while a student at Edinburgh University to his uncle, Prince Adam George Czartoryski, 1820–3. Translated from the originals in the Czartoryski Museum, Cracow, by M. Greenhill, with an introduction by J. M. Bulloch, 1936. *Typescript.* (Dc.2.78)

Theolectic Society. Minute books (2), 1820–6. (Dc.10.44$^{1-2}$)

Scots Law Society. Records, c.1820–1963. (Da. *Deposit*)

Papers concerning the Principal's claim for a house, 1824. (Da.)

Plinian Society. Minute books (2), 14 February 1826–6 February 1841. (Dc.2.53–4)

Brown Square Medical and Surgical Society. Transactions, 11 August 1826–23 May 1827, laws and regulations, 1826. Originally designated the Brown Square Emulation Society. (Dc.1.101/8)

Scottish Universities Commission. Papers relating to the University of Edinburgh, 1826–31. (Da.)

Returns by the University of Edinburgh in answer to the requisition made by the Royal Commission appointed for the visitation of the Universities and Colleges of Scotland, 1826–8. (Dc.1.78)

Classical Society. Minute books (2), 1828–33, treasurer's books (2), 1835–8 and 1841–2, lists of subjects for debates, 1836–8 and 1840–1, laws and standing orders, 1837–8, 1840 and 1842. (Dc.2.89–94)

Letter from the Home Office, Whitehall, to the Earl of Haddington concerning the memorial of the University of Edinburgh as to the exemption of students from the Militia Act, 26 March 1831.

(*In* La.II.511/1)

Letters from Samuel Lewis of Barbados written while a medical student at Edinburgh University to Mrs W. P. Hinds of Philadelphia, 1835–8. *Typed transcript.* (Gen. 1429/8)

Account of the snowball riot, University of Edinburgh, 1838. Written by one of the participants, R. Scot Skirving, fifty-four years after the occurrence. (Dc.1.87)

Original pen and ink drawing by Edward Forbes of a frontispiece for the *Maga*, symbolising the Oineromathic Society, founded by Forbes, 1838. (*In* Dc.4.101–3)

Reid Concerts. Accounts, tickets, programmes, etc., 1841–6.

(Da. Reid)

Hunterian Medical Society. Records, c.1842–68. (Dk.1.38–42)

Petition of the students to the Principal and professors against the introduction of academic costume, 22 March 1843. (Da.)

Edinburgh Philomathetic Society. Committee minute book, 1844–7. (Dc.10.39)

University of Edinburgh distinguished visitors' book, 1845–99.

(Da.)

Dumfriesshire Students' Debating Society. Minute book, 17 December 1847 – 28 March 1854. (Gen. 2032)

Letters from Thomas Cunningham to members of his family in Belfast concerning his medical education at Edinburgh University, 1847–9.

(*In* Dk.7.46)

Celtic Society. Minute books (7), 1848–95 and 1906–39.

(Da. *Deposit*)

Protest on behalf of the students, present and future, of the University of Edinburgh, against the present mode of managing the concert, commemorative of the birthday of the late General John Reid, n.d. (c.1851). *Printed*, with signatures appended. (Da. Reid 12)

'Journal kept by Thomas Laycock from 1833 including the time spent in London when a medical student, 1833–57.' Contains entries for December 1857 when he was professor of practice of physic at Edinburgh.

(Gen. 1813)

Letter from students to the Senatus proposing the adoption of academic dress, 29 July 1860. *Printed*. (Da.)

Petition of the students to the Senatus requesting an additional holiday on Friday, 21 December to increase the length of the Christmas vacation, 1860. A holiday had been declared for Thursday, 20 December to celebrate the tercentenary of the Reformation in Scotland. (Da.)

Rectorial election posters, 1865. The contest which resulted in the election of Thomas Carlyle. (Da.)

Letters (2) from Thomas Carlyle to the Marchioness of Lothian about his appointment as Rector of Edinburgh University, 16 and 28 November 1865. (*In* Dc.4.94²)

Letters (8) from Thomas Carlyle to David Laing asking him to be his Rector's Assessor and discussing his inaugural address, 16 November 1865–15 March 1866, with a copy letter from Laing agreeing to be Assessor, November 1865. (La.IV.4)

Letters (2) from Professor P. Kelland to David Laing about Carlyle's visit as Rector, 18 and 29 November 1865, with Laing's draft reply, 22 November 1865. (La.IV.17)

Edinburgh Association for the University Education of Women. Records, 1865–1960. Formerly the Ladies' Educational Association. (Gen. 1877)

Letter from J. Aitken Carlyle to Alexander Gibson, chairman of the Students' Committee, thanking him on behalf of his brother for Carlyle's reception as Rector, 19 April 1866. (*In* Dc.2.76³)

Robert A. Adam, of Lindsay, Ontario. Diary of his time as a medical student at Edinburgh University, 1866–71. (Dc.8.171–2)

'The Philomathic. A literary magazine conducted by a few of the members of the Philomathic Society,' May 1868–January 1869. Six numbers. *Manuscript.* (Gen. 825/4)

Scrapbook of cuttings, broadsides and posters for the Rectorial election, 1868. (Da.)

Letter from Thomas Carlyle to A. Robertson, student representative, regretting that he is unable to make a valedictory speech to the students, 6 December 1868. (*In* Dc.2.76³)

Round Table Club. Minute books (3), papers, photograph album, 1868–1908. A club founded 'to promote good fellowship among a number of young men in Edinburgh, most of whom were teachers in connection with the University or in the Extra-Mural Medical School.'
(Gen. 175–80)

Letter from Mary Edith Pechey to her aunt reporting the progress of the first women medical students, 23 October (1869). (Dk.7.62/1)

Mrs Isabel Jane Thorne. Autobiography, 1834– . Containing an account of medical education for women at Edinburgh University, 1869–70. *Xerox of a typescript.* (Gen. 1927/19)

Letter from the medical students of the summer session 1870 to the Chancellor conveying their thanks to the members of the University Council who successfully supported the amendment of Professors Christison and Laycock in opposition to the motion for the introduction of female students to the various classes of the medical curriculum, May 1870. (Da.)

Scrapbook of printed literature and manuscript notes on the Rectorial election, 1871. *Also* a copy of *Rectorial election sketches* (1883). (Da.)

Philosophical Society. Scroll minute books (2), 1871–3 and 1876–8, minute books (3), 1927–40 and 1945–6, printed syllabi, 1873–94 (incomplete). (Da. *Deposit*)

Queen's Edinburgh Rifle Volunteer Brigade, No IV (The University) Company. 'Our adventures at the Autumn Manoeuvres, 1872.' (Dc.2.60)

Musical Society. Membership receipt books (3), c.1871–3 and 1879–80, minute books (3), 1905–56. (Da. *Deposit*)

Valedictory address given by Robert Louis Stevenson to the Speculative Society, 25 March 1873. *Typescript copy.* (Dk.1.3.¹)

Letter from Sir H. S. Oakeley, professor of music, to J. Bennett concerning Professor J. S. Blackie's agitation for Scottish music at a university concert, 26 March 1877.   (Dk.7.38⁵/3)

Edinburgh University Athletic Club. Architect's drawing of the pavilion, Corstorphine, by J. Fairley, A.R.I.B.A., n.d. (? c.1878).

(S.R.C.1.9)

Essays (4) delivered to the Dialectic Society by W. K. Dickson, 1881–8.   (Dk.1.3⁶⁻⁹)

Papers relating to the Associated Societies, 1883–7. Including the text of a paper on international duties by W. K. Dickson, 1883, and letters from John Ruskin and Robert Browning, honorary presidents, to W. K. Dickson, 1883–7.   (Dk. 1.3¹⁰,¹⁴)

Records of the Tercentenary celebrations of the University of Edinburgh, 1884. Including minutes of the Tercentenary Committee, 1882–4, accounts, visitors' book and scrapbooks of printed tickets, publications and souvenirs, 1884.   (Da.)

Original drawings (12) by members of the Raeburn Club for the pamphlet *Tercentenary celebration. University of Edinburgh. The procession (progres medical), dedicated to the shades of James VI, George Buchanan, Regent Rollock, John Knox, Jenny Geddes, and to their modern representatives in 1884.*   (S.R.D.1.4/2)

Edinburgh University Students' Representative Council. Records, 1884– .   (Da. *Deposit*)

Original drawing by G. R. Halkett for a cartoon issued by the Tories during the Rectorial election, November 1885.   (Dk.1.3⁴⁽³⁾)

Total Abstinence Society. Programme of a conversazione, 21 January 1886. *Printed.*   (Gen. 733D/21)

Minutes and correspondence relating to the Rectorial election, 1887.

(Da.)

Innominate Club. Prospectus, 1887, *printed* and rules, *duplicated.*   (Da.)

Collection of press cuttings relating to student activities at Edinburgh University, with notes by S. W. Carruthers, 1887–8.   (Dc.2.76¹⁷)

Dissertation on aphasia, read before the Royal Medical Society by S. W. Carruthers, 1888.   (Gen. 1931)

Costs and sales accounts for early issues of the *Student,* 1888–9.

(Dc.10.18)

Edinburgh University Lecture Extension Association. Records, 1888–96. Including minutes, accounts and syllabi.   (Da.)

Records of University Hall, Riddle's Court, 1889–92. Including a record of social events, illustrated with sketches.   (*In* Dk.1.4)

Collection of printed literature from Rectorial elections, 1890, 1893, 1896, 1905, 1908, 1939 and 1951. (Da.)

Darwinian Society. Minute book, 1891–6. (Dk.3.3)

Valedictory address given to the Speculative Society by J.H.Tait, 1892. (Dk.1.3[11])

Women's Debating Society. Minute books (3), 1893–1914, committee minute book, 1909–14, printed syllabi, 1909–24 (incomplete).

(Gen. 160–3, 163*)

Masson Hall. Records, 1894–1969. Including also Edinburgh Ladies' Educational Association minute book, 1868–92, Women's Representative Committee minute and memorandum book, 1895–9, Zenith Ladies Amateur Swimming Club account books (2), 1928–39. (Da. *Deposit*)

Edinburgh Dental Students Society. Menu and toast list for the 14th Annual Dinner, 11 March 1898. *Printed.* (Da. *Deposit*)

Boat Club. Minute books (4), 1898–1961, log books (2), 1919–21.

(Da. *Deposit*)

Associated Societies. Papers, 19th and 20th centuries. (Da. *Deposit*)

Edinburgh University Club of London. Dinner menu and table plan, 1 May 1901. *Printed.* (Dc.2.96[85–6])

Edinburgh Indian Association. Papers, 1903–12. (Da.)

D.J.Cunningham, professor of anatomy. Edinburgh 'special' lectures and addresses, c.1903–9, several to student bodies. (D.J.Cunningham Papers.) (Gen. 2003)

Historical Society. Group photographs (2), 1906–7 and 1911–12.

(Phot. ill. 72–3F)

Blackie House, University Hall. Group photographs (7) of residents, 1908–14. (Phot. ill. 120)

Letter from G.A.Gibson to John Ross suggesting an approach to Mr Carnegie for help with a scheme for providing undergraduate halls of residence in Edinburgh, 20 January 1909. (AAF)

McEwan Hall bookings, 1910–18. Including papers relating to the planning of 'The Masque of Learning,' a succession of scenes from the life of the University devised by Professor Patrick Geddes to celebrate the semi-jubilee of University Hall, March 1912. (Da.)

Classical Society. Photographs of the cast of three plays, 'Plutus,' 1910, 'The Phormio of Terence,' 4 June 1920 and 'Adelphi,' February 1924. (P.C.93)

Edinburgh University Club of London. History for the first fifty years of its existence, extracted from the minutes by D.C.L.Fitzwilliams, 1864–1912. *Typescript.* (Dc.2.87)

'Reminiscences of the Edinburgh International Club, 1913, by an old member.' *Typescript.*   (Dc.4.104⁴)

Biological Society. Minute books (9), 1921–59. Originally called the Zoological Society.   (Da. *Deposit*)

Edinburgh Association of University Teachers. Records, 1922–67.

(Da. *Deposit*)

Edinburgh University Alumni Association. Agenda book, 1924.   (Da.)

James Dick. 'An account of the Dick family and of life in Scotland, 1863–79.' Written in 1924 as an account of his childhood up to the time he became a student at Edinburgh. *Manuscript and typescript.*

(Gen. 1941, Gen. 60)

Edinburgh University Settlement. Records, 1925–55. *Also* annual reports, 1905–77 (incomplete). *Printed.*   (Da. *Deposit*)

Correspondence of Charles Sarolea, professor of French, concerning Cowan House, 1929. (Sarolea Collection 225.)   (Gen. 265)

Cowan House. Album of annual photographs of residents, 1929–41.

(P.C.75)

'Life in Cowan House.' Reprinted from *The Scotsman*, 4 February 1930. *Printed.*   (Da.)

Address by John Orr, professor of French, to an Edinburgh student society about his first impressions of Edinburgh University, c.1933. *Corrected typescript.*   (Gen. 868/15)

Scrapbook record of the celebrations for the 350th Anniversary of Edinburgh University, compiled by A. Logan Turner, 1933.   (Dk.1.43)

A. Logan Turner. Notes and extracts for a work on the history of the Scottish universities especially Edinburgh to the early eighteenth century, with particular reference to the influence of the Netherlands. c.1937–8. *Manuscript and typescript.*   (Gen. 528–30)

Highland Society. Minute books (3), 1939–60, and miscellaneous papers. Formed by the amalgamation of the Celtic Society and the Women's Celtic Society.   (Da. *Deposit*)

Polish School of Medicine, University of Edinburgh. Records, 1940–9.   (Da.)

Album of snapshot photographs of Cowan House residents, 1941–c.1947, and of the 25th Anniversary, 1954.   (P.C.75)

Snapshot photographs (2) of the inspection of the S.T.C. by Principal Sir Thomas Holland and of the pipe band, under Major Campbell, 13 May 1944.   (Phot. ill. 101)

Sir J. S. Flett. Account of his student days, 1886–94, written down during the Second World War. *Manuscript and typescript.*   (Dc.6.116)

Col. R.B.Campbell. History of athletics and physical education at Edinburgh University, up to 1946. *Typescript.* (Da.)

Cowan House. Suggestions book, 1946–64. (P.C.75)

'The Bridge.' Paper of the Linguistic Society, February 1947–March 1956. *Duplicated typescript.* (J.Orr Papers.) (*In* Gen. 872)

James Eadie Todd, M.A. 1907. Autobiographical fragments, c.1949. Including notes on his student days at Edinburgh. *Typescript.*

(Dk.2.17)

Edinburgh University Chaplaincy Centre. Non-current archives, c.1950– . (Da. *Deposit*)

'Chance and circumstance.' The autobiography of R.J.A.Berry, professor of anatomy in the University of Melbourne, c.1951. *Duplicated typescript.* Including an account of his time as a medical student at Edinburgh University, 1886–91, as a house surgeon, 1891–6, and as an Edinburgh teacher and lecturer, 1896–1905. (Dk.2.36)

D.B.Horn, professor of modern history. Papers on the history of Edinburgh University. (*In* Gen. 1824)

Collection of printed literature from the Rectorial election, 1979.

(Da.)

The Other Side of the Counter

JAMES L. JENNINGS

Mention the Matriculation Office, and most former students think of the occasion when they went to the counter there to enter their names for degree examinations, but that transaction was towards the end of a long process of work which goes on at the other side of the counter.

The Office receives postal enquiries about admission. Certain letters are passed to Faculty and other offices, but some 10,000 per year are dealt with by the Matriculation Office. Each applicant for admission as an undergraduate must submit an application form to the Universities Central Council on Admission (U.C.C.A.). Photocopies of the application forms and relevant computer record cards are sent by U.C.C.A. to the Matriculation Office. These are sorted and distributed to the appropriate Faculty Officers who return the decisions of the selectors to the Matriculation Office for transmission to U.C.C.A. Most of this work is in coded form for the U.C.C.A. computer recording system.

After acceptance, and after consulting the Director of Studies, the new student matriculates and pays his fees to the Fee Office. (Since 1962 an annual fee has been charged to cover matriculation, tuition and one diet of examination.) Some of the Matriculation Office staff assist at the matriculation process. Student records are compiled from the matriculation forms.

But before the Autumn term begins, the Office starts preparations for the examinations which the students will take at the end of the Summer term. A list is prepared for each Faculty Officer showing the subjects for which a new external examiner should be appointed. (Each appointment is for a limited time only.) The Faculties send their nominations to the Senate for approval, and when this is given the Office sends letters of appointment to the new examiners.

The Office next asks Heads of Departments for lists of the Boards of Examiners for each subject. Thereafter, on behalf of the Dean, it sends to the Chairman of each Board details of the subjects which his Board has to examine, and of the procedure to be followed.

During the Autumn term the Office has to spend some time checking the information necessary for the production by the computer of the examination entry forms. If any new Honours examination paper has been introduced it is the responsibility of the Office to arrange dates and times of examination and to ensure that these do not produce any clash with times of existing papers. At the time of writing much preparatory work has been done towards a computer-produced Honours examination timetable. The provision of dates and times for new ordinary subjects is now the responsibility of the Associate Deans, but before the formation of the Examination Programme Committe that work also was undertaken by the Office.

Posters giving the last date of entry for degree examinations are drafted and distributed for notice boards throughout the University. Care must be taken in drafting these posters as students are quick to detect any ambiguity and to use it as an excuse if a fee for late entry is chargeable.

And so on to the busy days in the Spring term when students enrol for degree examinations. Most of this enrolment is now done by giving the student a computer 'print-out' to check and complete. While every endeavour must be made to deal quickly with the queue of students, care has to be taken to collect all relevant and necessary information about optional papers and such things as special subjects, offered by Honours students in their finals. Often student humour is much in evidence on these occasions. In the late 1940s, for some reason, a student could not complete his examination entry procedure. It may have been that he had insufficient money to pay the fees due. (At that time a fee was payable for every examination appearance and these fees were not included in the annual tuition fee, as is now the case.) The lady checking his entry form said she would put it under the counter until he called again. A great roar of laughter went up from all the students present because in those days of strict food rationing it was averred that shopkeepers kept any unrationed items 'under the counter' for favoured customers!

Student humour was much in evidence too when a notice was posted on the board at the entrance to the Old College giving details of a series of lectures to medical students by distinguished members of the profession. Under the title 'The unexpected in Obstetrics' some wag wrote the comment 'Mary had a little lamb'. Student society notices on occasion provide humour. One student society meeting was billed to take place in 'The *Old* New North Church'. Those with some knowledge of the history of ecclesiastical buildings in Edinburgh will know what was meant!

Although one is conscious of student humour, one often becomes aware of the difficulties, and even hardship and tragedy, encountered by some students, but this knowledge must be kept in strict confidence.

After all the examination entry forms have been collected and checked, the number of candidates for each paper is counted and the order is placed for the printed examination papers. The Clerk of Examinations is informed of these numbers to enable him to allot accommodation in the examination halls and to provide script books and other stationery for each examination.

While this is proceeding the Office sends lists of candidates to the examiners. When the examiners return the lists of results, certificates are prepared showing each student's result in each subject, except in Medicine and Veterinary Medicine, where the Faculty Offices prepare lists showing the names of those who have passed the professional examinations. These certificates are sent to the students in the envelopes that each has addressed at the examination. For Honours results, lists are prepared showing the classes awarded by the examiners. These lists are posted on the notice board and sent to the Press. All this work has to fit in to the preparations for the graduations.

These preparations are started early in the academic year. Posters, admission tickets, parchments and handbills of instruction about such matters as academic dress are printed. Among others, the Organist, the Robers, the Mace-bearer, the Servitorial Staff and the First Aid personnel are asked to provide their services.

When students receive their final examination results they register their names for graduation. The registrations are checked by the office staff to ensure that each student has completed the academic requirements for graduation. From these registrations the graduation programme is compiled and the parchments written by the office staff. The Deans of the Faculties are asked to call to sign the parchments. One Dean asked if he might smoke his pipe while signing. He explained that his output would be doubled thereby!

The printer's proofs of the Graduation Programme have to be checked in time to ensure that printed copies are available on the evening before the graduation. The time scale is so restricted that sometimes a Dean has little enough opportunity to ascertain the pronunciation of some of the unusual names with which he may find himself confronted. Next, the *Sponsio Academica* is prepared for signature by the graduands and the seating plan is drawn up. From it the appropriate seat number in the McEwan Hall is given to each graduand on signing the *Sponsio*. The seat numbers appear to be the more important at the time, but it may not be known that the University's oldest record of its Graduates is the original *Sponsio*, first signed in 1587.

I have found that the *Sponsio* sometimes becomes more important to graduates as they grow old. An example is the cheque for £500 sent to the University with a card 'With Compliments and in Gratitude from ...' The sender was a lady who had graduated some 60 years earlier.

In the Summer term there are three Graduations on consecutive days, and another in the following week. The Matriculation Office staff assist in the conduct of each Graduation, and are on duty in the McEwan Hall two hours before each ceremonial starts. Most of the examination result work and the graduation work has to be completed within *three* weeks before the Graduations. This involves a twelve-hour working day, and that it is a great strain is perhaps best illustrated by the story which has been handed down from pre-1939 days. A new member of staff was being instructed in graduation duties by the retiring member. The instruction ended with the remark 'And when the Dean of Divinity says "Amen" after the Benediction you'll say to yourself "Thank God" – *and mean it*!'

After the Graduations, parchments are sent to those who graduated '*In absentia*', and the work of recording each student's examination results is begun. Although students have written proof of their examination results, many require transcripts of their academic record and confirmation of their status as graduates. These documents are provided for employers and for other Universities as, of course, many graduates go on to further courses of study, sometimes abroad. This information is provided from the Office record of examination results.

The Office staff are often asked by their friends what they do when the students are on vacation. It usually comes as a surprise to the questioner to discover that there is a re-appearance diet of examinations in September for which all preparations must be made, including receiving the students' entry forms and fees. After the September examination results have been sent out, arrangements are made for the November graduation and for the payment of the external examiners.

The Register of Members of the General Council has been maintained in the Matriculation Office since 1858. This Register is produced annually and the current volume contains the names of over 60,000 living graduates. Addresses are known for approximately 40,000 of them. The Office makes arrangements for the despatch to them of the Annual Report and the billet for the half-yearly meeting. The Register is in use every day to identify the year of graduation, and therefore the correct volume of academic records, of those seeking confirmation of their graduate status as mentioned above.

There are printed volumes giving the names of graduates down to 1888, and a card index of graduates since 1889 has been maintained in the Office.

These sources are used when correspondents and callers seek information about their ancestors. Often the information they can provide is insufficient to identify the ancestor, but occasionally one has the pleasure of doing so and of hearing interesting stories. Before the earlier records were transferred to the University Library one lady came from U.S.A. to see her ancestor's signature in the *Sponsio*. She told me he was a Presbyterian Minister who had been a survivor of the ill-fated Darien Scheme in the 1690s. He settled afterwards in an American colony, where he established a branch of the Presbyterian Church.

In addition to the work already described, the Office provides a number of other services, perhaps because it was the original public office of the University. For example, it tells the engravers the names of those awarded class medals. It records the awards of Scholarships and Bursaries in order to know when the tenure of each falls vacant. Vacancies are advertised and applications for them are received at the office. It re-directs mail to students and to members of staff whom the servitors in the postroom are unable to identify. It notifies grant-making authorities if a student withdraws from study. It orders the stocks of Faculty programmes.

Over the years there have been changes, because within the basic essentials of admissions, examinations, graduations and records, the work is constantly being adapted and developed to meet alterations in regulations and situations. An example is the admissions procedure. Before the institution of U.C.C.A. in 1961, application was made direct to the Faculty by means of an application form, supported by a document bearing the grand title of 'Certificate of Attestation of Fitness'. It referred, of course, to educational fitness and was issued by the Scottish Universities Entrance Board on the basis of passes in the Leaving Certificate, Preliminary or equivalent examination. Law did not have a Faculty Office at that time, and only the services of a part-time typist. The admission applications for that Faculty were therefore handled in the Matriculation Office. All applicants who had the required passes on the Attestation Certificate were accepted – quotas appeared to be unknown then. Any application or enquiry which was doubtful in any way was referred to the Dean. After he had lectured to his class he called at the Office and gave his decision verbally.

I was told that application forms were introduced during the 1939–45 war in order to provide information to the Ministry of Labour and National Service. Students were sometimes permitted by the Ministry to defer 'call-up' to the Armed Forces, or to work of national importance, until they had completed part of their courses of study. I was also told that in pre-war years intending students just went to the Director of Studies, who gave each a fee pass if he or she had an Attestation of Fitness Certificate which showed passes in school certificate subjects which might be required for admission to the course. In those days students paid tuition fees to the University Factor and Law Agent, who set up a temporary office in the McEwan Hall for the purpose.

In pace with the increase in student numbers and the growing complexity of degree regulations the number of staff in the Matriculation Office has increased. Before 1939 there were three full-time members of staff and one part-time; in 1947 six full-time; now there are twelve full-time members of staff.

The Office was formerly situated in the room at the foot of the staircase leading to the room of the Secretary to the University. Like most of the Old College at that time, the artificial lighting in the Office was poor, as was the central heating, but it was well ventilated by the west winds which blew through the vestibule from the entrance in the south-east corner of the quadrangle. There were pewter inkpots on the counter. A well polished brass rail was fixed along the wall on the public side of the counter. Its use was obscure. Some said students used to hang their walking sticks and umbrellas there. Others said it was to keep them from rubbing against the paintwork – which had not been renewed for over a quarter of a century!

Before the expansion of the University and before the George Square complex was built, most committees met in the Old Senate Halls, beside the Matriculation Office. Few academic departments had a secretary, or a telephone, and on their way to committee meetings, or to the University Library, Professors and members of the academic staff frequently came to the Office counter with intructions or with enquiries or to make telephone calls, and one had an opportunity to identify them.

In August 1953 the Office moved to its present location in the rooms on the street level, in what was formerly the boilerman's house. I was told it was originally the Librarian's house. Before the alterations to provide the new Office there was a wine cellar near the bottom of the present lift shaft. However, the wine cellar then contained only old examination entry forms!

There was a great change in the Old College when the Library and Arts Departments moved to George Square. The population seemed to be reduced overnight, or rather, over a summer vacation. It took me a long time to get used to seeing fewer students around the quadrangle and to find no one in the empty Library.

Some parts of the work which I have described briefly extend in fact over several months and involve much detail. Although these lengthy tasks can in themselves be boring, interspersed with them is a great variety of absorbing work. The Office is always busy. Many interesting people – students, staff, graduates, members of the public – call at the counter with a variety of enquiries. One never knows what new work they, or the post, or a 'phone call will bring. On looking back, I think this has made the time I have spent behind the Matriculation Office counter pass very quickly.

Some Changes in the Classroom
in the Twentieth Century

GORDON DONALDSON

It would not be easy to find a single word or phrase to characterise accurately the manifold changes which have taken place over the last fifty years or so in the way of life of staff and students in the classroom and its precincts. The general reaction against authority and 'elitism' has led, in the university as elsewhere, to more relaxed attitudes on the part of the staff and to a novel emphasis on 'student participation', but, perhaps paradoxically, behaviour among students in the classroom has become more rather than less disciplined.

Some of the formality and almost ceremonial which used to surround lectures was fostered, if not dictated, by the structure of the university premises. There was a traditional plan, prevailing generally throughout the Old College and imitated in the Medical School and The King's Buildings and in some accommodation elsewhere which was taken over and adapted for university use. In this layout, lecture theatres were appropriated to particular departments or subjects. They were not numbered, but bore their names – 'Anatomy', 'Mathematics', 'Logic' and so on – and in each there was plainly visible an indication of the quasi-proprietary relationship in the shape of boards bearing the names of past medallists in the subject to which the room was assigned. Adjoining each lecture room there was usually an equally proprietary 'retiring room' for the professor, with one door opening into a corridor and another on to the platform from which lectures were delivered. Traditionally, therefore, the professor made his entrance not through the door used by the students but by his own private access. (And in those days it was almost invariably the professor who lectured to a large ordinary class, a duty regarded as too important to be delegated.)

While the professor was still in his retiring room before the lecture he prepared for his entrance with the help of a deferential servitor who was probably an ex-soldier and could be known to spring to attention and salute when his professor and he came face to face. The servitor, frock-coated, silver-buttoned and top-hatted, normally joined the professor shortly before the lecture was due to begin. He helped him into his gown (which on a cold day an especially considerate servitor might have hung over a chair before the fire) and then, at precisely five minutes after the hour, he ushered the professor through the communicating door on to the platform and closed the door after him, almost in the manner of a beadle showing a minister into his pulpit. At the end of the lecture, five minutes before the hour, the professor made his exit by the private door and returned to the seclusion of his retiring room.

The pattern of the quasi-proprietary suite of lecture-room and retiring-room, devoted exclusively to a single subject, had been in part disrupted before living memory begins. With the enlargement of the curriculum, subjects came to outnumber rooms, so that there were, so to speak, tenants as well as proprietors. Law classes, which normally met either in the first hour or the last two hours of the teaching day, were especially apt to make use of such 'tenancies', but other classes which did not have 'a room of their own' did so as well. Yet the prior rights were fully recognised and it was common enough to say that the 'X Class' would meet in the 'Y Classroom'. However, even when a teacher from another department was 'borrowing' a lecture room, he would still normally make his entrance through the retiring room (which the 'proprietor' probably used only before and after his own lecture). It simply never occurred to anyone that teacher and students could use the same entrance unless only one was available.

In the ancient accommodation plan, there was little provision for rooms for the staff apart from the retiring room adjoining each classroom, though a professor who did not have a classroom *might* have a retiring room of his own. As lecturers multiplied, they sometimes shared a room with their professor, but sometimes two or more – many more – lecturers had a room among them. It was rare, if not unknown, for a lecturer to have a room of his own unless he happened to be a Director of Studies, which gave him a special claim. This was all less of a hardship than it might seem, because in general a lecturer in those days came to the University premises to take a class and then went away again, so that all he needed was a place to deposit his coat and hat.

With the sharp increase in the numbers of staff and students after the Second World War pressure became still greater. In one department there was a time when a professor and two lecturers shared a room which served also as the departmental library and the reading room for Honours students. What made the congestion ultimately intolerable was a change in the habits of the staff, who now wanted and indeed needed more than a place to leave their coats and hats. They were spending far more of their time in the University, teaching loads increased, administrative tasks multiplied, secretarial assistance and telephones were provided and it was coming to be expected that teachers would be generally available on the premises. Whereas in the later nineteenth century a professor had remarked that the only property he kept in the University was his gown, cap and hood, teachers now wanted rooms where they could keep a proportion of their books and other possessions. Separate rooms became indispensable.

The traditional ritual accompanying lectures largely vanished as staff and subjects continued to multiply. In the buildings constructed since the Second World War, lecture rooms are anonymous, or rather known by letters or numbers and not by name – and, no doubt for the sake of administrative convenience, the rooms in the Old College were subjected to numbering not many years ago . Teachers have their individual rooms (or 'offices' as the Americans like to call them), in premises which do not adjoin the lecture theatre and may even be in a different building. Therefore the lecturer, unless he times his arrival with precision, must stand outside the main or only entrance as the students file in, then walks in unattended, sometimes making his way down from the back of the hall to the platform, and cannot even be sure that a servitor will close the door behind him. The old ceremonial has ceased to be practicable.

The wearing of a gown for lecturing outlived other formalities. Fifty years ago and less it was considered indispensable in some faculties to wear a gown, at least for lecturing to a large class, though even in the 1920s it was not general in Science, where a white coat sometimes took its place. If a teacher appeared before an Ordinary Class in Faculty of Arts without a gown – which he seldom did in the days when servitors attended to such things – students would demonstrate their disapproval. The conventional *riposte* when this happened was 'I assure you it's no sign of disrespect'. The academic cap was rarer than the gown, possibly because one seldom had to go out of doors between a retiring room and the classroom, though it is related of A. E. Taylor (Moral Philosophy, 1924–41) that he once entered his lecture-theatre wearing a cap from which clouds of smoke issued, as he had laid his pipe on it in his retiring-room.

Informality in dress has gone far beyond the general disuse of the gown (which, however, has not yet completely disappeared). The frock coat and top hat which so long remained the uniform of servitors – as formal dress has survived among menials elsewhere – had in earlier days been the garb of professors as well. It is reported that Alexis Thomson (Surgery, 1909–24) was a pioneer in adopting a lounge suit and a bowler hat instead,[1] but a morning suit was still worn by Barkla (Natural Philosophy, 1913–45) and Whittaker (Mathematics, 1912–46). The bowler was still not unknown in the Faculty of Arts in the 1930s, though it was even then much more common in Law, where, with the accompanying black jacket and striped trousers, it lingered on, to bring a remark from Richard Pares about 'those prosperous-looking hats that lawyers wear', and it is not yet extinct. For the less formal, a lounge suit and a soft hat were usual until after the Second World War. In the last twenty years even the lounge suit has become rarer, and more casual garb quite usual, while a cap or no head-covering at all is common.

The dress of students changed in much the same way, but on the whole went a good deal farther towards the casual. Between the wars lounge suits (often with 'plus-fours') were usual, especially in winter, for it was then thought that flannel trousers and blazers or sports jackets were appropriate only for summer wear. Law students, like their teachers, tended to be more formal, partly because in the offices where many of them spent most of their time they were expected to look like professional men, and they commonly sported hats and umbrellas, while headgear was out of fashion for most other students, though some wore a soft hat. After the Second World War various extravagances affected the dress of young males generally, and it became the fashion to look as scruffy as possible. From time to time attempts were made to popularise the scarlet gown for undergraduates, but never with much success, and it is many years now since the last of them.

Inside the classroom the changes in lecturing methods during the last half-century must be seen in the context of habits inherited from far earlier generations. We are always told that among the great changes which took place in the eighteenth century had been not only the abandonment of 'lecturing' in Latin – which almost certainly meant dictating material which the students could study at leisure to acquire full understanding of it – but also the abandonment of dictating, which might have seemed a logical step after the introduction of English. It would seem, however, either that the practice of dictating was extremely tenacious or, if it had ever been given up, it was to some extent revived in the first half of the twentieth century. It is evident from a number of reminiscences printed in the *Edinburgh University Journal* that dictating or semi-dictating was quite common: students seem to have expected to be able to 'get it all down' and were apt to feel aggrieved if they could not. Thus it was remarked of Scharpey-Schafer (Physiology, 1899–1933) that 'it was not easy to keep up with him but he was a lucid lecturer',[2] and of Gulland (Medicine, 1915–28) that 'one had to write very quickly to keep up with him and those who could do shorthand scored'.[3] Augustus Muir wrote of Saintsbury (English, 1895–1915) that he 'spoke rapidly – sometimes too rapidly – and his good things were always jerked out in parentheses, so that he was often in the middle of the next sentence before we realised that a pearl had been cast before us, and it was too late to acknowledge it. He never followed a script, like some professors, but used a series of cards on which were written bold catch-words for his guidance'.[4] Muir showed exemplary modesty on behalf of his fellow-students by using the metaphor of casting pearls! On the other hand, in Law in the early 1920s 'some professors were considerate enough to deliver at dictation speed' and Sir Ludovick Grant 'had . . . a way of repeating each phrase so that we could get it all down'.[5] One of the great merits of Lodge (History, 1899–1925), according to an admiring student who declared him 'the best lecturer in the University', was that 'you can take down every word he says'.[6] Lodge's technique of extremely deliberate and measured speech was imitated by others in the History department, including David Horn, Lodge's student and ultimately successor (1954–69). Dr Balfour-Melville, a lecturer in History, followed the same model, and D. P. Heatley, who lectured on British Constitutional History and on Political Science, also dictated, but at such breakneck speed that it was indeed possible, but no more than possible, to take down every word he said, at any rate for students who had developed some system of abbreviations. His wordage per lecture was about 50 per cent more than Horn's. Some teachers in the Faculty of Law likewise continued to dictate, and Professor A. C. Campbell has suggested to me that dictation was probably quite normal in Law until after the Second World War.

Some teachers, at least in the Faculty of Arts, compromised between dictating and lecturing, for they discoursed at large but interspersed summaries which they dictated. The students were not expected to take notes while the discourse was going on, and Kemp Smith (Logic and Metaphysics, 1919–45) would from time to time rebuke those who were doing so, 'Don't write'. R. K. Hannay (Scottish History, 1919–40) used exactly the same method, and with his gift for compression his summaries were masterpieces of their kind. This technique at least meant that students felt no obligation to scribble furiously for the whole 50 minutes and gave their professors a chance to see their faces and not only the crowns of their heads. Kemp Smith and others sometimes used the blackboard to carry the summaries which would otherwise have been dictated. It was often remarked that the lecturing system, especially when it took the form of dictation, was conducted as if printing had never been invented, and such a reproach became even more apt as facilities increased for methods of reproducing multiple copies, and the stencil and duplicating machine were followed by various devices of photo-copying. Even fifty years ago the summaries which were dictated could have been duplicated and circulated.

Nor was much use made until recently of any means of communication other than the spoken word, and 'visual aids' hardly extended beyond the blackboard and the map, the former more especially in some sciences and in mathematics and not so much in most Arts subjects, though the 'magic lantern' was used in subjects like Geography and Fine Art. But things which used to go on the blackboard can now be duplicated and circulated, and the use of projectors and screens have become everyday visual aids within the last twenty years or so in a wide variety of subjects. The blackboard, however, is still much used.

It is difficult to generalise about changes in lecturing style, because no individual's experience can cover both the range of lectures which a student might have heard fifty years ago and the range a student hears today, and without an individual's experience adequate comparison is impossible. One can, however, learn a certain amount at second-hand about university lectures and also make certain deductions from lectures given by university teachers outside the University. The impression one forms is that lectures have become less formal, more relaxed, more conversational in character, and one learns both from conversation with students and from admissions by teachers that some lectures have less structure than of old and are not always strictly tailored to the conventional 50 minutes so as to come to a real conclusion within the allotted span. It may be that the character of lectures has been influenced to some extent by the development of tutorial instruction to supplement lectures. Such tutorial instruction of one kind or another goes back at least to 1909 and was a change associated with the introduction of a real summer lecturing term.[7] Though 'tutorials' of about a score of students – common enough until fairly recently – hardly created an informal atmosphere or offered individual attention, they did encourage a more conversational style. Increased staffs have for many years now resulted in much smaller tutorials even in ordinary classes, and the proliferation of options in honours curricula has led to the small and intimate group for advanced teaching.

These are all changes on the part of the staff. But there have been great changes in student behaviour in the classroom, for students used to be far more demonstrative than they are now. According to all accounts the most rowdy scenes, as a habitual way of behaviour, belonged to a period now receding into the forgotten past, and few now remember the type of disturbance which was once common, but some of the reminiscences published from time to time in the *University of Edinburgh Journal* make it possible to build up a picture of what conditions used to be like. Perhaps especially in Medicine, where the content of lectures probably varied even less from year to year than it did in Arts, students who had failed in the previous year but had to sit through the lectures again were apt to make a group, high up in a backseat, whispering and giggling and occasionally dropping a marble which fell slowly down from tier to tier. Even when things were at their worst, of course, they varied from class to class, for there were always teachers who could and teachers who could not hold the attention of their classes, but it is clear that the personality of the teacher was not the only factor, for certain subjects and perhaps certain lecture-halls had their own traditions, and the size of a class made a big difference. Besides, even professors who had to endure a lot of rowdiness were recognised by their students as 'distinguished men, anxious to pass on with clarity their own enthusiasms and understandings of the subject' and the contemporary of mine who made that observation put it in the context of a remark that 'there were fewer universities then', into which various meanings could be read. On the other hand, students were often mystified as to why certain men had ever been appointed to their chairs and were conscious that it had not been because they were good teachers. It was *said* among students in history that Lodge recommended the appointment of Williams as his successor just to show how good Lodge had been!

Crum Brown (Chemistry, 1869–1908) seems to have been particularly unhappy, with a 'very unruly' class which gave him a 'very bad time'. He 'was incapable of controlling and holding the attention of the mob which greeted him each morning with a selection from the *Scottish Students' Song Book* and the *Church Hymnary*, the latter somewhat modified in wording'. The 'rowdy, genial disorder' sometimes became so intolerable that after expostulating in vain he withdrew to his retiring room. After an interval, during which the class might sing 'Will ye no come back again?' he would return and – incredibly – apologise for losing his temper.[8] Sir James Walker, his successor (Chemistry, 1908–28) used different tactics: 'If this noise goes on, not one of you will sit the exam'. And in an earlier generation, Sir William Turner's (Anatomy, 1867–1903) 'command of the rowdy first-year students was complete. If there was any talking, shuffling of feet or other noise, one glance was enough to produce absolute silence'.[9]

The milder type of demonstration lasted until much more recent times. A student in zoology in the early 1920s reported that 'Some of the more frivolous and exuberant of us could not contain our spirits, at times indulging in good humoured foot-stamping. One character, by name Corner, ginger-haired and with a broad grin, would frequently arrive late, to be welcomed by stamping and cheering to his seat'.[10] Similar conduct is well remembered by many, and it was not necessarily detrimental to the value of the lectures if the teacher was good. Sir Richard Lodge (History, 1899–1925) 'was born to lecture to large audiences: he confessed that the larger they were the more he liked it', and he 'had no difficulty over discipline', yet, although there was 'not a whisper of disturbance' in his large British Ordinary History Class, nevertheless 'the benches' expressed their feeling with their feet, and Lodge would make remarks in response.[11] Just how fortunate – and how skilled – he was, was brought home to him one day when he unexpectedly took the place of one of his assistants: 'As I entered the room, I was aware of a visible start of surprise followed by a mysterious shuffling, and I discovered that they were putting away their musical instruments and hunting for their notebooks'.[12] It could not be said with truth of many teachers, as it was of Scharpey-Schafer (Physiology, 1899–1933) that the subject was 'so interesting and practical, as well as being so exact and important, that the young audience had no thought to indulge in facetious outbursts'.[13] Scharpey-Schafer, who continued to lecture, with diminishing efficiency, into his mid-eighties, captured the imagination because he had discovered adrenalin in 1898 and had had a nerve cut just below his elbow so that he could measure the return of feeling down to his fingers and so the rate of nerve regeneration. Very different was Barger, 'the eminent biochemist, whose idea of lecturing was to pick up a text-book, ask where he had got to yesterday, and then gossip to himself over the next few pages'.

A medical student of fifty years ago pays tribute to the memory of 'two famous Professors of Surgery – Sir David Wilkie and Sir John Fraser – great surgeons and great showmen'. Here is one of his memories. 'The scene is the steep clinical theatre of Wards 7 and 8 in the Infirmary with the class and an admixture of surgeons from everywhere. Enter Sir John, fair, short, chubby and thick-set, in a white jacket with the sleeves out above the elbow, radiating command personality. Enter the first patient, an elderly man with a walrus moustache. 'Your name? Ah yes, Mr Mackenzie. And what is wrong?' 'Something at the back of the throat'. A quick look with a torch. 'Yes, indeed, there is a tumour there'. A pause for thought. 'What is your occupation, Mr Mackenzie?' 'A bagpipe maker'. Then followed a dissertation on the structure and function of the bagpipes. (Sir John came from Tain.) 'And the reeds, where do you insert them? And where do you keep the spare reeds handy. In your mouth, indeed. Show me how'. And then, turning triumphantly to the class, 'Just where the rear end impinges on the back of the throat at the tumour site. Thank you, Mr Mackenzie'.

By the 1920s the great scientific invasion of medicine had taken effect and practical training at the bench was a large part of the teaching and very well done. Agonising over the curriculum had left only a term in botany as the remnant of the old days of 'simples'. The changeover was exemplified in a little comedy. The Professor of Materia Medica up to about 1919 was Sir Thomas Fraser and the department was dominated by the museum with poisoned arrows from Brazil and the like. Then came Cushny, who dumped the stuff in an attic and used the space for experiments – to the great indignation of Sir Thomas. About 1929 came Clark, who changed the name to Pharmacology and threw it all out, Sir Thomas presumably turning in his grave.

'Disturbance' and reaction or response were not the same thing. Until well after the Second World War teachers invariably received a welcome from stamping feet at the beginning, and applause from stamping feet at the end, of a lecture. It was not entirely conventional, because the stamping on one's entry could indicate the degree of welcome one received, and it was quite noticeable that there might be exceptional warmth when, for example, one returned after an illness or when one had achieved some promotion or there was some other reason for feeling on the part of the students. Sir Richard Lodge, returning from a visit to a son dangerously ill with influenza in France, looked up in surprise when he was not greeted with the usual stamping feet on his entry to the lecture room; then realising that this was a mute tribute of sympathy he said gruffly 'Perhaps you would like to know that my son is much better'. The din which followed – short-lived, because no class took liberties with 'Dickie' – was a tribute to both the father and the professor.[14] One popular lecturer, after he received a doctorate, entered his classroom to find it decorated.

Equally, it is without question that the applause at the end of a lecture gave some indication of how well it had been received or at any rate how effective the peroration had been. Besides, conclusion on time – at five minutes before the hour and coinciding (in the Old College) with the ringing of the bell – was always well received, and prolongation much beyond that point was simply not tolerated. In addition, various remarks in the course of a lecture produced audible response: approval was marked by stamping of feet, disapproval of what was said by scraping, sometimes by booing or hissing. A lot of it – most of it – was perfectly good humoured. It was almost part of a ritual performance. A teacher knew perfectly well that certain remarks, even certain words, names and phrases, would call forth a predictable response and the students probably knew quite well what the lecturer expected. Exceptionally, and more serious, there could be a walk-out. This happened three times when members of the Scottish History Department gave lectures on the Scottish Reformation to British History

Ordinary, and Roman Catholic students, dismayed by revelations about the corrupt state of the pre-Reformation Church in Scotland, expressed their dissatisfaction in this way; of course after the first occasion we knew what to expect, but Professor Pares spoke so sternly on the third occasion that the practice ended. But the students sometimes detected reason for mirth which eluded the teacher. I was in the habit, when lecturing on the reign of James IV, to recite William Dunbar's lines about the many talented men who adorned that monarch's court, concluding 'Printaris, paintaris and potingaris'. But in the year when there had been a celebrated case about a civil servant called George Pottinger this caused quite unexpected hilarity. And it must be admitted that inaudible or incoherent speakers still had a rough time at the hands of a large class until about twenty years ago. Possibly students were sometimes unkind to inexperienced lecturers, but the only way a lecturer could discover whether or not he was acceptable was to face a class and sense the response. If he had any wisdom he would learn by experience.

All this traditional demonstrativeness went into a sharp decline and in some cases stopped quite abruptly. It was a startling experience for a teacher when his peroration and his exit took place in sepulchral silence, and he naturally thought, 'I didn't believe my lecture could have been as bad as all that'. One factor in the change was undoubtedly the physical alteration in the character of the premises. The austere wooden benches and uncarpeted floors in the Old Quad and similar buildings encouraged or at any rate facilitated noise, and more than one tradition was extinguished when removal took place. Some, but not all, of the new buildings have bells which ring at five minutes to the hour, but they lack the solemn majesty of the bell which tolled in the Old Quad. It appears that at an earlier stage things had become quieter in Science classes when they moved to The King's Buildings, and when Arts classes moved from the Old College to the upholstered and carpeted lecture theatres in the George Square area foot-stamping and foot-scraping – the audible demonstrations which it was easiest to make – became impracticable and it was not easy to operate a substitute, for example by banging desks. The significance of the environment on students' behaviour in class is confirmed by the fact that in the Law Faculty, which now alone conducts lectures in the Old College, the traditional barracking persisted longer. But, whatever the explanation, the fact remains that, by a curious paradox, in a generation which has seen students become so much more vocal and aggressive in their criticisms of University policy and their demands for a share in decision-making, and so militant in some activities to press their claims, they have become incomparably more docile in the classroom. It is perhaps another paradox that in rowdier times students were disciplined to the extent that attendance at lectures was checked from time to time: the servitor put up a notice 'Cards Today' and students were expected to deposit cards bearing their names. The practice was obviously never fraud-proof, and Sir Isaac Bayley Balfour (Botany, 1888 – 1922), 'always took cards himself, making quite sure that a second card for an absent friend ... was not proffered'.[15] The periodical demand for cards seems in general not to have continued after the Second World War, but the 'D.P.' certificate, which testified that the student had not only 'duly performed' the work of the class but had given regular attendance, long survived any general check on attendance by cards or other means.[16]

Reference has been made more than once to the Faculty of Law, and it deserves special mention because the changes in the way of life of both staff and students there have been in many respects greater than they have been elsewhere, and little short of revolutionary. Until after the Second World War all teachers in Law were part-timers who practised their profession each day, and most of the students were likewise part-timers, doing an office day as apprentices. This was why professors and lecturers in Law were especially apt to share retiring rooms with teachers in other Faculties as well as sharing rooms among themselves. Professor A. C. Campbell, appointed to the Chair of Public Law in 1946, and, he thought, the first full-time law teacher, declared that at one stage, after the staff began to expand, no less than 17 members of the staff had together the use of only a single room.[17] It was only with the new LL.B. degree in 1961 that full-time study became general for undergraduates and was followed by a great increase in the full-time staff.

Women students had become familiar and accepted before the end of the nineteenth century, and it has been suggested that their presence in classes had a somewhat mellowing effect by checking the more outrageous instances of student exuberance. Yet it may be doubted if women were fully integrated, and their equality with men completely established, until after the Second World War. It was not only true that there were still, for example, separate unions. Nor was it only true that until the 1930s the main reading-room in the Old College was divided into areas for men and women students, with less than a third allotted to the latter, fenced off by a scarlet rope extending from the counter to the opposite wall and with a separate entrance, so that there were distinct male and female queues at the counter. Apart from such formal segregation, though perhaps to some extent because of it, women still tended on the whole to sit together in class and to congregate with each other in the quad. There were even classes in which the women habitually occupied the front rows of benches, and it was not unknown for a professor to threaten that an unruly man should go and sit beside them. The years since the Second World War have seen many changes, in the University as elsewhere, in the relations between the sexes, and it would be hard now to detect any barriers between men and women students or any differentiation in their places in University activities. Women teachers, however, although they were not unknown even in the 1920s, have remained if not relatively rare at any rate very much in a minority.

Possibly the more disciplined behaviour in class owes something to the fact that there are ways in which students are regimented now to a degree unknown a couple of generations back or even less. Directors of Studies and the Advisers who preceded them had the effect of guiding students into certain stereotyped curricula, and with the growing complexity of degree structures and the ever increasing range of options their work was indispensable. Besides, regulations have been tightened up in various ways and this, added to the limitations imposed on most students by the conditions of their grants, have eliminated the 'chronics', as they were called, the well-nigh perpetual students, who repeated courses year after year and consistently failed. There was a legend, if it was nothing more, of a perpetual student in Medicine who had a distinct disincentive ever to qualify because he enjoyed a legacy for the time he was training to be a doctor.

Another innovation, much more recent than Directors of Studies, has been the formal arrangements now made to prepare first-year students, before the beginning of their classes, for what lies ahead, with programmes at University, Faculty and Departmental level. Fifty years ago and less, the freshman simply made a brief, usually quite formal, call on his Director of Studies, who approved (or dictated) his choice of classes and gave him a bit of paper to take to the Fee Office, where the fees were paid and class-cards issued. Then, on the day classes opened, the student simply went to the appropriate lecture-room at the appointed hour, to listen to the professor give the first lecture of the course. In practice, indeed, students from schools which regularly sent their products to the University had been in touch with their seniors, who had given them information about the idiosyncrasies of professors and about the techniques of note-taking and of methods of study generally. Knowledge passed on in this way frequently helped students to choose classes and when students who had come from the same school continued their friendship at the University (which they usually did for one year at least) their exchange of experiences might lead a student to change to what seemed a more attractive department or even faculty. But there was nothing done by the University, at an official level, to provide systematic initiation for the new students. Some think that more should now be done to arrange for the initiation of new teachers, which has not quite kept pace with that for students, though it is no longer quite true that there are no arrangements at all for instructing or advising newcomers on how to lecture.

It was not only in externals, either of dress or of behaviour in class, that the students' way of life changed. Fifty years ago a larger number than today were living at their parents' home, in or near Edinburgh, and spending most of their lives there. To many of them the University was simply a place to which they came to listen to lectures and to read in the library. If one lecture did not immediately follow another (with, that is, the statutory break of ten minutes) there might be time for a cup of coffee in an adjoining café as well as some work in the library before the hour of the next lecture. But students might go through their University years without ever joining other students in a meal, attending meetings of university societies of taking part in any form of physical recreation with their fellows. Despite their occasional exuberance in the lecture-room, they were in the main earnestly seeking to pass their examinations as a step towards a professional career and with considerable incentive to the extent that they had reached the University either through their parents' financial sacrifice or their own hard-earned bursaries. And of course they rarely even considered marriage while their University curriculum lasted. It was mainly medical students (who often came from furth of Scotland and tended to be better off) who had a not undeserved reputation for beer-swilling and billiard-playing at the Union. The attitude of the medical student before the Second World War, it has been suggested, was governed by two conditions that have now disappeared. First he had the spaciousness of the Empire before him. When he qualified he could if he wished kill wild animals with the Army in India or be a medical missionary in the Pacific or follow his father into general practice. And he had the confidence that he would do what his predecessors had been doing for two hundred years, supply the Army and the Navy and Britain and the English-speaking world with 'good Scotch doctors'.

The changes in the habits of the staff, consequent largely on the allocation of a room to every teacher and the tendency of teachers to spend most of the day on the premises, have facilitated contact with students, who now know that there is at least a good chance of seeing a teacher even if one cannot catch him immediately before or after a lecture. The relations between teachers and students at a social level have also become more relaxed. In the days when the atmosphere in the classroom was in many ways less cordial, many teachers did make an effort to entertain students in their own homes, and in the days when professors could afford one or two domestic servants there was no difficulty about having students in batches of twenty or so for afternoon tea on Sunday or for after-dinner coffee in an evening. Alcohol was not usual. These occasions were, it must be said, apt to be intimidating for the students. An undergraduate newly arrived, from a modest social background in town or country, received a formal invitation, which might specify 'morning dress' which he did not at first realise meant only a normal lounge suit. He was summoned to a much grander house than he was accustomed to, received at the door by a maid in cap and apron, and his hostess was the professor's wife, who was a complete stranger to him and with whom he might have little in common. Sometimes there was a musical entertainment: R. K. Hannay (who was a sufficiently competent organist to play in St Giles') would play the piano and Kemp Smith produced the son of another professor, who happened to be in the class, to play. It was difficult to find topics of conversation, and recourse was apt to be had to the exercise of asking each student in turn what he intended to do after graduation. While the answers given to such a question were certainly sometimes illuminating or even astonishing to fellow-students if not to the host and hostess, the occasion as a whole can hardly have been thoroughly enjoyable to either side. The proceedings were embarrassing to the end, because students never knew when to leave and often stopped too long. There was little personal contact outside the classroom and such formal parties. I recall that at my first meeting with the unconventional Vivian Galbraith (History, 1937–44), who had succeeded the ultra-conventional Basil Williams (History, 1925–37), he exclaimed 'Do you mean to tell me that Basil said all these nice things about you and never stood you a pint?' More recently it has become difficult for teachers to entertain in a formal way in their homes, but there are now some facilities within the University for informal encounters. Until after the Second World War if one wanted to have coffee or tea with a student the only place one could go was to a nearby restaurant or café, but some of the new University buildings provide cafeteria-style premises and, while they are used mainly by students, they do provide a common meeting-ground when one is required. However, increased accessibility or availability of staff within the premises of the department perhaps represents the most valuable change. One professor said, 'There is no need for formal machinery for staff-student liaison. My room has a door, on which students may knock, and very frequently do'. But fifty years ago Colonel Ronald Campbell, as Director of

Physical Education, had gone farther: his door had the notice, 'Don't knock. Come in.'

ACKNOWLEDGMENTS

I am very grateful for information, especially about the Faculties of Medicine and Science, from Dr James C. Lees, Professor Emeritus Neil Campbell and Professor Emeritus W. L. Edge.

REFERENCES
1. *UEJ*, xxvii, 265.
2. ibid.
3. ibid., xxiv, 129.
4. ibid., vi, 21.
5. ibid., xxviii, 61.
6. *SHR*, xxvii, 84.
7. ibid., 80.
8. *UEJ*, xx, 221, xxvii, 265.
9. ibid., xxvii, 120.
10. ibid., xxiv, 127.
11. ibid., xxv, 321, xxviii, 35–6.
12. ibid., iv, 106.
13. ibid., xxiv, 128.
14. *SHR*, xxvii, 85.
15. *UEJ*, xxviii, 265.
16. cf. Professor Hay's essay.
17. *UEJ*, xxviii, 63.

Some Changes Outside the Classroom
over the Last Half Century

DENYS HAY

The title of this short essay is somewhat misleading, since the author arrived only in January 1946, on the same train as his professor Richard Pares. They were both accommodated in the now perhaps fortunately defunct Queen Hotel. There the professor and the lecturer ceased to have similarities, for the professor was welcomed to chair his first Board of Studies whereas the lecturer was admitted to that board reluctantly as he had not been put on it by the Faculty, or the Senatus, or the Court – by higher authority at any rate, through which later on the lecturer was to make his way by stages until he had become so ancient a member of the establishment that the jargon which had so puzzled him at first had been replaced by a new and equally mystifying jargon. But Professor Pares had a room to himself in the Old College and (because a predecessor Sir Richard Lodge had had it years before) one of the few telephones in the building. The lecturer shared a kind of corridor room for a year or two with others, mainly the Edinburgh schoolmasters and schoolmistresses who came in to give a few tutorials a week. This last was a very unhappy arrangement. Like other departments, about a third of our intake came from Edinburgh schools and it was most dispiriting for a student to move from a teacher at school to meet the same individual as a tutor at the University; doubly unfortunate, one might add, since essay work at schools was at a very low level and teachers were used to being vehicles of information and not of inspiration. (Muriel Spark's *The Prime of Miss Jean Brodie* does not catch this aspect of the Edinburgh girls' school with her otherwise remarkable precision.)

Most departments were relatively small before 1939 and even smaller in the mid-forties. It took the University, and I suppose the U.G.C., some years to realise that we were faced with the student numbers the like of which do not seem possible again. Returning ex-servicemen and an annual intake from schools grew steadily when conscription ended, and, of course, conscription had not affected women nearly so much. Hence the need to recruit *ad hoc* tutors; hence their abolition as soon as funds permitted. At this stage professors and lecturers stopped teaching everything all the time, and there began, for good and for ill, greater specialisation in many departments. This began noticeably to affect teaching about 1950–2 and clearly varied enormously between faculties and departments. Faculties themselves, however, were not unaffected; the Dick Vet. came under the University umbrella in 1951, and even stodgy old Arts, which still had (and still in a sense continues to have) Maths, divided itself with infinite difficulty between Arts and Social Sciences by 1963. This last painful division took literally months of 6 p.m. meetings; it was forced on the undivided faculty because the latter had repeatedly aired its quarrels in Senatus much to the irritation of that body. The argument inside the faculty revealed that the only common ground of the two groups was that each wanted to have the philosophy departments (still two in those days, Logic and Meta-physics, and Moral Philosophy), in their share of the academic cake. Philosophers were in the event to be Arts men.

Many members of the two faculties thus created were shortly to be transported to new quarters in George Square, overflows being accom-modated in rooms in Buccleuch Place, although Languages and Maths still had rooms in Chambers Street. The most dramatic of these moves was undoubtedly contributed by the Library. This had been, in a way, the heart of the Faculty of Arts (and other faculties too, for that matter) and was situated in the south and west sides of the Old College; and on every floor from under the sub-basement to the attics where, in the 'Z' room, the ticking of the great clock reminded one of mortality and tea. Immortality might be obtained at a cost in the old library, though research was hardly encouraged and one has the impression that the great scholars had their own books in their own homes. But to buy a cup of tea on library premises one had to wait for Sir Basil Spence's new library building in George Square, opened in 1967. There is not much doubt that in the new airy and spaciously arranged premises students, perhaps younger staff too, are more at ease than they had been in the multiple mysteries of the Old College library. But the *smell* had gone, and the arcane knowledge that enabled expert penetration of dinginess and dust. And so, of course, had the books from the great Upper Library Hall, the heart of the early nineteenth-century library and one of the noblest rooms in Edinburgh.

It was, of course, not just the library that moved to George Square. For the first time in, it may be supposed, just under two centuries the humanities had new buildings. The poor best of them may be judged to be the David Hume Tower, apart from Spence's handsome library. Flanking it are William Robertson (History but a lot of Social Sciences including its Dean) and Adam Ferguson (mainly Social Sciences), and at one side of this complex the Appleton Tower, designed for first-year scientists. Between library and faculty buildings, a large lecture theatre was built which serves for dramatic performances as well. Some remarkable plays and operas, some very good lectures have taken place in the new theatre. Fine Art, incidentally, now also in George Square near the University Press and Archaeology, has suffered a remarkable change from the days of the Old College when it was in the Dome. Meanwhile new medical buildings are slowly marching across the north side of the Square.

When departments moved from their old quarters to new – from Old College and Chambers Street to George Square – they had room and (then) money to afford space for more secretaries. It is hard to remember how scarce these ladies were in the 1940s. In Arts, Professor Aitken (Mathematics) had a secretary (why?), a delightful person called Miss Leharivel who was so bored typing equations that she needed little persuasion to type an occasional piece in any other language; remember we are recalling a pre-computer age. The deans, the principal, the secretary and accountant had secretaries, and later some departments drew on a typing pool for secretarial help; but the bulk of one's formal dessemination of information was by hand-written, or self-typed, notices posted outside the main lecture room of a department, where students gazed at them to see how many marks they had gained in essay or exam, to see whose tutorials they were in. At some point this was regarded as an unwholesome encouragement of competition and lists were no longer posted, at any rate in some big departments. Now they have returned since they indicate who has got the equivalent of a D.P. or a merit certificate, as such documents seem now burdensome to collect by the students as they were certainly burdensome to prepare by the staff, and the final meeting of a big class no longer ends with applause for the medallist. He or she still gets the medal, but by informal application to the Matric Office. During the tumult of a Rectorial election the main factions, fighting it out in the Old College, as they had done for generations, not only flung fish heads and rotten fruit everywhere, but frequently tore down notices. The result was the closure of the Old College on the day of the elections (1954). Since then upheavals in any case died down with the increasing unimportance of the rector, especially when young graduates were elected – Edinburgh's mild share of the student troubles of the 1960s.

The rectorial installation in the McEwan Hall which followed the election grew so boisterous at the time of the troubles that the authorities washed their hands of it. Prior to that the great man came to deliver an oration and was either maddened or amused by the good-humoured uproar which greeted him. Occasionally (one recalls Alistair Sim in 1948, whose speech was alleged to have been written by the playwright James Bridie) the rector handled his audience magnificently. The most permanent (for how long, one wonders?) consequence of the demand for so-called 'democratic' procedures was the presence in various departmental and faculty bodies – up in the end to Senate and Court – of undergraduate and graduate students. This undoubtedly at first lengthened and multiplied meetings, and older members of departments had to say, as indeed they had to say to their younger colleagues, 'but we tried that five or ten years ago and it didn't work'. Repetition of such dismal sentiments by older members of a department led often to their not being spoken at all and the failed experiment was remorselessly repeated. Small departments, and soon large ones, sometimes found it hard to secure student representation. But at its height 'student participation' imposed a very heavy additional burden on members of staff trained to be teachers, not politicians.

Another development was the introduction of postgraduate work on an increasing scale. This was, indeed, no new thing in some subjects. The B.Ed. and the B.D. had a long history and, of course, the M.D. much longer still. In the Faculty of Science a B.Sc. (normally three years) was followed by a postgraduate year in honours; but the budding chemist or physicist aimed at a doctorate and a doctorate in any faculty was normally the only degree beyond that of Master; in 1921 the degree of Ph.D. was awarded for the first time in Divinity, Arts and Science. Two changes are to be noted here. Far from restricting graduate intake, a good many departments and faculties have introduced diplomas of various kinds (English is the one most familiar to the writer) or even, the latest move, one-year M.A. degrees – here an evident desire not to be cut out by English practice is surely the reason, for in England a three-year honours degree has, in most subjects, been the norm, and one-year graduate curricula were soon introduced. Equally interesting, the number of Ph.D. candidates, always high in Science, has grown very rapidly in Law and Arts. Here again, it is the larger departments which have had most of the graduate students, with their need for special orientation courses, supervision and examining; however, pressure has been heavy also in departments which have resources attracting students from all over the world, and an obvious example is Scottish history with the MS riches of the Register House as well as the vast printed sources of the great Edinburgh libraries). In most departments, it may be suspected, the young graduate is an incomer from England or North America or the Continent. Our own best pupils we have tended to chase away on the grounds that after four years in Edinburgh they were ripe for new horizons. All of this may seem pretty obvious. But the writer remembers the late university librarian Laurence Sharp telling him that 'we are not a research university'. Well, we are now. This has put a very heavy load on senior teachers. Encouraging students along lines one feels to be exciting is admittedly fun and often rewarding. But it is also extremely time-consuming, on top of what is often a heavy load of undergraduate lectures, tutorials, marking and so on (not to speak of the unspeakable meetings on which I have to say a bitter word later). It is salutary for one to move, as the writer has done for months, among American or continental academics, for whom a ten-hour week of 'contact hours' seems inconceivable, and who are also paid much more than their British counterparts and have a kind of cabinet of dogsbodies to help them. Our prospective Ph.D.s, at any rate in Arts and Social Sciences, have been predominantly foreign, as noted already, principally because Edinburgh is a relatively manageable town as to size, very beautiful, easy to lodge in and cheaper to live and move in than London or Oxbridge, the only places with remotely comparable libraries. But as these lines are being written it seems that general world economic decline and British government policy have begun drastically to erode postgraduate intake from overseas and also from British sources.

In broad terms, then, changes coincided with the movement of the Arts and Social Science faculties from the Old College and neighbouring buildings where they had for long existed, to the the 'airport architecture' of the new George Square, so that the changes were from the first, so to speak, moral and intellectual as well as physical. They went also with the new casualness in dress and manners which Professor Donaldson has mentioned, not all of which was detrimental to order and discipline, save perhaps for a short time of folly, but also went with an openness and willingness to approach teachers, even older and more venerable ones, which has sometimes seemed to be disappearing. This, one must suppose, is something that any way tended to happen to older members of staff. Even the word professor puts a distance between him and his pupils. It is now, however, happily very rare to hear a teacher addressed as 'Sir', which was certainly common in the later 1940s.

Somewhat paradoxically the move of a very large part of the University away from the Old College area took it away from what had become one of its focal points – the University Staff Club in Chambers Street. I recall (to slip into a more personal tone) my astonishment when I arrived in 1946 that the University had no Common Room. There had (I nearly said 'of course') been none then in Glasgow, my first University post in 1938–9, but they had one in University College Southampton, my second (1939–40), and my undergraduate life in Oxford had largely revolved around the Junior Common Room and other convivial and conversational places, just as senior common rooms were taken for granted by the teaching staff of all universities south of the border. Edinburgh was a large establishment of both teachers and taught, yet there was no Common Room for teachers or for taught: the men manned the bastions of the Union (except when they allowed women in for a dance), the women enjoyed the austerer amenities of a house in George Square – amenities of which they allowed other bodies, such as the Association of University Teachers' Discussion Group, to avail themselves, which resulted in some remarkable occasions there, such as Professor Max Born on relativity. But for the staff no Common Room and only a scattering of rather inaccessible lavatories – of which I suppose there were one or two for women (one was certainly created for the future Queen when she came officially in 1949). Within living memory there was in a New College retiring room a piece of furniture with a compartment for a chamber pot.

The whole staff (or a lot of them) met in May 1946 under the Principal Sir John Fraser, in the lecture room of the Psychology Department, the largest then available apart from the University's *Prunksaal*, the McEwan Hall, to prepare a submission for the U.G.C. visitation which was pending. As I remember it, the main call was for money to provide a Common Room; there were advantages in those days for those who liked the multiple amenities of local cafés and pubs (though 'ladies not admitted to the bar' discouraged some communal carousing, or even the modest half of bitter with a woman colleague); it meant that one went to J. & R. Allan's (or somewhere similar) for lunch or coffee and could meet students there informally, and even colleagues. Nevertheless there was universal agreement that a Common Room was a top priority, even among those who would soon be housed in the then small but soon to grow enormous complex of Science departments called 'The King's Buildings', so named because the foundation was laid by King George V in 1920. At any rate, the plea of the University was received with sympathy (perhaps with astonishment?) by the U.G.C., and so a large room in the north-east corner of the Old College became a Staff Common Room, where one could get coffee in the morning and tea in the afternoon. It was very much a Law and Arts affair. The doctors went, as of old, to the Union (or the nice cafeteria run by the nice nurses), and at K.B. I suppose suppliant secretaries brewed up when it was necessary (for lunch, I am told, many scientists went to the canteen in the Genetics Department). But we had not long had a Common Room such as was planned, I believe, by Adam in the University Building he intended to face the Old College, when on a fresh burst of enthusiasm and more government money, the University, now under Sir Edward Appleton, embarked on a Staff Club. This was cleverly (and expensively) constructed in Chambers Street, where the inside of an old clothing store was reconstructed by Sir Basil Spence to furnish all that the (non-academic) heart of the academic staff could wish for, and was opened in 1961. The committee at first tried to allocate a ground floor room for senior members exclusively but had to turn it later into a dining room with waitress service; on the same level there were, and are, a lounge and bar. Above there is a cafeteria and higher still a series of bed-rooms, as well as rooms for billiards, ping-pong and television. The basement houses a very popular squash court.

The construction of the Club at a time when there was a shortage of staff and teaching rooms, when the battle over the demolition of George Square still rumbled on, caused much controversy. But as a former disbeliever the writer feels that, however standards in the Club may have fallen, or failed to keep up with inflation, it has justified itself as a focus of entertainment for members of staff and their guests. There is no doubt that it is envied by many other universities. Now that it is open to virtually all members of staff, administrative and secretarial as well as teaching, it acts as a focal point, bringing people together from the scattered areas of the University, besides including some members of the public with a claim to the University's sense of indebtedness. Latterly it has also been open to members of the Heriot-Watt University; young lawyers (whose contact with the Faculty of Law seems occasionally somewhat tenuous) find its food cheaper by far than the New Club, and better value marginally at any rate than the refreshment facilities in Parliament House.

One of the disadvantages of the Club is that is has to be managed, which means several committees. The writer has been clever enough to avoid them, but others have not – choosing the abominable carpets and the (pretty good) wine. Especially admired by other universities is the possession of bed-rooms and bathrooms for visitors.

What has all this to do with a University? Probably not a lot in continental terms, but it is or in England has been for centuries of the essence for a mixed company of academics to swap scandal and story, entertain visitors, and occasionally (too occasionally?) postgraduates. Such facilities now exist at all the other Scottish universities and were indeed built in to the new ones. Of course it all has to be paid for, as it would probably not be so directly at Oxford or Cambridge, but, like the expensive car-parks, it seems to me worthwhile.

Mention of car-parks throws me back in memory to the Old College.

There, if one had a car, and I for one did not for many years, one could park freely, and there are still parts of the University (I am thinking of The King's Buildings) where payment for parking is regarded (or was till lately) as an unjust imposition, since pockets of government bodies are embedded there whose privileges include free parking. In fact in the 1940s and 1950s I would guess that the average lecturer used the trams and, when they disappeared, the buses; there were even a series of suburban railways, though of not much use for reaching the University. On the other hand many more younger men and women used bicycles, as they are now doing again for health reasons and perhaps economic ones too as a way of avoiding paying through the nose for petrol.

We were poorly paid. I don't know how much a professor got in 1945–6. I know I got £550 as a middle-grade lecturer; by then I was 30 and had a wife and two small children (I had been offered the job at £450 but had to explain that I could not live on this; the war had exhausted my savings and I had no other income; nor did the university make any contribution to removal expenses). Many other lecturers must have been in a similar position; some, the wretched assistants (on whom a word later) were paid much less and were not necessarily much younger. It was blandly assumed that you were expected to suffer for the privilege of working with good students and in a beautiful city. No one asked me, at any rate, what I had been earning, as interviewing committees would do now (I had been getting nearly £900 and came to Edinburgh under pressure from two older men, successively professors: Humphrey Sumner and Richard Pares; for anyone like myself who had had some teaching experience and had published a paper or two it was a seller's market, had I but known it).*

I confess that the maudlin remarks above give (in my own case) a totally wrong impression since I have been immensely happy here, and the university's bland ignorance of the financial realities of life after the war, though to my knowledge it lost the University at least one brilliant man, were accepted by pretty well everybody and were certainly not raised by the Scottish Association of University Teachers, not at that time linked with the English A.U.T. and rather poorly supported locally. Some dissatisfaction with money did emerge when salaries were taken up by the A.U.T. and membership figures reveal this, if I recall correctly. Even earlier there was the problem of Assistants.

An assistant was a young man or woman who taught very much as a lecturer though, in Arts, rather more tutorials and rather fewer lectures; in the sciences there were demonstrators about whose pay and duties I am

* See Appendix, pp. 175–6.

vague. The real difference was that an assistant had an appointment that terminated after three years (with a possible extension for a fourth). These posts, of course, were not peculiar to Edinburgh or Scotland, but when the terminal date arrived they could produce agonising interviews for the head of department who was obliged to say that the job was finished. Mostly assistants moved on to university posts with secure tenure, but some did not; altogether a very uncomfortable process which did not end at Edinburgh until 1960; it went on longer elsewhere. It was subject to other criticisms. The main one was that the appointment was virtually in the gift of the professor and the Dean as, indeed, were lectureships, for interviews were almost unheard of. No applications, *curricula vitae*, referees, were called for in the 1940s and 1950s. Perhaps for this reason assistants were treated rather like second-class citizens. But then, as indicated, it was not obligatory to interview for a lecturer's post, or perhaps even for a professor's; nowadays not even a professor would be appointed without being grilled by a committee. We got some admirable lecturers and professors in the old slap-happy way; and even strong committees can make dreadful mistakes.

Committees are, of course, the bane of the university teacher's life. He cannot bear to attend them and he cannot do without them. This is due to the curious 'we-they' syndrome where 'we' = the teaching staff and 'they' = the administration, or any part of it, including elected academics like deans. In fact the dislike generated by a principal, a secretary or an accountant (and I have no individuals in mind) is as nothing compared with the irritation provoked by someone elected who may be, like the master of an Oxford or Cambridge college, a candidate disliked by each of two powerful factions. Again I have no one in mind, although I think I have seen incipient symptoms of this *odium academicum* here and there. As for the committees, they multiply exceedingly, almost, I have sometimes thought, to the point of no return, to the point that is of just not being attended. For instance in the 1940s and 1950s Boards of Studies met once a year for formal business (mainly entries for the *Calendar*); now some of them meet monthly. And I have known professors who have not only never given an inaugural lecture but (different ones and not just medicals) who have never attended Senatus. When one reads the minutes of the Student Representative Council or the A.U.T. one gets the impression that virtually no one turns up, that meetings may be 'inquorate', a great S.R.C. word. And why not? Are the great distractions of the academic life not still with us, parties and pubs, girls and boys, and even libraries and work?

One totally enchanting aspect of the Edinburgh of the 1940s and 1950s has sadly diminished: second-hand bookshops. In the late 1940s there must have been six or seven in George IV Bridge alone, including the great John Grant with his policy of low prices and quick turnover, certainly the best bookshop for second-hand history (perhaps also Classics and Music) in the U.K. Now there are virtually only one or two shops remotely like this in the city. So that, at least on the Arts side, there were some compensations for low pay and a bicycle – if the latter had a basket. Alas, by the time of one's retirement (which I have now reached) accumulations of books, especially if in foreign languages, are largely non-saleable in Edinburgh and it is not much better in other parts of Britain. Anyway, even secondhand scholarship is pricey and one hardly needs to murmur *caveat emptor*.

Life in Edinburgh *was* cheaper, I believe, in the years after the war and not only because rationing persisted and salaries, of academic staff at least, were absurdly low. People entertained each other with tea and coffee – each other and students too. Now grown-ups expect their colleagues to supply stiffer refreshments and even students might be offended if one failed to open a bottle of plonk. Departmental gatherings are often (except perhaps in Divinity?) the excuse for nuts and, let us say, something called Valpolicella. In writing this I am trying to recover the atmosphere of 1979–80: I'm aware that financial stringencies are eroding this happy world. One should also add that before 1939 and in the immediate post-war period tea parties with one's professor were pretty stiff occasions, regarded with distrust by all concerned. Professor Donaldson has described how oppressive he found them as an undergraduate here before the war, and at Oxford so did I.

And it is important to make due allowance for the extraordinary development which followed on the realisation by the government and the universities that something had to be done to provide higher education for the generation born in the war and immediately post-war years. I mentioned a bulge immediately after the war, which was due to a coincidence of young people who were not conscripted plus an intake of returned ex-servicemen and women, who were mainly financed by the State. The next bulge was caused by the newly born children of 1943–55 or thereabouts and it led to a series of what have proved to be disastrous decisions by the Robbins' Committee. These resulted in much greater financing of existing institutions and the creation of dozens of new ones, besides rewarding certain aspects of the work of teacher-training colleges with university degrees.

All of this at Edinburgh resulted in larger undergraduate and graduate intake. The former were dealt with by enlisting staff, some of them ill-prepared for university teaching, some very immature and all by now in tenured positions, for it was almost unheard of to sack even the most disastrous or dishonest of teachers and for long the 'bar' for proficiency was neglected; indeed many people were recruited above it, a few coming in virtually at the senior lecturer level.

All of this led to discontents and none of it has been peculiar to Edinburgh. Edinburgh was, one might say, bidding against other universities for very limited qualified manpower. This was a somewhat frightening situation, especially in honours and post-graduate work, for the large numbers who were needed for the first-year classes were responsible for teaching students virtually their own age, and for supervising research when sometimes they had not completed their own. And they soon became accustomed to pretty liberal sabbatical and other leave arrangements, as well as departmental and equipment grants which may have been small in Divinity but were larger in the humanities and enormous in Medicine, Veterinary Medicine and above all pure and applied Science.

Retrospective thoughts like the above positively invite a concluding speculation about the future. Where do we go from here? Goodness knows. At any rate one should not assume that the Western European University forms part of a providential plan. The *universitas* meant a guild of teachers or students and as it emerged in the Middle Ages it produced enormous intellectual revenues during the twelfth and thirteenth centuries. Then it really ceased to be of much importance; it would not be unfair to say that from 1400 to 1800 (roughly speaking) the European university was increasingly moribund. In the early nineteenth century the university revived, beginning in Germany, and exercised enormous influence in all departments of knowledge down to the middle of the present century. But if it is to recover that influence, indeed if it is to survive it must justify itself without mystery to those not in the magic circle which gives academics the illusion that their world is *the* world, and it must demonstrate its relevance to the leaders of the distracted universe in which we all live.

ACKNOWLEDGMENTS

I have to thank a number of people for responding kindly to my queries. My chief debt is to the editor of this volume, my old friend Professor Gordon Donaldson. Others who have been most helpful have been Mrs Millar, Miss Dougall, Professor Rosalind Mitchison. The late Mr Charles H. Stewart kindly allowed me to read the typescript of his *History of the University* (from 1889).

APPENDIX

SCHEME OF TENURE OF OFFICE FOR READERS, LECTURERS, AND ASSISTANTS

(*Adopted by the University Court, 25th January* 1926,
and amended on 12*th December* 1927)

(NOTE.—These Regulations apply only to whole time Officers.)

1. Readers shall have the same tenure as Professors, but subject to an age-limit of 65: the Court reserving power to grant extension, by annual reappointment, up to the age of 70.[1]

2. All Lecturers shall be subject to an age-limit of 65.[2]

3. Lecturers now holding Lectureships of Grade C shall continue to hold office without further periodic reappointment. Subject always to the age-limit, their appointments shall not be terminable by the Court except after express consulation with the Faculty or Faculties concerned, and then only after at least six months' notice. Future appointments to Lectureships of Grade C shall be made on the same terms.

4. Appointments to Lectureships of Grade B shall be either (*a*) for a fixed period of years, or (*b*) upon the ordinary continuing annual tenure. By 'ordinary continuing annual tenure' is meant a tenure which continues without annual review, but may be terminated at the end of any Academical Year, upon six months' notice being given by either party.

5. Lecturers of Grade A shall be appointed in the first instance for a fixed period or periods, not exceeding five years in all, at the end of which they shall be reappointed only on the express recommendation of the Faculty or Faculties concerned, and if so reappointed, they shall have ordinary continuing annual tenure. The question of reappointment at the end of the fixed period or periods shall be decided not less than six months before the expiry of the same.

6. For the purposes of this scheme, a Lecturer whose salary is not more than £425 per annum shall normally be reckoned as belonging to Grade A; one whose salary is more than £425 and not more than £550 per annum shall normally be reckoned as belonging to Grade B; Lecturers whose salaries exceed £550 per annum shall be reckoned as belonging to Grade C. In exceptional circumstances grading may be given irrespective of the amount of salary.

7. Assistantships shall be held by annual appointment, normally for not more than three years; but in exceptional circumstances, with the approval of the Faculty or Faculties concerned, further reappointment may be made.[3]

8. The Faculties shall, in February each year, consider and report to the Court upon reappointments of Lecturers who would be entitled to six months' notice in the event of their services being dispensed with.

SCALES OF SALARY

Scales of Salary for whole-time Members of the Non-Professorial Teaching Staff came into force on 1st October 1930, as follows:—

*1/10/44

Assistants - - - - - - - - - £250 + 50	

Lecturers—

Grade A - £350, rising after two years by £25 annually to £425 + 50
  ,,   B - - - £450, rising by £25   ,,   £550 + 100
  ,,   C - - - £600   ,,   £25   ,,   £700 + 100

Readers, and Senior Lecturers in the Faculty of Medicine - £750 + 125

The salary is an inclusive one for all the duties which a Lecturer or Assistant may be called upon to discharge, as a whole-time Lecturer or whole-time Assistant, in the Department, e.g., the reading of Class Examination papers and, in addition, in the case of whole-time Lecturers, such assistance as may be required in respect of Degree Examination papers.

The salary of a Lecturer or Assistant will be paid only if the Course of Lectures is delivered.

Salaries are payable at the end of each quarter, viz., 31st December, 31st March, 30th June, and 30th September.

On a Lecturer or Assistant ceasing to hold office, only the proportion of Salary accrued at the date on which he ceases to hold office will be paid.

* See July 1944 Court Minutes p. 543.

REFERENCES

[1] Under resolution of the Court of 14th February 1921.

[2] Under resolution of the Court of 17th March 1924.

[3] On 17th June 1935, the University Court adopted the following recommendation of the Staff Appointments' Committee and resolved accordingly 'that heads of Departments should be notified that the normal tenure of the office of Assistant is three years, and that only in the most exceptional circumstances, and after special sanction of the Court has been obtained, will any appointment be continued beyond five years.'

INDEX

DESIGNATIONS
of Contributors

The Very Rev. John McIntyre, Professor of Systematic Theology, University of Edinburgh

Dr Christine Shepherd, Tutor with the Open University

Dr Jonquil Bevan, Lecturer in English Literature, University of Edinburgh

Professor Eric Forbes, Professor of History of Science, University of Edinburgh

Mr J. B. Morrell, Lecturer in History of Science, University of Bradford

Dr Ian Campbell, Reader in English Literature, University of Edinburgh

Mr C. P. Finlayson, Former Keeper of Manuscripts, University of Edinburgh

Professor G. A. Shepperson, Professor of Commonwealth and American History, University of Edinburgh

Mrs Sheila Hamilton, Research Assistant to the Dictionary of Scottish Business Biography Project, University of Glasgow

Mr R. M. Pinkerton, Lecturer in Humanity, University of Edinburgh

Miss Marjorie Robertson, Assistant Librarian, Department of Special Collections, Edinburgh University Library

Mr James L. Jennings, Senior Administrative Officer Matriculation Office, University of Edinburgh

Professor Gordon Donaldson, Professor Emeritus of Scottish History and Palaeography, University of Edinburgh

Professor Denys Hay, Professor Emeritus of Medieval and Renaissance History, University of Edinburgh